Together Bound

TOGETHER BOUND

*God, History, and
the Religious Community*

FRANK G. KIRKPATRICK

New York   Oxford
OXFORD UNIVERSITY PRESS
1994

Oxford University Press

Oxford   New York   Toronto
Delhi   Bombay   Calcutta   Madras   Karachi
Kuala Lumpur   Singapore   Hong Kong   Tokyo
Nairobi   Dar es Salaam   Cape Town
Melbourne   Auckland   Madrid

and associated companies in
Berlin   Ibadan

Copyright © 1994 by Frank G. Kirkpatrick

Published by Oxford University Press, Inc.
200 Madison Avenue, New York, New York 10016

Oxford is a registered trademark of Oxford University Press, Inc.

Library of Congress Cataloging-in-Publication Data
Kirkpatrick, Frank G.
Together bound : God, history, and the religious community /
Frank G. Kirkpatrick.
p.   cm.
Includes bibliographical references and index.
ISBN 0-19-508342-3
1. God—Knowableness.   2. History (Theology)   3. Faith.
I. Title.   BT102.K49   1994   231—dc20   93-18204

2   4   6   8   9   7   5   3   1
Printed in the United States of America
on acid-free paper

For Liz, Amy, and Daniel

Preface

This study is an exploration into the intelligibility of theological reflections on the Christian experience of God[1] as an Agent together bound with the believer and his or her community. It is not primarily an attempt to 'prove' the existence of God, or to evaluate the various arguments that have been offered for the credibility (or its lack) of trying to speak about God at all. I am assuming that most (if not all) of those who, on the basis of serious reflection, call themselves Christian have had (or would be willing to credit the testimony of others who have had) some kind of personal experience of a reality which they take to be so decisive, overwhelming, powerful, life-transforming, redeeming, and/or fulfilling that they are ready to name that reality 'God'. They are also, presumably, willing to affirm (at least to some significant degree) that the biblical picture of God conforms to their own experience of God or that of those people whose experience they are willing to credit.

This study, then, originates within and refers itself back to a community of persons who have had or believe they may be recipients of an experience of God that, for them, is most appropriately understood through the chain of interpretations that comprise the Christian tradition.

I do not intend to get into the question of whether such experiences are truly 'veridical', whether they correspond to the experiences of people in other religious traditions, or whether they are resistant to being explained away psychologically. These are all important questions and provide ample material for endless and significant studies. But my intention is more limited. I want to examine the apparently straightforward claims of many people, including the writers of Scripture, to have experienced the reality of God as a Person who encounters them, redeems and sustains them, promises them ultimate fulfillment, and, in the meantime, remains powerfully bound together with them individually but especially in community.

And, in a more limited way still, I want to argue that there is a coherent set of concepts drawn from our experience of ourselves and others as personal agents that can give rational meaning to, without substituting itself for, the experience of God as an infinitely powerful loving personal Agent together bound with us. If I am successful, then I will have provided an important piece of rational support for Christian claims that the experience of God (as depicted in Scripture and as accessible today) is congruent with our deepest rational convictions and claims about reality.

There is a great deal of scepticism today in academic circles about the credibility of speaking about objective reality at all, and therefore of speaking of God as an 'objective' reality who encounters and is experienced by other persons, and especially about the 'primitive' or 'anthropomorphic' God of the Bible. Deconstruction, linguistic analysis, relativism, a conviction that only subjectivity can be reflected in words and concepts, and the claims of 'modern' science have all been regarded as fatal to any enterprise intending to defend the rationality of claims about God as some kind of personal, objective, and rationally accessible 'Other'. What William Dean has called the "new historicism" in religious thought denies realism and the correspondence theory of truth (wherein rational statements more or less faithfully mirror a reality external to them). It rejects any nonhistorical reality and any absolute truth not found in history. There is no access to truth except through human interpretations of previous interpretations, all of which are socially and historically conditioned. As Dean puts it, "actual truths are entirely historical creatures, conceived within history, directed at history, and grown in a historical chain, as interpretation refers to interpretation which refers to interpretation on down through the reaches of history."[2]

There is much truth in many of these critical approaches to religious claims, but ultimately I think their quiver is spent on the *dualist* view of God, toward which I, too, will direct some serious criticisms. What can be said about God, according to most contemporary philosophers and theologians, can at best be said tentatively, cautiously, and in the spirit of entering into a conversation, certainly not dogmatically, absolutely, or imperially. While I do think that rational credibility can be restored to 'God-talk' (provided it is talk about a *particular* type of God), I want to enter a conversation, not pronounce a final judgment. I only hope the other conversation-alists are willing to listen to an argument that does *not* automati-cally assume the triumph of deconstruction, relativism, historicism, and subjectivity. Nevertheless, the conversation I want to enter is one that is central to the Christian community's 'historical chain'. It is a conversation about the encounter *in history* (personal and communal) with a historical force that those who have encountered it were bold enough to call 'God' and through which this God an-nounced/revealed the divine presence. I want to take the new his-toricists' claim that for the biblical traditions "there was no recourse beyond history" and that, consequently, "it is within history, within a plurality of tradition-events and interpretations, that God was to be found"[3] and explore what it entails for an understanding of God. I am convinced that in history and from history the Christian can build a coherent and intelligible claim that God is precisely that historical agent who makes all the historical difference in the world. Establishing that claim takes place within a historical conversation among Christians who believe that they have been touched by the actions of someone greater than themselves, who is as real as the other agents who make up the fullness of historical life in the world.[4]

In other words, if history is all we have, then there is, within history, enough material to sustain a Christian conversation about a reality who has been historically experienced as history's most decisive personal and communal historical actor. I want to push the logic of historicism beyond the a/theology and scepticism com-mon to many of its current practitioners. If history is "all there is," then a view of God, derived from historical experience, as a his-torically encountered agent becomes logically credible and coher-ent for those who have participated in that experience or whose current experience is congruent with the narrative of their community's past experience of God. I want to join a conversation among Christians about their knowledge of a God whom they claim to know primarily through God's acts in history. I want to explore the logic of what such a knowledge-base can and cannot reveal about God. I want to see just what can and cannot be said about a God who is known to us through God's purposeful, overarching, and specific acts in the history of those people who believe that God has chosen to act in especially revealing and decisive ways among them.

At the same time, I want to argue that our experience of this divine actor neither contradicts nor subverts the experiences that, when collected into systematic reflection, we have called modern science. Our knowledge of agents in and through history and our knowledge of the non-agential world (nature) are different enough to require significant distinctions but not so different as to force incoherent and conceptually muddy bifurcations between them. I want to argue, in effect, that within historical knowledge we find the appropriate space for a more limited knowledge of a world without agents. This latter knowledge we call science and, as a coherent part of a more inclusive knowledge of persons, it does not challenge, override, or contradict our knowledge of God.

There is ultimately something imperious and arrogant about rival claims that 'we' (usually affixed to the term 'moderns' or, more often, 'postmoderns') can no longer speak intelligibly about God or that the only 'authentic' God is one beyond the limits of human conceptuality. One of the imperial 'we's' is assumed to be rational people, schooled in the 'hermeneutics of suspicion', who can find no credibility in any claims that seem to violate the canons of natural science. Another imperial 'we' are those people who believe that no one can speak except through terms and concepts irremediably corrupted (or deconstructed) by the relativism of pure subjectivity. A third imperial 'we' are those who claim that 'of course' God is beyond all human conceptuality and therefore no human talk derived from the natural world and intended to refer to God can ever be credible by human rational standards.

Obviously these various imperial 'we's' are in disagreement with each other about what counts as the basis for credible or rational speech about God. The subjectivists reject the canons of natural science as hopelessly naive about the possibility of achieving 'objective' truth; the adherents of natural science charge the subjectivists with epistemological defeatism regarding the possibility of saying something true about the objective world, and those who espouse a transcendentalist view of God (in which the deity is treated as an exception to all principles of meaning applicable in the natural world) reject both the possibility of 'natural' objective truth and the limitations of subjectivity, holding out for the possibility of a transempirical truth in which the transcendentalized subject participates through revelation or intuition.

As the debates between these various contenders for cognitive supremacy swirl through the intellectual academy there are many people (who certainly do not think they are any less rational than the spokespersons for the major intellectual currents of the day), who feel as if their experiences are not being fully represented by the different imperial 'we's'. These people find themselves often left voiceless, or, at best, lumped together with the chorus of voices emanating from antirational, dogmatic forms of fundamentalism or anti-intellectual fideism.

I wish to provide a voice, which is my own voice as well, for those who feel both that they are faithful to the canons of reason and that they have experienced a supremely powerful, ultimately decisive power whom they are audacious enough to call 'God' and whom they see represented faithfully in the words of the Christian Scriptures and the traditions of the historical Christian communities. This voice can speak intelligibly in the terms of reason but it can also speak convincingly in the terms of the deepest and most intimate religious experience. One of the most striking characteristics of the intellectual debate about the intelligibility of 'God-talk' today is its virtual indifference to the talk about God that seems to fill the pages of Jewish and Christian scriptures. All pay lip service to the obvious—namely that the God of those scriptures is described as a personal being with individualizing and distinguishing characteristics, the chief of which are love, compassion, and justice, and that this God manifests those characteristics through concrete actions intentionally carried out empirically in nature and history. But virtually no one believes that this picture of God can stand up to the contemporary canons of rationality. Even those who claim to be interpreting Christian theology often speak as if no one today would claim an experience of such a God. The natural scientific approach rejects this view as inconsistent with the canons of natural cause and effect. The subjectivists reject it as fatally naive in its belief that it has reached any kind of objective reality in and of itself. And the transcendentalists reject it decisively as a caricature of the 'real' God who 'must' be completely beyond all such limiting and individualizing attributes.

I want to take seriously the elements of the experience that has historically constituted, and continues to constitute for many people today, a conviction that God is a personal Agent together bound with the believer and to put those elements into a rationally coherent framework that can reveal their metaphysical intelligibility. The link and the linchpin will be a fully developed concept of God as Agent who acts both overarchingly as well as specifically in history and in the lives of individuals and communities.

There is no reason why the experiences of people who feel that a living, acting, loving, and individual divine being has encountered them cannot be given the same serious consideration as the experiences of those who feel that only a reality 'beyond' all human cognition can merit the name 'God' or those who feel that there is no reality, either mundane or transcendent, who so merits that appellation.

The argument of this book rests on two propositions: one, that it is possible to develop a rationally coherent, metaphysically respectable concept of God as a personal Agent in dynamic relation with and to the world, and, two, that such a God is worthy of worship and discipleship. To the canons of natural science it will be necessary to show that such a God can interact with the other agents of the world without violating, fundamentally contradicting, or having divine action reduced to the causal laws that constitute the natural sciences. To the canons of subjectivity it will be necessary to show that such a God is no less 'objective' than other realities that even subjectivists are willing to concede have at least plausible objectivity beyond themselves. And to the canons of transcendentalism, it will be necessary to show that a 'limited' God is neither an affront to reason nor a diminution in the fullness and mysteriousness that God must have in order to be an object of devotion and awe.

At the same time, it will be necessary to argue that there are limits on the 'reach' of causal law in its attempt to explain everything that happens; to argue that some degree of objectivity is achievable, both in experience and in thought; and to argue that the urge for a sense of the unconditioned and the unlimited is neither to be explained away nor made the sole basis for a concept of God.

The task I have set myself is to situate a particular understanding of God within the context of a particular set of experiences (reflected in Scripture and Christian community). At the same time, I have to show that such a view of the divine Agent is rationally coherent. The argument will revolve around the credibility of extending the experience of personal agents who are together bound through action to the experience of another personal Agent worthy of the name 'God'.

Hartford, Connecticut   F.G.K.
June 1993

Notes

1. Throughout the text I use the word 'God' only, and not gender-specific pronouns, such as 'His'. This may seem awkward at first but I

think it is necessay in order to avoid the traditional but subtly gender-exclusive masculine pronoun usually affixed to 'God'.

2. William Dean, *History Making History* (Albany: State University of New York Press, 1988), p. 1.

3. Ibid., p. 38.

4. The general thrust of my argument would apply equally well to Judaism and possibly Islam insofar as they root their basic understanding of God in God's historical acts. The argument would part company with them, of course, at the point of interpreting the significance of that one divine historical act that is central for Christians, the life-death-resurrection of Jesus of Nazareth.

Acknowledgments

In many ways this book was written in isolation, except for the companionship of my word processor. The bulk of the writing was done without much direct scholarly consultation except that which occurs as one reads and rereads the published work of others. Nevertheless, nothing that I have written has been unaffected by the many teachers I have had, especially Edmund LaB. Cherbonnier and William A. Johnson, and the colleagues with whom I work, both in my college and in the larger scholarly community. I would especially like to acknowledge the influence of the many people who constitute the recently formed International John Macmurray Association.

Some chapters have found their way, in different versions, into print, including chapter 6 ("Together Bound: A New Look at God's Discrete Actions in History," *International Journal for Philosophy of Religion* [1991] and chapter 10 ("The Logic of Mutual Heterocentrism," *Philosophy and Theology* [Summer, 1992]). I have also received some critical comments on chapter 6 from William P. Alston, which I acknowledge gratefully, as I do those of the anonymous reviewer of the first draft of this manuscript. Finally, I would acknowledge the generous time and comments given by Lee Wallace and Amy Limpitlaw in reading portions of the manuscript as they took shape.

Contents

Together Bound

I come with Christians far and near to find, as all are fed, the new community of love in Christ's communion bread. And thus with joy we meet our Lord. His presence, always near, is in such friendship better known: we see and praise him here. Together met, together bound, we'll go our different ways, and as his people in the world we'll live and speak his praise.

Brian W. Wren, Hymn no. 304, *The Hymnal 1982 according to the Use of the Episcopal Church* (New York: The Church Hymnal Corporation, 1982).

1

Situating Our Knowledge of God in Relationship

At the heart of the Christian experience is the fact of relatedness: being together bound with other Christians in a community of faith, celebration, and responsibility. The foundation of that relatedness is the conviction that there is a loving God who creates and sustains the conditions of reality that make relatedness possible and who, in particular, is in a decisive personal relationship with that community of belief and its individual members as they celebrate the divine presence and seek to be responsible to the divine intention, as they have discerned it, for the world.

Relation and Reflection

But the heart and the foundation have often been in conflict, at least in many of the reflections (which, in their systematized form we call 'theologies') that have emerged from the historical experience of Christian community. The understanding of relatedness to the divine being is often in rational tension with some traditional theological claims of who God is and how God is to be conceived. As the Christian community tried to affirm God's majesty, transcendence, mystery, and sovereignty, it developed conceptual categories that increasingly tended (of logical necessity, given their philosophical assumptions) to separate God from the world God had created and with which God was also assumed to have some deep relation-

3

ship. Consequently, it became increasingly difficult to speak of God's together-boundness with the world and God's community in any way that would be both rationally coherent *and* faithful to the assumption that God must be absolutely transcendent.

In recent years there has been a significant attempt to restore rational credibility to traditional theological propositions. But much of this new work has *assumed* the supremacy of a theological position in which God, *by definition*, is understood to be omniscient, omnipotent, immutable, and transcendent of time, space, and 'finitude'. On this definition, any notion of God that qualifies these attributes is to be dismissed as either "not what we theologians who are faithful to the tradition mean by God," or as unintelligible. In one sense the argument of this book is a challenge to the traditional definition of God. But in another sense it is an attempt to show how an alternative understanding of the divine as personal agent is faithful both to the underlying religious experience of relatedness to a supreme power, especially as it is given expression in Scripture, and to the canons of rationality. Whether my argument is successful or not, it should not be dismissed *a priori* simply because it doesn't accept, without qualification, the traditional assumption of what God *must* be in order to be God in the theological tradition. That tradition is itself the product of a great deal of dualist thinking, as I shall define it, and thus is subject to the critique of dualism. At the same time, it is derivative from and therefore subordinate to the authority of the *experience* of God as narrated in Scripture and as found in the lives of religious people.

In one sense, of course, the lack of rational coherence in many of the traditional theological propositions about God was not fatal to the expression of Christian belief and certainly not to the life of the community in worship and practice. Christians, like other people, can navigate the waters of experience without *always* having to reconcile the theoretical maps in the pilot house with their 'feel' of how to steer their ship successfully. In the short run, it may seem more vital to experience the acts of navigation or to enjoy the destination itself than to reflect abstractly on what they are and what makes them possible. Christianity is primarily a religion of experiences, namely of estrangement, reconciliation, empowerment, hope, awe, and fulfillment in relation to others and to God. Its reflective or theoretical dimension is secondary to and derivative from the experiences that constitute its core. Even theologies that ultimately project a highly abstract concept of God can be, as a recent writer on the relation between religion and psychology has put it, "bearers of an intense, passionate, and lasting bond with the sacred."[1] A Christian need not pass through the portals of philosophy before being admitted to the hall of new life that God promises.

In this sense, the notion of God is less important than the experience of God. Millions of Christians have experienced the divine presence without being able to articulate a conceptually coherent concept of the God whom they are convinced they have experienced. Even when such a concept has been developed it has often seemed, in comparison with the experience, to be a pale, distorted, limited, and limiting thing.

There is something 'foundational' in the Christian experience of God that cannot be explained away by or even made derivative from a 'philosophy' of reality *into* which the idea of God is fitted and conformed. Apart from the basic experience of the living God, Christian 'philosophy' builds its conceptual schemata in abstraction and, ultimately, in futility.

Nevertheless, the struggle to understand God in conceptual terms has never been entirely abandoned by the Christian community as a whole. Part of the reason is that the Christian experience of new life reaffirms the goodness of the divine creation of genuinely human life, which includes the delights and integrity of the human mind. Christians know, at a deep level, that the celebration of God's creativity would be in contradiction with the denigration of that dimension of human beings that can reason and reflect on what has been created good by God.

Maps of the Way to God

Another reason that Christians have been reluctant to abandon the integrity of rational reflection is that it has proven indispensable, and not only in the realm of spiritual experience, as a guide to more fulfilling living. While it is possible to guide a ship through smooth waters without *constant* attention to a navigational chart, more dangerous and unknown waters usually prove unnavigable without the skills of one who knows how to read the charts that are the result of reasoning and reflection. Even in smooth waters, the charts are necessary if one is to have some sense of where one is sailing. A 'feel' for the immediate situation will not, in and of itself, provide either foresight, purpose, or knowledge of what to expect further ahead.

The Christian's knowledge of God is an integral part of the map by which she seeks to navigate through life. If God is real and if that reality is in fact encountered as being, in some ontological sense, distinct from the sojourner herself, then the reality of God as 'Other' must be mapped accurately if the journey to and from God is to be successful. A map detailing a car trip from Hartford to Boston must include an accurate (true) depiction of Interstate 84 if it is to be relied upon successfully. That is not to say that one could not get to Boston without going on Interstate 84, but even to go another route requires knowledge of the fact that the Interstate exists and must be gone around if another route is chosen. In other words, knowledge of Interstate 84 is crucial because Interstate 84 is a decisive reality in the geography between Hartford and Boston.

Now if we believe that God is a decisive reality in the actual journey of the human person toward fulfillment (or the wholeness of life), then not only must God be encountered as a reality in God's own right, but, if that encounter is to be properly prepared for, understood, and integrated into the journey, the map of the journey must include an accurate (true) depiction or representation of God, at least with respect to those divine actions and attributes that affect our fulfillment. That is to say, we do not necessarily need a *complete* or *exhaustive* depiction of God but we do need an accurate depiction of God *insofar as* God's reality is decisive for the completion of our journey. (God need not exhaust the fullness of God's nature in God's relationship with us, and thus our representation of God's reality need not be exhaustive of God's full reality, but if God's reality is to be decisive for us, what we experience of it or what acts upon us must be accurately depicted if our conceptual representation of God is to be an indispensable ingredient in our relationship with God.)

In making these claims I am not taking a stand for or against contemporary philosophical arguments regarding whether we can ever truly 'map' external reality. I am not assuming the ancient truths of the 'correspondence' theory, in which it is believed that our concepts 'mirror' or represent what is 'out there' in some direct, immediate, and noninterpreted way. Nevertheless, I don't think one has to accept the correspondence theory of truth in its initial and naive form in order to hold to the idea that there is some reality external to our minds with which we have to 'deal' through our actions and that our ideas provide us some kind of guidance system for dealing more effectively than we could without them. These ideas do not have to 'mirror' reality in a completely undistorted and isomorphic way but they must give us the kind of help that maps give in aiding us to negotiate our way around the terrain through which we have chosen to travel. In this sense, my use of the map metaphor permits a wide variety of interpretations as to how maps literally model the reality they depict. Nevertheless, I do want to hold out for a modeling that permits us to apply to God in a straightforward manner the same notions of act and agency as we apply to ourselves. In fact, by grounding my claims about God on the experience of agency, I will be suggesting that knowledge of reality through action is more fundamental than knowledge of reality through reflection, the latter being only a derivative of the former.

A true conceptual representation of God is not a substitute for God, nor is our knowledge of God a substitute for a living relationship with God. But that relationship is itself incomplete without the contribution that knowledge makes. I will press the following analogy in more detail later, but I think it will be sufficient at this point to note the importance in any genuine human relationships of the knowledge one person has of another. That knowledge, at least in its conceptual dimension, is an essential ingredient in maintaining the fullness of the relationship, but it is not more than an ingredient. It is not the wholeness of the relationship but rather contributes to it. If I am woefully ignorant of your intentions and character my actions with regard to you will be clumsy, misdirected, and hit or miss. Only if my map of our relationship includes accurate conceptual knowledge of you can our relationship develop beyond theory into the fullness of which it is capable.

Our knowledge of God, then, is justified, at one level, in the same way we would justify a knowledge of any other reality with which we have to deal as we negotiate our way around in the world. If God is real and if God's reality is essential to our fulfillment, then our knowledge of God is indispensable to (though not sufficient or a substitute for) that fulfillment. A false or misleading understanding of God will eventually disrupt our journey to ultimate fulfillment precisely because it will lead us to act in ways that are out of harmony with reality as it is.

Now if God were only an inanimate object, it might be possible to form an accurate understanding of God that would enable us to work around God without any contribution from God's own self, as it were. Even the most massive and complex natural objects are eventually susceptible to the manipulation or avoidance of rational people, as our encounter with atomic reality makes clear. But if God is animate, a living being with not only intentions but power, then God is much less likely to be manipulable or avoidable. And if God's intentions are enacted with infinite power in the world we inhabit, then our intentions must take account of the divine intentions. And if God's intentions include our willing acceptance of them, then our intentions must take account of the divine intentions by seeking to be in conformity with them. But we can be in conformity to God's intentions only if we know what they are, and we can know what they are only by having a sufficiently accurate understanding of the God from whom they issue.

A false view of God can only, ultimately, produce a failure to act in such a way as to be in conformity with God's intentions. This does not mean that a person with a false view of God is necessarily doomed to frustration or unfulfillment. An intentional divine being certainly has the power to choose to 'save' or fulfill any one God chooses, including those who are woefully ignorant of God. But it does mean that someone with a false view of God is less able to *act* and *intend* successfully in relation to God than is one who has a truer picture of the divine being.

Historically, most religions have claimed to provide a truer picture of divine reality than other religions. It is certainly the claim of Christianity that in its historical experience it has been given a 'picture' of the living God that is, despite occasional distortion and incompleteness, essentially accurate insofar as God's existence, power, acts, and intentions are concerned. That picture is of God as creative, sustaining, nurturing, loving, forgiving, reconciling, merciful, just, and, finally, triumphant (in the sense of being able ultimately to fulfill God's intentions).

I am not unmindful of the debate that has gone on for centuries, and especially now in the age of philosophical analysis of language, over whether our 'maps' of reality truly 'represent' reality as it is or only provide us with an interpretive overlay that simultaneously hides reality while enabling us to work our way around in it. At this point I am not concerned to enter that debate.[2] Nor do I think its resolution directly affects the point I wish to make, which is simply that without maps that are more or less accurate depictions of a world that is in some sense 'external' to us, even as we participate in it, we have no way, conceptually, of knowing the world.[3] In this respect, I am at one with the thrust of what has been called 'the new metaphysics'.[4] Like it, I believe that "there is no truth without *radical otherness . . . the real otherness of things within the world must be acknowledged unless truth itself is to vanish into a set of merely conceptual relations.*"[5] I am not disputing that we can know the world in nonconceptual ways (as I 'know' the pain in my left ear or that I am now hitting keys on a keyboard). But if God is assumed to be in some basic way 'other' than myself (even if in intimate relationship with me), then some 'picture' or map of God is required and is required to be accurate. And, historically, the Christian picture of God is of a Being or Person or Agent who stands as Creator, Redeemer, and Sustainer of the world.

The Centrality of Agent Language about God

In this Christian picture of God, God's together-boundness with the world God has created, and, in particular, with the people God has called into covenant and whom God has graced with new life, is reaffirmed time and again. And what makes together-boundness capable of being reaffirmed is the capacity of the divine being to *act*. All the language that paints the Christian picture of God rests on the experience of divine *action*, which in turn justifies the notion that God is an *agent*. To create, sustain, nuture, love, forgive, reconcile, show mercy, do justice, and achieve the fulfillment of one's intention are all *actions* emanating from an *agent*.

It is literally impossible to find a picture of God in Christian Scripture, liturgy, and even in those theologies that intend to transcend the notion of God as Agent that does not presuppose as well as employ the language of divine agency. The language of agency is the highest form of human language in which to express the power of doing or achievement. It is also the language of encounter between living beings and it is the language of intimacy between living beings who seek to live in each other's presence.

It would be superfluous to dwell on the centrality of agent/action language in the traditional Christian imagery of God and God's together-boundness with the world and God's people. Nevertheless, despite the prevalence of agent/action language in Scripture, liturgy, and theology, there has been a persistent strain in Christian reflection away from too heavy a reliance upon such language if applied too 'literally' or straightforwardly to God. Even agent language used of God has been felt by most theologians to be limited, limiting, and distorting. The limits of agent language as applied to God have been felt to consist in its reduction of God to the limits of 'worldly' conditions, especially those that have to do with the constraints essential to any relationships of interdependence between agents and with the material infrastructure that undergirds their actions.

Agent language is inherently the language of beings together bound with each other and with a common world. It is the language of interdependence and interaction. It is, therefore, inherently limiting language insofar as agents together-bound respect some degree of autonomy on the part of those other agents with whom they are in active relation.

But these limits have been felt to demean, denigrate, or diminish the majesty of divine reality, despite the fact that the language of praise, devotion, intercession, and prayer is inherently agent language and the language of the Christian experience is inherently the language of feeling together-bound with a loving (and acting) God. Historically, much of Christian theology has been devoted to the task of retaining enough of the agent language of God so as not to destroy the language of liturgy and worship while at the same time pushing beyond that language in the realm of theology to forms of expression that are not bound by its perceived limitations. Two of the most important alternatives to agent language are what I shall call simply monism and dualism, the views, namely, that God is the one and only reality (and thus not subject to the limits of a language that *distinguishes* God from other things), or that God is a reality so radically, absolutely, and utterly *other* than anything in or of the world as to be beyond all forms of human thought and expression. Despite the prevalence and appeal of these two different ways of looking at God, I intend to engage in the rational act of elaborating and defending not only the religious significance but also the rational coherence of a straightforward, literal use of agent language to describe God's reality, at least insofar as it *can* be known by us and is encountered by us. One dimension of the new metaphysics, as expressed by Nicholas Capaldi, is its insistence that the "primordial reality is man's relation with the world." The new metaphysics, in order to articulate this relation, "has adopted the perspective of the agent, the engaged participant."[6] And since agents make history, this means that all reflection on what agents do is rooted in history. "Metaphysical thinking is therefore historical," not eternal.[7]

There have, of course, already been important and helpful explorations of the notion of God as Agent. The work of Gordon Kaufman, Thomas Tracy, Robert King, Robert Blaikie, Maurice Wiles, Austin Farrer, Frank Dilley, William Alston, Brian Hebblethwaite, Mats Hansson, and, in their own way, of process theologians such as John Cobb, David Griffin, and Lewis Ford, has examined the applicability of agent language to God.[8] Much of this work is indispensable for my own project. However, I intend to go at least one step beyond these studies in order to make the rather audacious claim that agent-act conceptuality is not simply the best model or symbol we can have of God, but that it is as 'literally' true of God as it is of any other reality we know; that it is a more accurate depiction of God's reality than any other language we have; and, in particular, that it is the only language we have for depicting God's specific and particular acts in history.

It is this latter claim that has rarely, if ever, been made *without qualification* by Christian theologians. Even those who want to employ some version of agent language shy away from using it to refer to concrete divine acts *in* history. The belief of some scholars (e.g., Bultmann and Gilkey) that scientific causal law has replaced traditional talk of God acting in history has seemingly eliminated any credibility of language about particular unique divine acts within the causal infrastructure known (presumably exhaustively) by natural science. I want to restore that credibility by showing that agent language is not only compatible with scientific description of the causal patterns of nature, but is also transcendent and inclusive of it in the sense that it depicts beings whose reality (as agents) is greater than the reality found solely within a causal law description of the 'natural' world.

In short, I intend to show that the language of God as an agent who acts in history is philosophically or rationally coherent and well grounded *and* that, by virtue of that fact, it provides a metaphysical ground for the Christian language of experiencing a together-bound relationship with God including the language of its Scripture as the book of the acts of God. I am not suggesting that the language of Scripture or of experience is *intended* to be metaphysical. Rather, I am suggesting that while the intent of the language of Scripture and experience is to express the together-boundness of God with God's creation and, in particular, with those God calls into worship and service, there is an implict and metaphysically sound rationality to that language and to the reality that it reflects.

I hope it is clear by this point that an appeal to 'metaphysics' is not meant to suggest that the Christian faith is reducible to or even to be identified with theoretical abstractions. Metaphysics is the rational schema through which we attempt to reflect the basic structures of reality. All agents who act intentionally do so with an implicit picture of reality—that is, they have some sense of what there is 'out there,' which their actions will encounter. Of course, reflection helps us to deepen, extend, and develop that sense—to move it from the implicit to the explicit. Metaphysics as a particular field of study focuses on that development and on the coherence of the various elements in our reflective schema and with the reality they are intended to represent. In our reflections upon experience we do not, of course, necessarily intend to bring out the underlying metaphysics of what we have experienced or what makes such experiences possible. Nevertheless, underlying all reflections on experience are implicit metaphysical principles (regardless of whether they are made explicit in a metaphysical *system*). When the Bible and the liturgies of the Christian community talk about encounters with God in history and in the personal lives of those who have been renewed by God, an implicit claim is being made that the structures of reality are such that personal agents exist, act, encounter each other, transform each other, and, through those moments of direct together-boundness, create history. This claim is radically reflective of a metaphysics even though that metaphysics will remain only implicit in the actual language describing or giving thanks for the moments of relationship between God and human agents. In the reflections that constitute the act of writing this book, I will be attempting to make explicit the metaphysical principles of agent/action relationship that I believe constitute the underlying metaphysics of the Christian community's encounter with God, and its language, especially liturgical and scriptural, about God. And if that metaphysics is truly representative of the reality that it reveals, then it is implicitly rational as well.

The importance of that implicit rationality is that it provides the Christian with the firm undergirding in reality that can deepen and sustain her commitment to carrying out the intentions of God. Those intentions can then be seen as the stuff of reality itself, as the foundation for all life and action. By conforming ourselves to the intentions of the God revealed in the language of worship and Scripture, we are conforming ourselves to the heart of reality. And if our picture of that reality is true (accurate), then we are assured that our intentions cannot fail to be fulfilled provided God remains true to God's own intentions. The metaphysical adequacy of the picture of God as loving Agent is the ontological foundation not only for Christian life, but for eschatological hope as well. It provides the basis for the endurance of the Christian community in times of travail and the imperative to keep up the struggle for peace and justice because the conditions for their achievement are 'wired into' the heart of reality precisely because they are the intention of God.

Notes

1. See James W. Jones, *Contemporary Psychoanalysis and Religion: Transference and Transcendence* (New Haven, Conn.: Yale University Press, 1991) p. 132. Jones notes that Paul Tillich's abstract notion of God as 'being-itself' has to be seen alongside Tillich's passionate collection of sermons, such as *The New Being* and *The Shaking of the Foundations*.

2. If I were to do so it would be on the side of the 'realists', who contend that reason is capable of reflecting with some degree of accuracy, though never as a mirror, the world out of which it arises through the approach taken by Edward Pols in his new book *Radical Realism: Direct Knowing in Science and Philosophy* (Ithaca, N.Y.: Cornell University Press, 1992). Pols, whose work in the philosophy of action I will draw upon later, argues that the antirealist or relativist position is ultimately self-contradictory because to assert it as true is to deny the absolute, and not just relative, truth of opposing positions. Radical realism, on the other hand, starts with the fact that knowing is an activity "that completes itself in the independently real" (p. 155).

3. For a persuasive critique of the deconstructionist attempt to undermine realist assumptions about knowing, see John M. Ellis, *Against Deconstruction* (Princeton: Princeton University Press, 1989). Among other telling points, Ellis argues that deconstructionists who insist that there is no correct way of viewing the world nevertheless know how to identify false or incorrect constructions of deconstructionism, especially when they respond to critics who have somehow gotten the meaning of their text wrong.

4. Robert C. Neville, ed., *New Essays in Metaphysics* (Albany: State University of New York Press, 1987).

5. Carl G. Vaught, "Metaphor, Analogy, and the Nature of Truth," in *New Essays in Metaphysics*, p. 221.

6. Nicholas Capaldi, "Copernican Metaphysics," in *New Essays in Metaphysics*, p. 47. As Charles Sherover, another contributer to this volume, has stressed, "all thinking is temporally structured in specific historical situations that entail a continuing dynamic of all components comprising an experiential situation in continuously changing relations with each other. . . . What is presupposed in every act of consciousness is its intrinsic involvement in and reference to what has variously been termed intersubjectivity or community" ("Toward Experiential Metaphysics: Radical Temporalism," p. 81). I am trying to draw the full implications of this aspect of the 'new metaphysics' for our understanding of God as an Agent in a world of intersubjective or mutual community.

7. Ibid., p. 48.

8. For a full bibliography of sources on act(s) of God in the world, see the Appendix.

2

Alternative Views of God: Monism, Dualism, Pluralism

While the agent-act metaphysics is, I believe, most truly representative of the Christian's experience of God and the world, there are two other alternative metaphysical views of God that have, historically, found important places in the Christian tradition. While they share with each other some important metaphysical assumptions, especially those that entail that God is beyond the reach of human reason, they are significantly different in enough respects that they should be treated separately before being compared to the third view of God as Agent.

The first of these two views I call simply 'monism'. It is found especially in many of the mystical traditions around the world, including those within Christianity. The other view, discussed in detail in chapters 3 and 4, I call 'dualism'. It is implicit in most, if not all, of the traditional theologies of Christianity and is, more often than not, a touchstone of orthodox Christian thought. In challenging the adequacy of dualism I may appear to be challenging orthodox Christian belief itself. That is not my intent, however, except insofar as I believe a case can be made that this particular dimension of orthodox belief is itself incapable of metaphysically sustaining the fundamental conviction of the Christian community that God is a personal agent together-bound with it through direct and loving acts. In short, I want to argue that the dualist view, in order to preserve what it understands to be the essence of God's transcendence, resorts to a set of metaphysical principles that, in the end, eliminate any metaphysical basis for an active, agent-centered relationship between God and God's creation.

In treating dualism and monism, I will be regarding them metaphysically as ideal types, as systems of understanding that have a systematic internal logic and coherence that transcend the particular formulations they have received by individual theologians. I want to explore the systematic and logical implications of the assumptions that God is either the only reality or an absolutely transcendent reality. In practice, of course, the use of the monist and dualist logics has been mixed with other concerns on the part of the theologian with the result that the monist or dualist logic is submerged or compromised to some extent. This is not scandalous on the part of the theologian. Rather it may well be a testimony to the fact that most theologians are so committed implicitly to the conviction that God *is* a personal agent bound in relationship with other agents that they are willing to sacrifice logical consistency rather than give up that conviction even when it conflicts with the implicit logic of either monism or dualism.

Both monism and dualism are ultimately in metaphysical conflict with 'pluralism', the general name I give to that metaphysical view that includes the notion of God as a personal agent. That is not to say, however, that dualism, especially, *intends* such a conflict. In fact, I believe that dualism in many of its traditional forms *wants* to talk about God as a personal being who acts in a multitude of ways (who creates, cares, loves, forgives, reconciles, reveals, empowers, etc.) just because this is the picture of God in the Bible and worship that it wants to protect from rational attack from other quarters. However, the philosophical principles that it employs in defense of its God are such that, when carried to their logical conclusion, they wind up removing the metaphysical support necessary for employing language about God as a personal being.

Divine Transcendence

The difficulty, which both monism and dualism intend to address, is that talk about God as a personal being *seems* to limit and diminish God, to destroy the mystery and transcendence that seem to be essential to God's status as Creator of the universe and Redeemer of all humankind. At the root of the worship of God is the experience of standing before the 'Holy (and Wholly) Other', that reality that is not simply greater than all other realities but so great and overpowering that it cannot be compared with anything other than itself without reducing it to the level of the object of comparison. Comparisons, even between the greatest and the least thing, still presuppose some common ground on which the comparison is made (e.g., power, beauty, goodness, etc.). But there seems to be something in the experience of worship that compels us to seek that reality that is so much greater (still using comparative language) that its greatness shares no common ground with that over or with respect to which it is great. This is the foundation of the notion of transcendence.

To transcend something is to surpass it, to go beyond it, to be in no way subject to its limitations. Out of the communal and personal experience of being profoundly transformed by the power of God it is natural to want to express that power in words that underline its transcendence of our own limitations. We want to reflect and give praise for the surpassing, excelling power and love of God. One way to do this is to allow the intellect to postulate a reality that surpasses *every* limitation that is inherent in the spatio-temporal 'world' of multiple, distinct, and individual beings, including those who are personal agents.

There are, clearly, limitations inherent in the world of beings. At one level, of course, each being is a limitation upon all other beings simply in the sense that no single being can literally *be* another being. I cannot be you or the book in front of me and neither can you or it be me. In that sense a pluralistic world of beings is shot through with limitations. The ontological authenticity of each being limits the ontological 'reach' or inclusiveness of other beings.

Within a spatio-temporal context other limitations are equally obvious. If I exist *in* time, then I am limited in not existing now in the past or in the future. I am limited to the present: I cannot go back now and live in the past (except in rememberance), nor can I now live in the future (except in anticipation or imagination). Also, as a spatial being I cannot be in all spaces simultaneously as long as there are other, distinct beings occupying some of those spaces. And as a spatio-temporally limited being my power of action is also limited. Even in the present, I cannot do everything I could imagine doing—my powers are limited both within me as well as externally by the powers (both passive and active) of other beings with whom I am bound in some set of relational networks.

Because spatio-temporal, pluralistic being is so limited it is understandable why both monism and dualism, in their own ways, have sought to remove God entirely from the restrictions of the universe (understood as the totality of space-time) as we know it.

Not only must God not be a limited being like we are within the universe, God must be completely beyond or transcendent of the universe as a whole, unable (though it is insisted that this is no limitation) even to be compared to the universe since God and it share no common features or underlying principles.

Affirmations of divine transcendence are intended to protect God from the defects and limitations of beings who are relationally interdependent in the world of spatio-temporal experience. Nevertheless, such affirmations cannot sufficiently exhaust the story of the Christian experience of God. Any reality that *is* experienced by us is, in some basic sense, *within* our universe of being and, in that sense, not *entirely* transcendent of it. And so, the language of divine transcendence has had to exist side by side with the language of relationship, of together-boundness in the encounter between God and human persons that constitutes the story of redemption.

The theological obligation of pluralism is to preserve those things about God that the traditional notions of transcendence have tried to preserve, but to do so in a way that does not disconnect God from the community that has experienced God's reality. I believe the metaphysics of agent/action can fulfill that obligation in a way that is faithful both to rational coherence and to the experience of the Christian community with its God.

Pluralism must not simply jettison those dimensions of God's reality that are truly 'beyond' or 'transcendent of' the limitations of human existence. Pluralism must not attempt to flatten out the notion of God so that it becomes nothing more than a single piece in the jigsaw that represents reality as a whole. The reality of God *is* distinctive, unique, and decisive in a way that is not true of other individual beings. But the *character* of God's uniqueness must not be represented in such a way as to divorce it completely, exhaustively, or metaphysically from the reality with which our experience convinces us it is bound in some kind (as yet undetermined) of mutual relationship.

If we push the logic of the metaphysics of agent/action, I believe we can find a set of metaphysical principles that provide for the uniqueness of *all* agents, including God, and that also justify a conceptual representation of at least one Agent as sufficiently different from other agents (without ceasing to be an agent) to be worthy of our worship, praise, and moral response. At the same time, this metaphysics of agent/action can coherently relate the principles of science and intraworldly representation to the principles of divine action without logical paradox or unintelligibility.

In order to appreciate the power of the agent/action 'map' of reality, however, we need to understand both the power and the logic of monism and dualism insofar as they have attempted to represent both the transcendence of God and the experience of the Christian community. Only if we can show that they ultimately fail to make that representation in a fully coherent manner, can we open up space for a consideration of an alternative form of representation.

Monism

At first blush it might appear as if monism is so fundamentally at odds with the Christian conviction that God is together bound with the world that it would have no credibility as a Christian way of understanding God. And in fact in many of its manifestations, especially in some forms of mysticism, monism has been associated with heresy. Nevertheless, monism represents an important response to some assumptions about the nature of God that lie close to the heart of the Christian experience and that are still present in nonmonist concepts of God.

In treating monism, I will be looking at it as an ideal type, as a logically consistent schema for articulating a view of reality given its presuppositions. I am not interested in showing (nor do I think it *could* be shown) that the monistic ideal has been found in an unadulterated form in any Christian theologian. In fact, I believe that one reason for its failure to be perfectly represented in Christian theology is precisely its inability to account satisfactorily for the experience of God as being in relation to other persons, an experience that remains at the core of Christian life even if its reflection in thought is not always consistently developed or preserved. I am also mindful of the fact that a case can be made that *Christian* mysticism, at least in the work of its major expositors, never went the final step into monism proper by collapsing the difference between God and the individual human person. Grace Jantzen's recent "'Where Two Are to Become One': Mysticism and Monism," argues that the most extreme form of unity in Christian mysticism is one of love, not of substance (as monism would require).[1] A union of substance (a denial of distinction or difference) might well occur with*in* the Godhead, but not between the Godhead and human beings. If Jantzen is correct, then while mysticism has a tendency toward monism (and while that tendency is realized in some non-Christian religious traditions), Christian mysticism never relinquishes the fundamental distinction between God and all that is other than God (thus avoiding monism in the strict sense).[2]

Nevertheless, monism as a metaphysical system pushes us to consider what happens to our map of reality if we push to their logical conclusion some basic assumptions about the 'otherness' of God, assumptions that are driven by the fear of limiting God in any way whatsoever. The power and appeal of monism derive from the way in which it tries to drive the human mind beyond all forms of limitation and restriction. Monism has the virtue of working through all the explicit and implicit conditions that could be restrictions on the absoluteness of God. I believe, actually, that monism is perfectly correct in drawing out what it would mean to try to think of reality without limits or conditions of any sort.

Whether that reality is what Christians mean by God is another question. And, if it is not God, then a second question emerges, namely, What is God's relation to this unlimited, unconditioned reality?

In the Christian tradition, a tendency toward monism is found most often in mysticism. Mysticism is itself a highly complex, variegated, and individualized set of experiences and reflections. There is no single, underlying, uniform 'system' of Christian mysticism to which all Christian mystics conform. Most Christian mystics fall closer to what has been called theistic, as opposed to monistic, mysticism because they wish to retain some notion of God as an 'Other', no matter how intimate and close the union between the believer and God becomes. Theistic mysticism comes closer to the ideal of dualism than to monism, even though I believe that, in the end, both forms of mysticism have great difficulty in articulating a coherent understanding of God as an Agent, even one who acts to produce the effects for which mysticism of whatever form yearns. Nevertheless, there are tendencies or vectors of thinking within all forms of mysticism that often arise from and culminate in principles found most clearly and starkly in the monistic ideal. This is especially true with regard to the attempt to remove any and all limitations from God.

Differentiation

At the heart of the monistic view of God is the conviction that only by transcending all *distinctions* or forms of *differentiation* can God's absoluteness be preserved. Or, to put it negatively, differentiation and distinction are the hallmarks of inferior, less than absolute being. The prefix *dis*, which appears before so many words that draw distinctions between things comes from a Greek word for twice. (This suggests, of course, that ultimately dualism and monism have the same root and, as I will argue, come to the same conclusions, though by different trajectories, regarding the nature of God.)

Differentiation is the division into at least two things and, by extension, into many things. Thus differentiation is the ground of pluralism. But monism wants to overcome distinction and differentiation or duality by pointing us toward an absolutely undifferentiated, undivided, nondual, nondistinct reality.

The fundamental deficiency in a differentiated reality is that one being stands 'over-against', divided from, and therefore limited by that which is 'other' than it. Otherness (alterity) constitutes the fundamental defect of reality because each thing that is 'other' than other things to which it stands in relation is limited and conditioned by those other things and they by it. Its being is not their being and their being is not its being. In this sense they mutually condition and exclude each other. Their very existence as other than each other is a sign of their less than absolute or pefect status.

Some monists have used phrases such as the 'curse of thisness and thatness', meaning that to be a 'this' is necessarily to not be a 'that'. The curse is that not being something other than what you are is a limitation: that one thing stands 'out there' as a silent rebuke to another thing's desire to be unlimited and unconditioned by any reality other than itself. The force of monism rests on its appeal to our experience of frustration, incompleteness, or insufficiency *as* beings who exist within spatial and temporal limits and over against other objects. At some very deep level monism believes that we simply 'know' that it is more perfect to be unlimited and unrestricted in all respects. We 'know' this presumably because we feel frustrated, thwarted, blocked, and therefore less than 'absolute' because there are 'others' out there who are not us and who do not automatically conform to our intentions and desires. Carried to its logical conclusion, the belief that perfection consists in the removal of all limits results in a vision of God as absolutely unlimited, unrelated to anything other than Godself, and 'beyond' time and space. From our experience of limitation, God represents absolute freedom, completeness and self-sufficiency. Ultimately, 'other' beings must be regarded as having no 'real' independent status but rather as being simply 'modes' or aspects of God's infinite being.

What monism cannot give any credibility to is the experience of being fulfilled, complete and sufficient only in *relation to* other beings. Nor can monism accept as metaphysically sound the claim that the limitations of the multiplicity of other beings and of time and space are not *inherently* frustrating (though they often are for other reasons).

The philosopher Hegel actually developed a metaphysical scheme in which the entire goal of history was for God to come to consciousness of Godself as the *only* reality by coming to see that all other 'distinct' entities were really Godself in some objectified form. The underlying assumption is that the truly ultimate reality must *include* within itself anything that otherwise appears to be external to itself. Monism is the claim that, essentially, there is only one reality, undivided and undifferentiated.

To call God 'infinite' is, in effect, to assert that there can be no beings 'outside of' God or distinct from God. To be infinite, in traditional theological language, is to be exempt from all the limitations of finite being. It is to have nothing limiting one's being, whether it be time, space, matter, or other beings. Therefore, God's infinity rules out the independent existence of beings external to God's infinite being. God's infinite being is the *only* reality, in which, in some way, apparently 'other' beings are included but not as distinct or differentiated from God.

Monism knows, however, that this claim is not easily grasped by the human mind precisely because our thought structures and the language through which our ideas are expressed presuppose distinction and differentiation. Thus the articulated claims of monism are inherently paradoxical and impossible to state fully in the forms of discursive logic. When we think, we think *of* something *as* something or *in relation* to something else. We characterize things, states of affairs and their relations. To do so, we need to differentiate what we are thinking about from everything else as well as to distinguish one characteristic from others. I cannot think of another person (in order to characterize her as kind) unless I can in some way differentiate her from other persons and characteristics (e.g., as her father and vindictive). Sentences, through which we make truth claims about reality, reflect this fact. They require subjects and predicates. A subject is the 'thing' that we have differentiated from the rest of reality and the predicate is the characterization we have made about that subject. And so, thought and language presuppose differentiation.

Monism does not deny this. Rather it acknowledges it as a justification for insisting that truth must ultimately go beyond what can be grasped in discursive thought and expressed in nonparadoxical language. As W. T. Stace has put it, "All words in all languages are the products of our sensory-intellectual consciousness and express or describe its elements or some combination of them. But as elements (with the doubtful exception of emotions) are not found in the mystical consciousness, it is felt to be impossible to describe it in any words whatever."[3] The mystical consciousness, to which Stace refers, is at the heart of monism. It involves an "apprehension of *an ultimate nonsensuous unity in all things,* a oneness or a One to which neither the senses nor the reason can penetrate. In other words, it entirely transcends our sensory-intellectual consciousness."[4] It is an experience whose core is "an undifferentiated unity—a oneness or unity in which there is no internal division, no multiplicity."[5]

What this means for a concept of God is that God cannot be conceived of as a being alongside other beings, no matter how much power, wisdom, and goodness are ascribed to (the character of) God. Given its presuppositions, monism rightly insists that God stands in no comparative relation to other beings, not even as the most high, most mighty, most loving. To be compared to other beings presupposes both a distinction between God and those beings and a common basis for comparison. It is precisely the differentiation assumed by such a distinction and comparison that monism seeks to transcend.

In the Christian tradition, Paul Tillich has probably done the most to work through the negative implications of viewing God as *a* being above other beings. Tillich has pointed out that even an absolutely superior God is still limited by the conditions of being that God shares with lesser beings and, in particular, by those other beings themselves insofar as God is *not* them. Tillich has argued that the conception of God as a singular entity is always subject to doubt since any 'object' external to us can be doubted by us since its existence can only be known by us indirectly through external evidence in the differentiated world. On the other hand, according to Tillich, if we can affirm that God is 'Being-Itself' or the Ground of Being, that which metaphysically explains singular beings because it is the source of the being which they possess, then that affirmation is beyond doubt since it is presupposed in every claim that we make about particular beings.[6] All particular beings 'have' being and therefore participate in the source of being. But the Ground of Being in which they participate and from which they draw their being is not itself a being nor does it have being since it must transcend the limitations of 'finite' or limited being, including the limitations intrinsic to all singular beings, such as having being but not from themselves.

The Incomprehensibility of God

This means that our ability to conceptualize such a God is virtually nonexistent. As Stace has said, "the mystery of God is essential, absolute, and irremovable . . . the logical intellect is incapable of apprehending Him. . . . God is not a part of the universe . . . and to say that His being lies in a plane, order, or dimension, wholly different from the system of things which constitutes the natural order is to say that God is not capable of being apprehended by concepts."[7] If by 'literal' language we mean words that refer in a straightforward way to the objects about which they intend to communicate, then no 'literal' language refering to God is possible at all. When I use the word 'cat' to refer to the feline creature on my sofa, I am using language in a 'literal' way, at least insofar as we have agreed that this word 'cat' in the English language has a specific kind of denotation that we can exemplify, ostensibly by pointing to the object to which it refers.

The word 'God' is not literal in this sense because 'literally' there is no 'object' out there to which one can point (or even that one can experience *as* an object). If God is not an 'object', then no language, except paradoxical language, is appropriate in referring to God. Stace speaks of a consciousness of undifferentiated unity but is quick to point out that ordinarily we think of consciousness as being 'of' something or other. But the monist consciousness of God is a consciousness with no object: it is not consciousness 'of' anything at all. It is a consciousness with no content. It is not even a consciousness of consciousness, "for then there would be a duality which is incompatible with the idea of an undifferentiated unity."[8] Stace should also acknowledge, of course, that the 'idea' of an undifferentiated unity is also nonliteral, not logically possible, since an idea or concept of that which transcends all concepts is a contradiction in terms.

A great deal has been written about the cognitive coherence of claims about a consciousness of undifferentiated unity.[9] It is not my purpose to subject those claims to the same kind of scrutiny. I am primarily interested in what they imply for a notion of God as a being in relation to other beings. In the end, I believe that if God is not an "Other" in relation to us, then claims 'about' God cannot be cognitively different from claims about those 'states' or experiences whose origin and referent is only themselves and not something external to them.

There is, of course, one sense in which God is an 'Other' in monism. That is the sense in which 'God' is totally unlike the beings that we experience in the universe of differentiation and limitation. God is radically 'Other' than any entities that comprise the finite world of our experiences. But this sense of Other is meant precisely to exclude the concept of God as *an* Other, as a distinct and separate *being* or entity since distinctness and separateness are the very essence of that which God is 'other than'.

Some monists have consistently adopted what has been called a negative theology, insisting that nothing 'positive' or affirmative can be said of God since such affirmations build upon the characteristics of a differentiated world. Even to call God wise or good is to use language drawn from our experience of wisdom and goodness *in* the world of differentiation and thus is to *mis*-characterize God. We get closer to the truth when we insist that God is *not* wise as we are wise, *not* good as we are good, than when we say that God is the wisest or best of all beings.

Even to speak of God as characterizable is to fall closer to theistic mysticism. Monism would prefer to stay closer to the limits of the experience of undifferentiated unity and the consciousness without content or object. Hewing to those limits enables us to see more clearly that monism, as such, has no place for God as 'an Other', but only for the notion of an *experience* that is totally other than our ordinary experiences.

The key to the monist insight is to see the fundamental distinction (the paradox is intentional) between an experience that is totally other than all other experiences and an experience of something or someone that is totally other than all other things or ones. As long as our experience is 'of' something or someone it falls into the inferior world of differentiation and distinction. Thus the experience of God as an Other, no matter how other than us God is in a multitude of ways (e.g., power, goodness, wisdom, etc.), is still an inferior experience compared to one of undifferentiated unity.

Oneness with God

Does this mean, therefore, that God is not together bound with us? In one sense, no. According to monist logic, if 'God' is the term we wish to use to refer to the experience of undifferentiated unity, then 'God' (i.e., the experience itself) and 'we' are together bound in the sense that we are one reality. In the experience of undifferentiated unity the distinction between us and God disappears: if we are now experienced as truly undifferentiated, then there *is* no self to be related to another (God), but only a single, undifferentiated One. This could be taken as the extreme possibility of being together bound—bound, that is, so closely that what is bound becomes literally one, not two in relation.

In another sense, of course, this understanding of boundness so completely dissolves the 'relation' between what is bound that boundness is no longer a meaningful notion. If two things literally become one thing (and not just two things in intimate relation) then there are no longer two things at all: their distinctness is now abolished and only one thing remains. Though the analogy may not be exact, we can think of a drop of water that has been lifted out from the ocean. While it remains apart from the ocean, it and the ocean are differentiated and distinct. But when the drop is returned to the ocean it does not enter into 'relation' with the ocean, nor is it bound with the ocean. 'It', as a drop once differentiated, loses its 'itness', its distinctness, and, once returned, the ocean remains the 'one and only' reality.

There is much debate within and about monism as to the 'status' of the selves who think monistically and seek the experience of undifferentiated unity. Are these selves 'real' or are they only illusions? If they are real, what is their reality compared to the reality of the only 'one', namely undifferentiated unity itself? If they are not real, 'whose' illusions are they? These questions are fascinating and constitute much of the reason for the attraction of monism throughout the centuries. They exercise the deepest parts of the human mind.

In fact, I believe that monism's appeal often rests on its ability to call us beyond the everyday kind of thinking that constitutes our attempts to get around in a differentiated world. Monism suggests to us that there is a new way of thinking that transcends the limitations intrinsic to intramundane reflection. This new way of thinking stretches the limits of thought to their breaking point and then opens up to us a 'world' beyond thought as we know it—it offers an experience of incomparable 'otherness' precisely by transcending the distinction between one thing and another.

But the question is not whether monist thinking is stretching or exciting or new or simply different. The question, for Christians, is whether it is capable of representing the Christian experience of being in relation with another Person who has created, redeemed, and renewed them. Clearly, my argument suggests that it is not. A different conceptuality is needed to do that—one that is able not only to represent God as a personal Other but also to do so coherently, without violating the criteria of meaning and truth (though without being simply reduced to them) that we use in the everyday world of action and experience.

But what does monism's logic reach? Surely the sophistication and appeal of monism are not simply to be dismissed as useless or as fanciful. I find the study of monism intrinsically satisfying—there is a genuine delight in following the challenging and paradoxical conclusions of monist thought. But in the end, I think those conclusions tell us more about the delights of stretching the mind than they do about the reality they admit cannot be thought. They tell us about the possibility of an experience seemingly without limits of any kind. It may even be possible that there is such a thing as an experience of undifferentiated unity. How one could tell, however, even to oneself, that it is that experience and not another, is not easy to see. To know something as an experience of *this* kind rather than of *that* kind requires some kind of prior awareness of what an experience of *this* kind would be like and that, in turn, requires the ability to discriminate and differentiate this experience from other experiences. And once one has 'come out of' the experience, especially one that is alleged to have transcended all concepts, how can one tell which concepts and words are appropriate for referring to it? There is a host of problems, voluminously pored over in the literature on mysticism, about these kinds of issues.

All I am suggesting is that there may well be an experience of such a radically different nature that it compels those who have had it to try to refer to it according to the logic and in the language of monistic mysticism. But that experience need not be taken to be the experience of God. (Of course, one has the right to name an experience anything one wants and one may choose to call it the experience of God as many mystics do). But as long as God is in some residual and irreducible way experienced by Christians as an 'Other', as a distinct, individual being with whom they are in relation (no matter how complex that relation is), the logic and language of monism are inappropriate for fully representing that God.

The charge has been made that to consider God as anything other than the experience of undifferentiated unity is to reduce God to something less than ultimate. It is to put God 'back' into the world of limitation and thus to limit God. That is the charge to which both dualism and pluralism must address themselves. As we shall see, dualism attempts to answer the charge by insisting that God is without limits even while trying to preserve some sense of God's otherness from the world with which God is in some kind of primordial as well as ongoing relation. Pluralism attempts to answer the charge by observing that even dualism ultimately falls into some of the monist's logic, thereby qualifying in a seriously damaging way what it *wants* to say about God as a being in relation to the world. Pluralism, in the mode of conceiving God as a personal Agent, then goes on to argue that only if God is in literal relationship with other beings can God be together bound with them and be the agent of their creation, redemption, and renewal.

Notes

1. Grace Jantzen, " 'Where Two Are to Become One': Mysticism and Monism," in Godfrey Vesey, ed., *The Philosophy in Christianity*, Royal Institute of Philosophy Lecture Series no. 25, supplement to *Philosophy*, 1989 (Cambridge: Cambridge University Press, 1989), pp. 147–66.

2. Jantzen even suggests that the 'pervasive self-deception' of so many interpreters of mysticism as monism in Christianity may well be due to their desire to utilize the sexual imagery of much mystical literature in order to devalue the feminine. Because they read the sexual imagery as a symbol for the complete loss of the soul in God, and the feminine as a symbol for the soul, this reading reinforces the notion that maleness ultimately triumphs over the feminine by annihilating it.

3. Walter T. Stace, "Subjectivity, Objectivity and the Self," in Jacob Needleman, A. K. Bierman, and James A. Gould, eds., *Religion for a New Generation* (New York: Macmillan, 1977), p. 414.

4. Ibid., p. 415.

5. Ibid., p. 419.

6. See especially Paul Tillich, "Being and God", and "The Reality of God", in *Systematic Theology* (Chicago: University of Chicago Press, 1951), 1:211–89; and *The Courage to Be* (New Haven, Conn.: Yale University Press, 1952), pp. 155–90.

7. Walter T. Stace, *Time and Eternity* (Princeton: Princeton University Press, 1951), pp. 153–55.

8. Stace, "Subjectivity, Objectivity and the Self," p. 420.

9. See especially William J. Wainwright, *Mysticism: A Study of Its Nature, Cognitive Value and Moral Implications* (Madison: University of Wisconsin Press, 1981).

3

Dualism

While monism has *a* form which is intentionally theistic, dualism by and large intends to be theistic in all its forms. Dualism is the logical model of reality in which God is affirmed as the ultimate reality upon which all other, nondivine beings depend, but which is Itself distinguished from them in a basic, qualitatively different, ontological way. Dualism does not try to escape from distinction or differentiation, at least in the first instance. It accepts it as the very condition necessary for affirming the superiority and absoluteness of God over against a temporal, finite, and limited world of creatures. Ultimately, however, dualism tends toward monism to the extent that it recognizes that differentiation of creature from Creator suggests ontological limits on the latter.

In my treatment of dualism I will be regarding it as I did monism: a logical construct of ideas about God, intending to be both coherent and logically consistent. Again, there is probably no Christian theologian who perfectly embodies the logical schema of dualism in all respects. However, dualism has been more central to most mainstream Christian theologies than either monism or pluralism. I believe this is so because dualism does intend to preserve the distinctness, the 'otherness', of God that is at the heart of the Christian *experience* of God. Dualism also intends, as does monism, to remove offending limits on God that might appear in false or immature notions of God. In other words, the strength of dualism lies in its attempt to represent simultaneously both God's limitlessness and God's distinctness, since the latter is a precondition for God's *relation* to that which is not Godself.

The issue for coherent, rational reflection is whether dualism, in its most logically consistent form, *can*, without contradiction or incoherence, affirm both God as absolutely 'Other' than everything else and the possibility of genuine relationships between God and human persons. In short, can dualism maintain both the condition for relation (which is distinction between beings sharing *some* identical ontological conditions) between God and others, and the 'absolute' Otherness of God, that is, God as radically unlike, wholly Other than, anything else?

I will argue that dualism ultimately falls incoherently between the two extremes that it wants to maintain. If it stresses the possibility of relationship between God and others it must necessarily qualify God's absolute "Otherness" and if it stresses God's absolute "Otherness" it must necessarily abandon the possibility of God's relationship with those others. If it goes too far in the first direction, it reduces God to 'anthropomorphic' levels. If it goes too far in the second direction, it makes God into an absolute 'mystery' completely beyond human comprehension. And if it tries to find a middle ground between these extremes it winds up in a form of monism in which all 'things' participate in God's Being without distinction and differentiation.

Divine Otherness and Knowability

Referring to our knowledge of God in the dualist tradition, David Burrell has put it nicely:

> If the status of intentional creator places God outside 'all things' as their 'beginning and end,' then divinity must be said to be outside that universe which forms the context for all that we know and do. . . . And so God must be deemed unknowable, since we will not be able to characterize the divine essence as we do things in the world such as events, objects, species, [or] numbers. . . . So the quintessential theological task becomes one of formulating that 'distinction' so as to assure the required transcendence, while allowing us to have some notion of what it is that we are referring to in addressing 'the Holy One,' [or] 'our Father'[1]

Burrell goes on to note that we cannot treat the distinction between God and the world "as though it were one *in* the universe" for that would lead either to denigrating the world (God being the only *real* reality—monism, in short) or making God *part* of a larger whole in which God is less than Absolute and thus caught within the limiting conditions of the finite universe. But at the same time, Burrell argues, God cannot be *completely other* than the universe "if we are to use the name *creator*, or if divinity is to be in any way accessible to our discourse." The solution to this dilemma, for Burrell, is to "articulate the distinction between God and the world in such a way as to respect the reality appropriate to each."[2] He believes that in the work of St. Thomas Aquinas one can find the appropriate distinction between God and the world to enable us to conceive created beings in relation to their creator, as well as to articulate "what distinguishes the source of all from everything else which is."[3]

Burrell is right in believing that in Aquinas one can find both the premise of dualism and one of the most ingenious and influential ways of articulating it. It is, therefore, worth our time to examine Aquinas' project and its result in order to determine whether he (or Thomism generally) has, in fact, provided a coherent and adequate treatment both of God's distinction from the world and, more importantly, of God's loving relationship to and action upon that world. At the heart of our examination should be the Thomistic understanding of God's 'act' of creation, or God as creator of finite creatures.

Aquinas makes it absolutely clear that God is not to be conceived as simply one more being in a series or set of finite beings. The clarity of his position should not be clouded by a superficial reading of his famous proofs for the existence of God. The second proof, the one that appeals to our experience of causality, sometimes appears to be proving the existence of God as a 'first' cause in a series of causes, but this is misleading.

The proof, briefly stated, argues as follows. We experience and therefore know that a cause must precede its effect. Nothing in our world causes itself. But we cannot go back to infinity in the search for causal explanation, for then there would be no intermediate causes and no first cause, and thus no ultimate (i.e., present) effect. But this is plainly false—there are intermediate and ultimate effects. "Therefore it is necessary to admit a first cause, to which everyone gives the name of God."[4]

Critics have rightly pointed out that if we understand by 'God' that cause that temporally precedes all other causes and effects, we have merely found the first cause *in time*. But a first temporal cause is still a cause *within* the universe of temporal causes and effects and thus not adequate as an explanation of why there is a universe of temporal cause and effect at all or in the first place. The adequacy of explanation for the very existence of the universe as such appeals, of course, to the principle of sufficient reason, which holds that everything must have an explanation not only as to why it is what it is but also as to why it is at all, and that the explanation must be from 'outside' itself. That is, nothing explains itself. (As Thomas notes in his 'proofs', nothing moves itself and nothing causes itself.) The explanation for what and why something is is always 'external' to the thing itself. Thus, if we are seeking the explanation of the universe, the principle of sufficient reason demands that it be found in some reality 'outside' the universe. A temporal first cause only explains other, later temporal causes and effects but cannot explain why there *is* a sequence of temporal causes and effects in the first place.

It is generally assumed by most Thomists that Thomas did not intend to prove only a first temporal cause. He wanted to reach a reality beyond temporality, spatiality, and everything else that comprises 'finitude'. His proofs begin to point us away from finitude, even if, taken literally, they do not carry us cognitively 'into' what is beyond it.

But this is precisely the problem. The principle of sufficient reason demands a God wholly other than the conditions of finitude that comprise the universe, but reason, logic, thought, and language (being part of the universe and subject to its finite limitations) cannot bring us (in thought) beyond that which conditions them. We need to speak of God as the explanation of the universe, and yet the universe constrains the meaning we can attribute to any such explanatory speech when it attempts to convey meaning about that which is transcendent of the universe in which that speech occurs.

Yet, as long as we do not deny the reality of the universe, we are forced to affirm the ontological gap that must separate the universe from its explanation—and this gap is the premise of dualism. The dualist rightly sees that to deny the ontological gap is either to collapse God into the world or to eliminate the distinction between God and God's creatures, which lies at the heart of the experience of worship and adoration.

Paradoxes abound once we try to speak of that which explains the universe from outside itself. We speak of God *as if* God were a singular being in relation to other singular beings. Even though we refer to God as *the* most powerful, *the* most wise, most holy, most loving, and so one, we speak as if God is in a category of being in which comparisons from the lowliest to the most exalted are appropriate. But the premise of such comparison is precisely what must be negated if we are to do justice to the ontological gap that separates God from everything else. To compare beings to each other *at all* presupposes that they have enough in common to be comparable. But if God and human persons had enough in common to be compared, then they would comprise, together, an ontological set that would need an explanation from outside itself, thus eliminating the very function that God's ontological otherness (as the explanatory principle) was intended to provide in the first place.

For many people one strength of Aquinas and Thomism generally is that they take these criticisms seriously and try to find a way to deny a basis for comparing God with creatures and to affirm God's reality as an explanation for the universe in which comparisons do occur. At the same time, they try to find a way in which to preserve the biblical and Christian language of a God who creates, sustains, loves, and saves the very creatures whose being God explains. Thomism is not content to leave God as an abstract and arid explanation. It is committed to defending God as in some sense a 'personal' reality, caring for God's universe.

Divine Predicates and Negative Language

One paradox that emerges from the attempt to affirm God as ontologically other than everything else in and including the universe is that such affirmation must be essentially negative. Most Thomists have conceded that no literal, affirmative language can apply to God. We cannot say that God *is* wise, good, loving, and so forth in the way that we are because the *meaning* of these terms originates within and is bounded by the finite experience of their finite employers. As David Burrell has said, in speaking of Aquinas' view of our language about God, such language "lacks the structural isomorphism requisite to any statement which purports to refer to its object."[5] Thus, we can never say what God is, only what God is not. Let us take as an example the term 'loving' because it has a clearly relational implication. If we say of another human person that she is loving, we generally mean that she is both interiorly disposed to care for others and that she will act toward other persons in ways that exemplify her disposition. She will both 'feel' loving and act lovingly. We know the meaning of the word 'love' in this case by its manifestations in her life and we know it in our own lives by how we feel as well (a feeling that we can infer in someone else whose actions seem similar to our loving deeds). Love is irreducibly relational and manifests itself in the way one person treats another.

Now it is clear that we cannot apply 'loving' as a literal ascription to an ontologically transcendent dualist God because its meaning as relationally manifested is not adequate. God is not simply another being acting alongside us, exemplifying a feeling of care for and attraction to other persons in ways that we can observe. Dualism requires that God not be understood as a being alongside other beings. At best God is affirmed as the power that makes possible the existence of finite beings standing alongside other beings, but God is not one of those beings. Thus 'loving' as we use of it of human persons is not an appropriate ascription for God. We can, however, insist that God is *not* loving as we are loving and by this negative affirmation we can begin, according to Thomism, to get a 'sense' of God. God is *not* good, wise, loving, powerful, and so on, *as we are,* yet God's reality is necessary if we (as well as these qualities) are *to be and to be loving, and so on* at all.

Some Thomists have gone so far as to say that we can only say what God is not in order to affirm that God is 'to be' itself. God is the power of being but is not *a* being. As Etienne Gilson has said, "beyond form which makes a being be such a being belonging to a given determined species, we must . . . place 'to be', or the act-of-being, which makes the substance thus constituted a 'being'."[6] The 'act-of-being' is God, or being-itself. It is the very principle of reality but it is not a singular entity *within* reality (at least as reality is construed by us to be coextensive with the 'universe' of finite being which we inhabit). God is the pure act of existing, not a 'something' that exists by the power of something else alongside other 'somethings'.

As *not* a being, God is *not* changeable (mutable), temporal, spatial, limited in knowledge, wisdom, love, and goodness even though God is *in God's own way* knowing, wise, loving, and good. This is despite our inability to see or say *how* God is these things because God can be these things only in God's own way (appropriate to an ontologically transcendent reality), which is radically different from our way of being these things. We can affirm that God is not any of these things *as we are* and at the same time affirm that God is the power of being that enables them *to be* at all. As the power of being that underlies them, God is somehow rightly attributed these qualities but the 'somehow' is irreducibly opaque to us because it belongs to a reality whose being we do not share in.

The difficulty emerges when we try to say in different words what we think we are saying when we affirm that God is 'act-of-being' but not *a* being linked in a similarly constituted ontological chain with other beings. The difficulty is language itself and con-sistent Thomists recognize this, pointing us toward paradox, anal-ogy, or silence. Before plunging on into this murky terrain, how-ever, we need to spell out briefly why language as such is the source of our difficulty in speaking about God.

To speak or write *at all* presupposes that words used in one context have a meaning that carries over into at least one other context, both for speaker and for hearer. The use of words presup-poses some minimal shared ontological context that can provide the basis for the transfer of meaning from one 'place' within that con-text to another. When I use the word 'chair' I, as speaker, know the context from which I have drawn that word. Having learned it in one or more contexts as a child, I now know that what I am sit-ting upon (another context) is (or can be meaningfully referred to as) a 'chair'. I also know, or hope, that your learning has led you to move from the contexts in which you learned the meaning of the word 'chair' to the present shared context in which you and I are looking at the same object. My ability to communicate with you about this object (by referring to it as a chair) depends upon our mutual ability to transfer meaning from context to context against a background of similar ontological conditions (e.g., that which we call a chair must meet certain basic ontological expectations, such as bearing the weight of one who sits upon it). In other words, the transfer of meaning from one context to another presupposes a gen-eral background of shared ontological meaning and experience.

By employing negative language ('X' is *not* this or that) we are trying to eliminate any shared ontological context between the object to which we want to refer and the objects from which we originally learned the meaning of the concept or ascription we want to deny of 'X'. Thus, when we want to speak of God in a dualist perspective, we want to eliminate as much of a shared ontological context as possible between ourselves and God (without of course denying that God is somehow 'responsible' for our context in the first place). We want to insist, along with Aquinas, that no literal attribution to God of qualities in our context is possible through human language. Our discourse about God, as Burrell puts it, lacks the "structural isomorphism requisite to any statement which pur-ports to refer to its object."[7]

Now if we were willing to stop at this point, the demands of consistency would have been met. God simply cannot be referred to at all. But virtually no one except the mystic who seems willing to retreat into silence (the only alternative to the use of language) *is* willing to stop here. As the language about God as 'act-of-being' makes clear, *some* words continue to be used with respect to God. And it is interesting to note that these words have at least a superficial resemblance to the kinds of words whose intitial context of meaning is that of beings *who act*, the very kind of beings who are capable of loving relationships and decisive action with respect to others, the kind of beings, in short, who seem to be at the heart of the Christian *experience* of God.

But the dualist perspective is scrupulous in reminding us that while there are words which we *will* use in referring to God, these words are not to be understood in such a way that we can simply transfer meaning from one context (the finite) to another (the infinite) against the background of shared ontological conditions without some significant loss of meaning. This reminder is, I believe, the fatal block to using the dualist approach to express our experience of being loved by God. For in the end its use of action/agent language is not sufficient to provide a basis for an understanding of God as a loving Agent who acts to create, sustain, and fulfill us *in* our ontological context. Even the doctrine of analogy, which is traditionally called on to provide some kind of alternative between completely equivocal and univocal language about God cannot override the barrier to meaning that the lack of 'structural isomorphism' erects. I share in the judgment of another of the 'new metaphysicians', George Allan, who has said that "the assertion of something at the extremes of experience that is of a different sort than what constitutes the heart of experience is no more than a failure of nerve, a flight from reality into comforting illusion."[8]

God as Act-of-Being and as Creator

The notion of 'act' or 'act-of-being' is not identical to what we ordinarily understand to be an 'agent' who acts. *Actus* is, in fact, according to Burrell, a 'master metaphor' guiding Aquinas' 'grammatical' treatment of God.[9] It must be understood by reference to its counterpart, potency. Something is in potency if it is not yet complete, if it has not yet achieved the fullness of its 'potential' or being. By contrast, a being is in act when it is complete, when it is full being, lacking nothing. As 'pure Act' God lacks nothing—God is the fullness of Being Itself. Using 'Act' in this fashion is a way of pointing to the uniqueness of God—to God's lack of structural isomorphism with any other beings all of whom are still in potency to some degree. God, as contrasted with everything other than God, lacks nothing, and is therefore limitless. God is absolutely transcendent, not even "a prototype within the genus of substance, but the prototype of all being, transcending all genera."[10]

'Act,' however, also carries the connotation of 'doing'. Burrell insists that for Aquinas 'act' has an intentional, active dimension to it. But what, in fact, is it, that God, as pure Act, *does*? This is the heart of the matter. Certainly, as Thomists insist, part of God's 'action' must consist in God's creation of everything other than God. In addition, God, as far as Christians are concerned, 'reveals' Godself and 'saves' them. God 'loves' them and 'cares for' them. These certainly seem like actions of an Agent. But are they?

Let's look at one example of a divine action, that of creation. In one sense this is the most basic kind of divine act since it is the very act by which God brings into being everything other than God. In speaking of creation Aquinas is quite clearly using agent language. It must be, Aquinas says, that "all things . . . are caused by one First Being, Who possesses being most perfectly."[11]

To speak of God as agent or cause is, of course, precisely what we *need* to say if we want to have God as the 'source' of all that is —that is the intrinsic meaning of the notion of 'act-of-being' as well as of the initial distinction between God and the 'universe' in the first place. Unless God were somehow to be affirmed as the 'ground' or explanation of the universe, God's reality would be irrelevant, at least to us and our universe.

But already we have fallen into a confusion of language by employing words such as 'cause', 'creator', 'source,' and so on. All that we have said previously now comes back to remind us that these words do not share a similar ontological context with God. They are drawn initially from our finite, human experience of causing and creating and they presuppose that finite ontological context. What does it mean to use the same terms in a radically different, ontologically transcendent context? Certainly God is not 'cause' or creator as we are cause and creator. At the very least we know that we create out of preexisting material. But God creates *ex nihilo*, out of nothing. We don't literally know what that means since we have no experience of it and can conceive of no analogue to it that does not already presuppose a shared ontological context within which it *is* an analogue.

But beyond the difficulty of grasping creation *ex nihilo*, there is the problem of getting a conceptual grasp of 'create' or 'cause' when it is applied in a totally different ontological context. When I cause something to come to be I stand in a relationship with that which is now 'other' than I. In some sense that which is now 'other' conditions and limits me in at least the minimal sense that it exists 'over-against' me, as 'not-me'. But can this be said of God? No, not if God is understood to be limitless, not bounded in any way by anything other than God. Creation seems to be an act by which one being enters into relationship with another being (which it has created and which is dependent on it). And relationships have a limiting dimension to them in the sense that the partners in the relationship limit each other insofar as the one is not the other (even though one partner may have had to make the initial decision to become self-limiting). But the limiting, relational aspect of creation would seem to be unacceptable to the dualist notion of God, which received its impetus in the first place precisely in order to avoid limitation and relationality. Thomas is quite clear that while God's effects have a relation to 'Him', 'He' has no relation to 'His' effects. "Since, therefore, God is outside the whole order of creation, and all creatures are ordered to Him, and not conversely, it is manifest that creatures are really related to God Himself; whereas in God there is no real relation to creatures."[12] If a relation were predicated of God as really existing in God, it would follow that God would be changed as the relationship itself changes, which is, of course, incompatible with God's being immutable. Therefore, God has no real relations with anything other than God, and we attribute relations to God as cause or creator, according to Thomas, because we can do no other, according to the creaturely limitations of our intellects.

But dualists do not want to give up the Cause-effect, Creator-creature 'relation' between God and the universe because it is the very basis for belief in God in the first place. At this point, they usually appeal to the notion of *analogy* to justify the continuing use of 'cause' and 'creator' to refer to God.

Notes

1. David B. Burrell, *Knowing the Unknowable God: Ibn-Sina, Maimonides, Aquinas* (Notre Dame, Ind.: University of Notre Dame Press, 1986), p. 2.

2. Ibid., 17.

3. Ibid., 18.

4. St. Thomas Acquinas, *The Summa Theologica*, part 1, question 2, article 3, in Anton C. Pegis, ed., *Basic Writings of Saint Thomas Aquinas* (New York: Random House, 1945), 1:22.

5. David B. Burrell, *Aquinas: God and Action* (Notre Dame, Ind.: University of Notre Dame Press, 1979), pp. 13–14.

6. Etienne Gilson, *The Christian Philosophy of St. Thomas Aquinas* (New York: Random House, 1956), p. 33.

7. Burrell, *God and Action*, pp. 13–14.

8. George Allan, "The Primacy of the Mesocosm," in Robert C. Neville, ed., *New Essays in Metaphysics* (Albany: State University of New York Press, 1987), pp. 26–27.

9. Burrell, *God and Action*, p. 116.

10. Ibid., p. 25, referring to Aquinas, *Summa Theologica*, 1.3.6, reply to second objection, and 1.3.5.1.

11. Aquinas, *Summa Theologica*, III 44.1, in Pegis, *Basic Writings*, p. 427.

12. Aquinas, *Summa Theologica*, 1.13.7, in Pegis, *Basic Writings*, p. 124.

4

Refining Dualism

The Doctrine of Analogy

Realizing that language about God can be neither univocal (trans-
ferring meaning without qualification from one context to another
against the background of shared ontological conditions), nor
equivocal (having radically different meanings, completely unable
to transfer meaning from one ontological context to another, since
this would vitiate the purpose of having God as an ontologically
transcendent principle of *explanation*), Thomists generally resort
to a doctrine of analogy to give meaning to language about God.
An analogous term is one that is neither univocal nor equivocal. It
presumably conveys some nonliteral but nonequivocal meaning
from one ontological context to another. "Whatever is said of God
and creatures is said according as there is some relation of the creature to God as to its principle and cause, wherein all the perfec-
tions of things preexist excellently. Now this mode of community
is a mean between pure equivocation and simple univocation. For
in analogies the idea is not, as it is in univocals, one and the same;
yet it is not totally diverse as in equivocals."[1]

But problems arise with the doctrine of analogy. It seems
unproblematic at first blush to attribute wisdom to God (provided
we can justify thinking of God as a cause of wisdom), but there
seems to be nothing to prevent us from attributing speed or color
to God since God must be the cause of these attributes in finite

things as well. But if we can attribute to God *any* finite attribute (except those, perhaps, that imply a *lack* of being or virtue), then it seems as if we have not gained anything in our search for some minimal knowledge of God. It is even more troubling to be reminded that in God there is no distinction of attributes since God is primordially simple (i.e., not complex and differentiated).

It is not without significance that the primary justification for using analogous terms is the conviction that God is the 'cause' or source of the ontological context in which the analogous term first takes on meaning. For example, we can call God 'wise' because God is the cause of wisdom in human persons. God is not wise as we are wise but as 'act-of-being', God is the source of human wisdom. As source God can be called wise analogously. We do not know *how* God is wise but we do apparently know that God's wisdom is related to God in the only way appropriate for something to be related to that which is infinite, just as our wisdom is related to us in the only way appropriate for something finite. Thus God's wisdom is analogous to ours in that God's wisdom and our wisdom are similarly related to their analogates appropriate to the respective but different ontological status of each.

But this doesn't really get us very far because if, as Eric Mascall, a proponent of analogy, concedes, "there is, literally, all the difference in the world between the relation between two analogates in the finite realm and that between God and a creature,"[2] then we have gained nothing in terms of our knowledge of God by asserting what has been called the analogy of proportionality. In fact some have argued that this analogy ultimately must fall back on the analogy of attribution, which is the first one we mentioned. The analogy of attribution assumes God as the cause of what is being attributed to a finite analogate (e.g., wisdom).

But the problem here seems equally insurmountable. The concept 'cause' must itself be regarded as an analogy. God cannot be a cause in a univocal sense since that would make God a cause *as we are* causes, inasmuch as the initial meaning of cause derives from our finite experience of being causes. Nor can God be a cause in an equivocal sense because this would eliminate the very 'connection' between God and the world that our analogical language is attempting to establish. Therefore 'cause' must be treated as an analogy. But if the doctrine of analogy depends upon the cogency of the preanalogical notion of God causing in us the attributes which we then attribute to God analogically, we have moved into a vicious circle of reasoning.

We cannot justify using the concept of 'cause' for God unless we can first justify our belief that God is a cause similar enough to us to be understood as 'causing' in us the attributes that we want to attribute to God, however analogically. But we cannot justify our belief that God's causality *is* similar enough to ours unless we assume the truth of the doctrine of analogy in the first place, and that we cannot do without assuming what we are setting out to prove.

Burrell has suggested one way around this problem. If God is 'act-of-being' or Pure Act, then God does not have to *do* anything (such as cause something to happen). Whatever is *in act* is already the source of other things in that their very being depends on its Being. But its Being does not need to *do* anything to, about, for, or with respect to the situation of other beings. It is enough that Pure Act simply *be*. Finite beings, by the mere fact of their dependence on Being, are sufficiently 'caused' by Being and no further 'action' by Being is necessary.[3]

Burrell's suggestion may make sense at the level of conceptual abstraction, but it forfeits any notion of God as *an acting being*. Burrell admits this (divine creation for Aquinas, he says, is not a question of action but of a relation of dependence).[4] A God who plans, loves, decides, reveals, and fulfills is an acting being and not simply Being on whom all other beings are ontologically dependent in the sense of participating in the power of being that it is. But *an* acting being is too similar to acting beings in the finite ontological context to be the basis for an analogy for God understood as Pure Act or act-of-being.

The result is that analogy does not truly help us to articulate a belief that God acts to create, sustain, and save us. The problem with analogy, in the Thomist, dualistic perspective, is that it cannot adequately hook on to or provide a logically continuous transition into a radically different ontological context from the one in which it originated. The difference in the contexts is so radical, so qualitative (and, necessarily so, given the function God is asked play, namely as explanation of all that is ontologically other than God) that no term or concept can transfer meaning from one context to the other.

Thus the logic of dualism plays itself out into what Aquinas himself seems to have accepted near the end of his life. Looking back on his writing, after some kind of mystical experience, he declared it all to be "but straw," and is reputed to have thereafter lapsed into silence with respect to God. Dualism does not intend to collapse the fundamental difference between God and the finite realm. In this sense, it wants to avoid the monist conclusion that there *is* only one realm, namely the infinite. But the logic of dualism requires that God explain the finite realm by being absolutely and completely other than the finite realm. And in this sense it reaches the monist position of denying context-comparable meaning to all finitely derived and grounded terms and concepts when applied to the infinite.

Transcendental Thomism

In what has come to be called 'transcendental' Thomism, the argument is made that a careful examination of the human intellect reveals a sense of God as the 'absolute horizon' of human thought. Our intellect is dynamically driven toward this horizon as toward an unrestricted act of understanding (completing what in the human case are always restricted and conditioned acts of understanding). God is 'revealed' as the absolutely 'unconditioned' on which all conditioned acts are grounded. What we know in the ontological context of proportionate being (i.e., proportioned to our limited ability to know) is, in Emerich Coreth's words, "possible only under condition of a simply unconditioned presupposition. Thus the conditionally unconditioned presupposes ... something which is unconditionally unconditioned. ... Therefore, the mind's dynamism can reach the existent in its unconditioned validity only if it always anticipates the simply unconditioned; the intellectual dynamism, through which we grasp being in its unconditional validity, is possible only on the basis of the intellectual anticipation of the simply unconditioned within whose horizon we are able to know beings in their conditioned unconditionality."[5] But our minds cannot stop with knowing finite things. The dynamism of our intellect "proceeds necessarily beyond every finite object ... towards the infinite itself. It can reach its fulfillment only in the unlimited."[6] And Coreth insists that our "original immediate knowledge" of Absolute Being "demands the Absolute Being as its first cause, that is, it stands with respect to Absolute Being in a relation of causal dependence."[7]

It may be true that the human mind requires some kind of pointing beyond or below the totality of the finite. There may be what transcendental Thomism has called a demand of reason that we postulate an infinitely other, qualitatively different ontological reality than the one we are and inhabit. But pointing and postulating are not in themselves justifications for attributing objective reality to that which we take to be what we postulate or point toward. It may be that the most we can do is point mutely and postulate emptily. And it may be that our pointing and postulating do not get us any closer to the reality of that which we experience as creating, sustaining, and fulfilling us. It may be that the demands of reason culminate only in an intellectual abstraction which does, in fact, fulfill the dynamism of the intellect but the identity of this abstraction with a living God is not demonstrated or even self-evident. It is certainly not obvious that the 'horizon' demanded by our intellectual dynamism can in any way be understood meaningfully as the 'cause' of the ontological context out of which that demand has arisen.

It is not insignificant, with due respect to Tillich, that transcendental Thomism insists that what is reached by the intellect as it drives toward the absolutely unconditioned is in no way a being alongside other beings.[8] In this sense the concept of God as an active agent has no particular standing in our attempt to understand God. Nevertheless, God is affirmed as distinct or differentiated from all objects *within* the divine horizon. "The differentiation between the ineffable term or 'horizon' of human transcendence and all finite being is precisely what allows us to perceive objects *as finite*, and thus to differentiate them from the absolute horizon itself and from each other. For this reason, the absolute horizon, as the condition for the possibility for all categorical distinctions, cannot itself be differentiated by the same categorical norms that apply *within* the horizon."[9] In this sense God is distinct from the world, but transcendental Thomism insists that this distinction is *not* a duality in the sense of there being two entities that form part of a larger whole. Karl Rahner says that the difference between God and other beings is a difference 'in' God, or even 'is identical with God'.[10] As Richard Viladesau explicates this view, it seems as if it wants to affirm simultaneously God's absolute distinctness from 'his' creation and the real 'otherness' of the world, which is really related 'to' God (classical dualism), and God as the fullness of being, apart from which there is nothing, and who contains the world's 'otherness' in himself (pantheism). It is interesting to note that there are some Hindus who believe that Aquinas' view of God as 'pure act' is the same as the monist view in the *Advaita Vedanta*.[11]

At the very least, one would have to say that transcendental Thomism leaves us with a sense of both paradox and some confusion. It wants to draw distinctions in order to differentiate God from the conditioned world of proportionate being and then wants to deny those distinctions (through a Tillichian appeal to a notion of finite being 'participating' in infinite being) in order to avoid too radical a separation of God from the world. What is not clear is whether the resulting notion of God provides the religious believer with a reality who can enter into creative and nurturing relationship with the self over and above its 'role' as intellectual resolution of an intellectual drive.

It may be possible, even desirable from the point of view of worship, to tease apart 'that which' seems 'indicated' by our demand for a 'wholly other,' ontologically distinct,' reality and that loving, active Person who seems 'indicated' by our experience of being loved and acted upon by someone who has made all the difference *in the world* to us. There is something tantalizing, haunting, mysterious about what Rudolf Otto called the *mysterium tremendum*, the numinous.[12] But we don't need to hypostatize it into something that we need to think about *as if* it were an acting being while at the same time vigorously *denying* that it *is* an acting being. It may be possible to accept the cognitive attraction to what is cognitively inaccessible without accepting the identification of 'this' with God.

Process Theology's Concept of Creativity

Alfred North Whitehead's original vision of process theology included a concept of God as the chief 'exemplification' of the underlying Ultimate, Creativity. There is much in this notion that speaks directly to the issue at hand. Whitehead regards creativity as the 'given' force or drive underlying the universe. It is the "universal of universals characterizing ultimate matter of fact. It is that ultimate principle by which the many, which are the universe disjunctively, become the one actual occasion, which is the universe conjunctively."[13] But as such, creativity is not 'actual', that is, it is not an efficient cause, not an actual entity or occasion. It does not create, but is the context within which creation by actual entities takes place. Creativity "is without a character of its own in exactly the same sense in which the Aristotelian 'matter' is without a character of its own. *It is the ultimate notion of the highest generality at the base of actuality.*"[14] So in one sense, creativity is more basic than God ("God is the primordial creature"),[15] but God is the chief, and therefore actual, exemplification, instantiation, embodiment, or actualization of creativity. God is the 'aboriginal instance' of creativity, the aboriginal condition that qualifies its action. God is the 'eternal primordial character'.[16] The only 'real' things are actual occasions of which God is the chief. Compared to creativity, God is *actually* effective (in the peculiar sense that process theology gives to the notion of action) because only exemplifications of creativity have ontologically 'real' status ("agency belongs exclusively to actual occasions").[17] Creativity is, in one sense, nonexistent, since only *actual* entities exist. It does not *do* anything, it is not a distinct subject *in* the world in which action and relationship occur. There is, in Whitehead's view, "no meaning to 'creativity' apart from its 'creatures'. . . ."[18] It does not even explain why things are the way they are. It is the given in and on which individual beings operate. It is the ontological 'context' in which the 'existence' of beings occurs. In this sense, as an individual being, God exists, as do all the other actual entities, even though they are, as such, actualizations of creativity. And, Whitehead reminds us, "creativity is always found *under conditions, and described as conditioned.* . . . The non-temporal act of all-inclusive unfettered valuation [God in his primordial nature] is at once creature of creativity ['the primoridal created fact'] and a condition for creativity."[19] God, in short, is the entity with which we have to deal. It is God's actions that make all the difference in the world, since creativity is not an agent. Creativity has a metaphysical priority but not an actual priority in affecting the lives of all other entities. God's priority is more real and more effectual than the metaphysical priority of creativity, even though the latter is the metaphysical presupposition of the former. Religiously, then, God is what matters. It is only with God (again, in the sense peculiar to process theology) that we can have a real relationship, not with creativity.

Now I would suggest that if we want to retain the notions of Horizon, Act-of-Being, Ground, or Unconditioned we do so by identifying them with something like Whitehead's creativity, leaving God as the actualization (i.e., the reality) of creativity, or horizon, or ground. In this way we can retain all those characteristics that many theologians want to attribute to the Unconditioned Ground or Horizon, namely ineffability, mystery, and transcendence of all forms of knowledge or cognitive apprehension. There may turn out to be an ultimate, irresolvable mystery about why there is any ontological context at all (the old question of why there is something rather than nothing). And if we cannot answer that question (through the principle of sufficient reason) by 'going outside' that context entirely, then we may have to accept as a not-to-be-further-explained given the reality of the ontological context as such, and find God *within* that context as the single most important, powerful, decisive, but actual, loving, individual Agent. We could affirm the ontologically transcendent *as* ground without claiming knowledge of it or identifying it with the God who creates the specific forms that the given takes in time and space, and who sustains, redeems, and loves. After all, it is only individual agents who act and through their action determine, decide, cause, or explain what is going on in the world.

John Shepherd has made the point rather tellingly that an ideal God "must be beaten hands down by an otherwise inferior but actual deity. What matters is which exists, not which is abstractly ideal."[20] Shepherd is responding to the charge of J. N. Findlay that it is "wholly anomalous to worship anything *limited* in any thinkable manner."[21] Clearly, a particular individual God (such as Whitehead's) is in a 'thinkable manner' limited as compared to creativity, or by analogy, to the Unconditioned, the Horizon, the Absolute, and so forth. Shepherd quotes P. C. Appleby that a reasonably intelligent person would choose to worship something between a "feeble, stupid or malevolent" god, and "the ineffable Absolutes of many metaphysical systems." What falls in between are *actual* beings, deities (or ultimately *a* deity) "of great power, knowledge and goodness, one who is not subject to the usual vicissitudes of time, and one who is capable of personal communication with humans."[22] Appleby's and Shepherd's point is simply that there is a broad range between the outer limits of metaphysical absolutes and the tawdry idols of more primitive religions in which to find a God worthy of our worship. What we should do is find a god we can believe in and about whom we can know some things from the evidence at hand, especially that which derives from personal experience, rational analysis of the world around us, and inference from historical investigation. At the very least we should not predicate our belief in God on what we presume, ahead of time, is the *only kind of God* worthy of worship. For Christians, belief in and worship of God emerges not primarily from metaphysical abstractions derived from speculation, but from the concrete experiences of redemption, reconciliation, and liberation.

Therefore, even if the ontologically transcendent can be affirmed at some level, it is not clear that it 'explains' what needs to be explained, namely our experience of redemption and salvation. It is not even clear that the concept of explanation itself can transfer meaning from the finite to the infinite ontological context, even though the postulation of the latter is presumably justified because we think we need and can find an explanation of the finite context from 'outside' itself. But we cannot do so, at least in any direct or unambiguous way, since the finite context limits what counts as explanation. To go beyond it is to go, as the mystics and dualists ultimately know, into mystery and holy silence, the total blindness of the intellect. And to enter into that abyss is to leave behind any straightforward cognitive understanding of the active, loving ministrations of the particular Person we experience as God.

What I am now going to propose is that there is a notion of God as *an* acting being, within the same general ontological context as human beings, that can explain what needs explaining (though it cannot explain what cannot be explained) and that rationally, coherently, and adequately reflects the actual experiences of those who have felt renewed and graced in their lives by a power which they can only affirm as decisive and ultimate for them. This notion is the notion of God as an Agent acting in and upon the world, and revealed to rational but religiously sensitive minds through God's acts and the witness to those acts.

But, it might still be objected, I have not adequately resolved those feelings and drives within the heart and mind to find a reality wholly Other, ontologically transcendent to our own. In a sense that is true. I don't believe, however, that we must be committed to identifying the wholly Other with God. If our minds and hearts drive us toward the postulation of the ontologically transcendent, perhaps that tells us more about our hearts and minds than it does about whether there really 'is' an ontologically transcendent reality that is dynamically decisive for our lives. Kant may have been right when he conceded that the understanding demands a completeness that no object in the finite world can fulfill. But Kant was also honest when he admitted that the Idea of 'God' was transcen*dental*, and its 'object' not thereby transcendent. 'God' understood as ontologically transcendent may resolve some inner mental need, but God, as a living reality, need not be identified with 'God'. With 'God' (a transcendental Idea), we may find an outlet for mystery, paradox, profundity, and the sheer delight of transrational speculation. But it may also be the case that only in God, a living personal Agent, can we find an answer to our need for the kind of love, wisdom, and goodness that alone can save us.

Dualism and the Problem of Human Freedom

One important consequence of adhering to the traditional dualist point of view is that the nature of God's 'together-boundness' with the world seems to leave little room for human freedom. In its desire to assert God's limitlessness, dualism insists that God be omnipotent and omniscient, that God have infinite scope for the exercise of divine power and knowledge. If there were occurrences that were not under the direct control of God, then some things might happen that God did not cause to happen. And if God did not cause them to happen, then their happening would be beyond God's causal power and thus they would have a kind of 'ontological' independence from God, an 'otherness' that would limit God's infinite power and control.

Of course, if the negative theological approach is used to articulate God's relation to the world, it would be appropriate to deny that God literally 'causes' anything to happen in the world, since such a claim seems to entail thinking of God as an efficient cause alongside other, finite, efficient causes. But, as we have seen, dualism, at least in the Christian tradition, is loath to give up some kind of residual notion of God's causal efficacy, even if it cannot be conceptualized as coherently consistent with the assumption of God's absolute, ontological otherness.

Divine Omnipotence, Omniscience, and Human Freedom

As long as God's causal efficacy is retained as a conceptual necessity, the independence of some of God's effects vis-a-vis God is problematical. Through creating it, God is clearly bound in some way to the world, but the bond is usually assumed to be so tight that the relative independence that true partners in relation must have if their relationship is to be mature often seems to be in jeopardy.

On the one hand, Christian dualism does not want to compromise a conviction that God, to be God, must be omnipotent (understood in the minimal sense of able to do whatever can be done). Nor does it want to leave open the possibility that some nondivine beings can do things which God does not ultimately determine, since such openness would imply an unacceptable limitation on God's power.

It might, of course, be open to the dualist to propose the possibility that an omnipotent God could choose to relinquish part of divine omnipotence in order to permit some degree of human freedom. But this kind of self-restricted omnipotence carries a high price. It requires that those who assert that God is absolute and limited in no way accept that there will be some limitations on what God both can do and can know. A self-limited God would, in some sense, not control or foreknow some things that happen to human beings. For some dualists this price seems too high to pay. There is also the conceptual difficulty of articulating what it means for a being that is essentially an omnipotent/omniscient being to 'choose' self-limitation. An absolutely perfect infinite being would not need to choose anything, since perfection entails immutability and choice assumes change. At the very least there are some conceptual hurdles that a strict dualist view would have difficulty surmounting in order to conceive an absolutely perfect infinite being coexisting with events over which it has no control or foreknowledge.

As implied above, the notion of God's omniscience or foreknowledge of all that is still to happen is generally added to the notion of divine omnipotence, since if God determines everything God must know 'ahead of time' that which God has determined. But on the other hand, Christian dualism generally does not want to abandon completely the notion that human beings have some relative degree of freedom, both in their moral actions with respect to other finite beings and in their responses to God's action. The difficulty is in bringing the two hands together in a coherent way.

Virtually no defenders of God's omnipotence would deny that God cannot do that which is logically contradictory, such as create a round square, cause the past not to have existed at all, or make a stone too heavy for God to lift. It is not that God cannot do these things: it is better to say that they simply cannot be done at all. It follows that if God creates persons with some freedom of will, God cannot simultaneously determine each and every choice they make since such determination and freedom are logically incompatible. This is what William J. Wainwright calls the "presumption that God's power and sovereignty have normally been understood in such a way as to accommodate human freedom."[23] This is not to say that God cannot determine the outcome of all events, but *if* that outcome is at least partially determined by the choices of persons who are not themselves completely determined by God, then God is not omnipotent with respect to those particular outcomes. Urban and Walton have made the interesting argument that a God who can create a world in which free beings exercise some control that God doesn't exercise is actually more powerful than a God who can *only* create a world in which he has complete control since the former has the power to create two different worlds and the latter only one kind of world. "Hence a being who could create beings over which he has no control has, paradoxical as it may seem, a greater measure of control than one who cannot create free and independent beings."[24]

The notion of divine omniscience might be assumed to permit us to pry apart God's omnipotence from the relative freedom of human persons. God, it might be said, does not predetermine every human act but does know ahead of time all that is going to happen, and thus retains power over all that is creaturely. But, as innumerable objectors have pointed out,[25] if God truly knows what I will do then I have no real option as to whether I will do it or not. I might deliberate mentally, I might think I have a genuine choice, but because God cannot know truly what will turn out not to be true, if God knows that the act will happen, then it will have to happen necessarily, no matter what contribution to its happening I think my free choice has made. Thus my belief that I am freely choosing (and thereby making a difference to the occurrence, a difference without which it would not occur in that way) is an illusion.

Nelson Pike, who takes what is called the incompatibilist position (that divine omniscience and human freedom are incompatible)[26] argues that "it is not within one's power at a given time to do something that would bring it about that someone who holds a certain belief at a time prior to the time in question did not hold that belief at the time prior to the time in question" and "it is not within one's power at a given time to do something that would bring it about that a person who existed at an earlier time did not exist at an earlier time." Pike concludes, "therefore, if God existed at t1 and if God believed at t1 that Jones would do X at t2, then it was not within Jones's power at t2 to refrain from doing X."[27] In other words, Jones could not have decided to change his mind and do something other than X at t2 *if* God knew at t1 that Jones would do X at t2. Otherwise, God's knowledge at t1 was not knowledge or, if it was knowledge (infallibly true) then it couldn't contain a falsehood, namely that Jones would do something other than what God knew he would do.

Nevertheless, Marilyn McCord Adams argues that Pike has not shown that God's omniscience is inconsistent with the voluntary character of some human actions.[28] As long as there are 'soft' facts, namely, ones that are at least in part about any time future relative to 't', those facts are soft. As long as God's existence is still relative to the future of present time 't', then God's existence (and omniscience) is a soft fact (i.e., God does not yet exist in the future). Adams contends that Pike's argument holds only on the assumption that God's existence is a hard fact (a fact that is solely about the past and not relative to a future time). But her argument entails that God's prior belief about my present activity is a soft fact about the past and hence not fixed, and even that the very existence of God is also a soft fact.[29] But John Fischer contends that God's prior belief is a hard fact about the past. A soft fact is a fact *in virtue* of events that occur in the future. If a human being knew at t1 that Jones would do X at t2, this would be knowledge if Jones did X at t2 but would not count as knowledge if Jones did not do X at t2. But with respect to God, the only way in which God's belief at t1 about Jones at t2 could be soft would be if one and the same state of mind of the person who was God at t1 would count as one belief if Jones did X at t2 but would count as a different belief (or not a belief at all) if Jones did not do X at t2. But surely God cannot have two different states of mind with regard to the same future event. This would "seriously attenuate" the notion of God's omniscience.[30]

Another response to the issue of divine omniscience holds that God has no literal *fore*knowledge in a temporal sense since God is not a temporal being (temporality being a finite limitation, which, on the dualist view, must be denied of God). In this sense God knows nothing 'ahead of time' since for God there is no ahead or after in any temporal sense at all, God being eternal in a nontemporal or timeless sense. But this response leads one to ask, How then is God omniscient? The answer is by knowing everything all at once from the point of view of an eternal present. In other words, God's knowledge is eternal, not temporal, and God knows everything, as it were, as having happened, happening, and still to happen at one single (though nontemporal) instant. But this reply is probably incoherent since it assumes that we can give some rational meaning to the notion of knowledge all-at-once or eternal knowing. But we can't do this precisely because of the premise with which dualism begins, namely that God's ontological state is totally beyond the reach of our mental faculties, imprisoned as they are within our completely other finite ontological state.

The result of the dualist's understanding of God's relation to the world is that God is both together bound and radically other than the world. The radical otherness is the premise on which dualism operates, but the together boundness is the given that it must accept if it affirms the reality of both the finite and the infinite 'realms'. As long as there *is* an ontological state of finitude (or whatever one wants to call that which is *not* God), God must be bound to it as its ultimate 'explanation' or causal source. But the

notions of divine omnipotence and omniscience, understood dual-
istically, define that boundness in such a way as to make suspect
the reality of human freedom and power vis-a-vis God's power.

The Christian experience of God certainly seems to include the
experience of radical dependence upon God's power, a dependence
that the notions of divine omnipotence and omniscience try to capture. The question is whether it is possible to preserve the centrality of human dependence on a divine Creator and Sustainer without sacrificing some relative degree of human freedom, power, and
independence in the relation with God. Can one modify notions of
divine omnipotence and omniscience and still retain the experience
of dependence upon God? Can one abandon the notion of God's
radical otherness and still preserve the experience of God's freedom
and mystery? Can one assert God's together-boundness with the
world and still affirm a mutual freedom for those in relation to affect
each other without God's wholly subsuming the human partner in
relation? The answer to these questions can be 'yes' if we are willing
to consider the fruitfulness of notions drawn from our experience
of act, agency, and agent.

Notes

1. St. Thomas Aquinas, *The Summa Theologica*, part I, question 13,
article 5, in Anton C. Pegis, *The Basic Writings of Saint Thomas Aquinas*
(New York: Random House, 1945), p. 120.

2. Eric Mascall, "The Doctrine of Analogy," in Ronald E. Santoni,
ed., *Religious Language and the Problem of Religious Knowledge*
(Bloomington: Indiana University Press, 1968), p. 160.

3. David B. Burrell, *Aquinas: God and Action* (Notre Dame, Ind.:
University of Notre Dame Press, 1979), pp. 132–34.

4. Ibid.

5. Emerich Coreth, *Metaphysics* [English edition by Joseph Donceel]
(New York: The Seabury Press, 1973), p. 173.

6. Ibid., p. 174.

7. Ibid., p. 175.

8. Richard Viladesau, *Answering for Faith: Christ and the Human
Search for Salvation* (New York: Paulist Press, 1987), p. 39.

9. Ibid., p. 41.

10. Ibid., p. 42.

11. John Hick, "Mystical Experience as Cognition," in Richard Woods,
ed., *Understanding Mysticism* (Garden City, N.Y.: Doubleday Image
Books, 1980), p. 429.

12. Rudolf Otto, *The Idea of the Holy: An Inquiry into the Non-rational Factor in the Idea of the Divine and Its relation to the Rational,*

trans. John W. Harvey (New York: Oxford University Press, 1958), chaps. 1–5.

13. Alfred North Whitehead, *Process and Reality* [Corrected Edition, David Ray Griffin and Donald W. Sherburne, eds.] (New York: The Free Press, 1979), p. 21.

14. Ibid., p. 31 (emphasis added).

15. Ibid.

16. Ibid., p. 225.

17. Ibid., p. 31.

18. Ibid., p. 225.

19. Ibid., p. 31.

20. John Shepherd, *Experience, Inference, and God* (New York: Harper and Row, 1975), p. 114.

21. Ibid.

22. Ibid., pp. 114–15.

23. William J. Wainwright, *Philosophy of Religion* (Belmont, Calif.: Wadsworth, 1988), p. 87.

24. Linwood Urban and Douglas N. Walton, "Freedom within Omnipotence," in Linwood Urban and Douglas N. Walton, eds., *The Power of God: Readings on Omnipotence and Evil* (New York: Oxford University Press, 1978), p. 207.

25. See especially Anthony Kenny, "Divine Foreknowledge and Human Freedom," in A. Kenny, ed., *Aquinas: A Collection of Critical Essays* (Garden City, N.Y.: Doubleday Anchor Books, 1969), pp. 255–70.

26. Nelson Pike, "Divine Omniscience and Voluntary Action," in John Martin Fischer, Ed., *God, Foreknowledge, and Freedom* (Stanford: Stanford University Press, 1989), pp. 57–73.

27. Ibid., p. 63.

28. Marilyn McCord Adams, "Is the Existence of God a 'Hard' Fact?," in Fischer, *God, Foreknowledge, and Freedom*, pp. 74–85.

29. John Martin Fischer, "Freedom and Foreknowledge," in Fischer, *God, Foreknowledge, and Freedom*, p. 86.

30. Ibid., pp. 93–94.

5

Persons and Agents

Despite the caution that dualism lays against any use of concepts of God drawn from the finite ontological context, the concept of 'person' has historically been used by Jewish and Christian theology for the One whom they regard as Lord and Savior. The fact that such personal imagery has not only been regularly employed but also that it has the highest orthodox credentials is not in question, even for a dualist. What is in question is the precise meaning 'person' has when applied to God.

Personal Symbols of God

At one extreme are those who insist that personal symbols of God are inescapable insofar as human persons will always symbolize the deepest and highest dimensions of reality, not least because it is persons who engage in the act of symbolizing. Since we are persons, we cannot help but conceive of God as a person. When this claim is then further qualified, it is usually said that we cannot help but conceive of God as *not less than* personal, meaning that God cannot 'contain' or 'be' less full of 'being' than are persons. And persons are, clearly, fuller beings than are subhuman entities (e.g., they have consciousness and intelligence, which is apparently lacking in less than human beings). The horizon or limit of human conceptuality is the personal, but since God lies beyond the horizon and transcends all limits, the personal image captures only the furthest reaches of human conceptuality but not the reality that lies beyond them. Nevertheless, it won't do to use any symbols of God (if we expect them to represent God literally and unambiguously) drawn from any portion of the finite ontological context that fall short of the horizon itself. Therefore, the personal symbol for God is the best we can do, even though it is not ultimately adequate.

Another way of employing personal symbols of God is to insist that God *is* personal inasmuch as persons participate in the Being of God and, in order to do so, God must have the power of personhood in God's own Being. This is the position set forth by Paul Tillich and by some transcendental Thomists. But even though God must *be* personal in this sense, God cannot be only personal, or be limited to being personal. The fullness of God's Being goes so far beyond the personal that no personal concept or symbol can ever represent it adequately. The truth of symbols used of God lies, ultimately, in their subjective power for the user, not in their ability to represent God objectively in any direct way. The power of symbolizing God as personal is felt subjectively more intensely and meaningfully than the power of any other symbols of God. But this power is not due to the symbol's depiction of God's being as it objectively is in itself.

Another variation on the theme of using personal symbols for God is to insist that God *reveals Godself* to us in personal ways, and that on the basis of these revelations we are compelled to use personal imagery to refer to God. But, it is quickly added, these personal symbols are determined by the form of the divine revelation and cannot be assumed to represent God as God is in Godself. The form of God's revelation is separated enough, ontologically, from God's Being that no direct ontological connection can be drawn between God's Being and the ways in which those beings 'less than' God receive and interpret manifestations of God in nondivine ontological contexts. God may *appear* to us as a person, but between the appearance and the reality (between what Kant called the phenomenon and the noumenon) is an ontological gap unbridgeable by any human concepts taken in a literal way.

A variation on this theme is to say that God is person*al* but not *a* person. That is, God is grasped by us at the deepest levels of our personality as one who encounters us personally, but the form of the encounter is not a solid foundation on which to erect an ontological claim that God is *a* person. Another way of putting it would be to say that if God *is* conceived as a person, God is not a person as we are persons. (This is related to the dualist use of analogy). We are persons finitely, and God is a person infinitely, or transcendently. And since the difference between the infinite and the finite is itself infinite, what it means to say that God is 'a' person infinitely is infinitely different from what it means to say that God is a finite person.

Underlying these thematic uses of the concept of person as applied to God are two major assumptions: the first is that human conceptions must not *anthropomorphize* God and the second is that no human language about God can be *literal*. To anthropomorphize God is to think and speak of God *as if* God were a human being, a finite reality, a being alongside other beings within the finite ontological context. If God is thought of in this way, then God's *transcendent* reality is compromised. The fear of anthropomorphism is rooted squarely in the belief common to dualism and monism that any reality that is subject to finite ontological conditions cannot be worthy of worship and metaphysical supremacy. The fear of literal language about God is based on the same belief. If we understand the word 'literal' in this particular context to mean simply a word employed within the same ontological context referring to two or more objects in that context in exactly the same way or in the same respect, then no word can literally represent God, who is both beyond our ontological context and unable to be represented in exactly the same way as any object within it. We can say that Fred and Mary are literally 'agents' if we mean exactly the same thing by 'agent' when we apply the term to both of them assuming both are human beings. But no term can apply literally to God if it is initially drawn from and exhaustively receives its meaning from an ontological context other than that appropriate to God and applies literally to finite beings.

It follows that if we want to make a case that God *is* an agent or person in a literal sense, then we will have to acknowledge a similar ontological context for both God and other agents and persons, and we will have to admit to some mimimal form of anthropomorphism. The metaphysical question is whether, in doing so, we so diminish or degrade God's majesty, power, and divinity as to render God unworthy of our worship, praise, and ultimate commitment. The task that lies ahead of us is to develop a metaphysics of agency and persons such that conceiving of God as literally an agent and person both preserves the experiences of being in mutual relationship with God and reflects the forms of rational understanding appropriate to the highest possible reality.

For the sake of convenience, and without sacrificing crucial metaphysical distinctions, I will from now on use the terms 'person' and 'agent' interchangeably. For our purposes, persons are necessarily agents (they must act to express their personhood), and agents always seem to be persons (since agency requires intentionality, a trait that seems unique to persons). It may be possible to develop a conceptuality of persons and agents that more finely distinguishes them from each other, but those differences are not essential to the thrust of our argument.

At the same time, care must be taken to avoid two dangers that have often been associated with, if not logically implied by, anthropomorphism. One is to conceive of God as a tyrant and the other is to conceive of God as one's 'buddy'. The notion of God as tyrant is directly related to the belief that if God is simply the mightiest being in relation to all other beings, God will be their puppet-master, controller, dictator, and determiner. Paul Tillich assumes this will necessarily be the case. In speaking of a God who is a being alongside other beings, he says that God

> makes me into an object which is nothing more than an object. He deprives me of my subjectivity because he is all-powerful and all-knowing. ... God appears as the invincible tyrant, the being in contrast with whom all other beings are without freedom and subjectivity. ... This is the God Nietzsche said had to be killed because nobody can tolerate being made into a mere object of absolute knowledge and control."[1]

The notion of God as buddy is directly related to the belief that if God is in personal relation to all other beings then God will be as exploitable and manipulatable as other persons often are. God becomes simply one's 'copilot' as one flies through life. God is just like us though somewhat steadier, wiser, stronger, and so on. Such a concept of God profoundly diminishes the majesty and glory of the God encountered in the biblical traditions. In either case, the 'mystery' of the divine will have been lost.

Now these two views contradict each other. They both cannot be correct and, I believe, neither of them is ultimately right. Nevertheless, the metaphysical *possibility* of either being right is real because they both presuppose a common ontological context in which God and other beings are in real relationship to each other. The ontological question is whether the *character* of God revealed through God's acts sustains either view or whether it is revealed as something that retains a mysterious dimension while at the same time is known truly as loving, compassionate, and graceful.

Another issue that will have to be faced directly is that of establishing the metaphysical basis not just for an 'underlying' or 'overarching' divine act through which the world comes into being and is sustained, but also for *specific, particular* acts of God *within* the world. The notion of particular acts of God, which can be distinguished from the particular acts of other agents, is one that even the most personal and agent-based understandings of God have generally shied away from. These 'particular' acts of God are either elevated to the status of 'supernatural' interventions into the natural order that are beyond rational understanding or are reduced to epiphenomenal occurrences ontologically coincident with the acts of other agents. I want to establish that God can perform specific, particular acts attributable uniquely to God's agency *and* that these acts are subject, in principle, to the *same* principles of explanation as actions by nondivine agents. To have established the rational coherence of divine acts will have been one of the most important contributions of this study.

Finally, and most troublingly, precisely because one can establish the rationality of divine action within the world one will be confronted head on by the problem of evil. Evil really is a problem only on the assumptions that there is a being with sufficient power, sufficient agency to exercise that power, and sufficient desire to exercise power for the benefit of those who are beloved, and that there are things that happen in the world that are not beneficial to its inhabitants. A God who acts with mighty power and who loves what God has created is, *prima facie*, complicit with the evil that exists. Any notion of divine reality that cannot literally attribute power, desire, and agency to God would not have nearly the same difficulty in responding to the question of evil.

Concepts of Agent, Act, and Agency

Now, in order to get a handle on the host of issues I have identified, I need to begin with notions of agent, act, and agency that will form the explanatory basis for our treatment of God as agent.

Over the past few decades an enormous literature in the field of analytic philosophy has appeared dealing with the concepts of action, act, agent, and agency. It is not my purpose to survey or utilize the full range or depth of that literature. Nevertheless, many of its insights can be helpful to us as we try to sort out what (human) agents are, what an act is, and, ultimately, what a divine act and agent would have to be if they are to be understood by us as existing within our ontological context. But our purpose, it should be remembered, is not in the first instance to reduce God to the limits of human understanding but rather to provide from within those limits a concept or model that expands and deepens the freedom, majesty, decisiveness, mystery, and love of God while maintaining God's *relationship* with us. The concept of act/agency does just that.

While almost every definition of act/agency and every shaded nuance within each one has been the subject of endless debate in the philosophy of action, most of us would agree that at least at first glance, before deep reflection, we know what agency is because we *experience* ourselves acting as agents. We wink at someone across the room, intending to make contact, to indicate that we are aware that he is there and that we are interested in establishing or renewing a relationship of some kind. Our wink is a deliberate *act* intended to accomplish an end or purpose that would not have come about without our having undertaken this particular action.

But we also know, because we experience it, what it is to have the same eyelid close over the same eye in the very same physiological way as in our intentional wink but without our having intended it. This physiologically identical closing of the eyelid over the eye occurs regularly many times in the course of a single minute as part of the biological infrastructure of our body. We normally are not even aware of this regular blinking pattern of occurrences because it goes on without our needing to intend it. And we normally do not think of this kind of blinking as an act that we have chosen to perform in order to accomplish the end of keeping the eyeball watered.

And so the very same physiological occurrence can be either an act or a non-act (what I will call simply an event), and the difference seems to lie in whether or not *we* intended it to happen and, having intended it, brought it about or caused it. In other words, our knowledge of action, as something capable of being distinguished from occurrences that are not actions, is based on our *experience* of agency, of *doing* some things intentionally as distinguished from undergoing events brought about by something other than our intention. This appeal to a distinction that is based on our own experience is crucial to a full development of the notion of an act as distinguishable from an event.

In the most minimal sense possible, then, we can understand an act as a doing by an agent who is responsible for it. It is the bringing about of something, the exerting of some kind of (causal) power, for the purpose of producing an effect or effects in something that can be distinguished from the purpose itself. My intention is for something to happen "in the world" (which may include my own body or thought processes), which is more than simply entertaining the intention mentally, and the means for making something happen is the act. (The act could, of course, be in and of itself what one intends to happen, e.g., making a loud noise 'for its own sake', or it could be the means for making something else happen, e.g., warning someone of an imminent danger).

Now all this may seem so obvious as to be trivial and uninformative. But I stress it in order to establish a couple of basic, and ultimately very nontrivial points. First, the concept of action is rooted in one of the most basic dimensions of our experience. Therefore, any true picture of human being must not explain away or eliminate the reality of action since it is one of the bedrocks on which any true metaphysic of human reality must rest. Second, the concept of action requires us both to accept the reality of intentions or purposes and to distinguish them from nonintentional, nonpurposive occurrences. And third, the concept of action presupposes the reality of something other than the solitary agent: it presupposes a single, common, inclusive pluralistic world consisting of a multitude of relationships between the agent and other agents and/or non-agents.

The importance of these points will prove, ultimately, to be that the concept of act/agency cannot be reduced to any explanatory categories that explain away or deny the primordial, basic reality of agents who act, a reality we know first and foremost in and from our own experience of acting. Agents will be the basic 'power-units' in the world and any *exhaustive* (complete without remainder) explanation of what happens in the world must make reference, in a nonreductionist way, to the activity of agents (even though many portions of that same world include no agents). An activity of thinking that concludes that action is impossible is a contradiction in terms. This activity presupposes the freedom of choice or intention that is an indispensable dimension of action. Thus no explanation of occurrences, if they are intentional acts, relying exhaustively and solely upon physical laws of cause and effect that eliminate any reference to the freedom of the human will, can adequately represent that 'part' of the real world in which action by agents takes place. (And thus, causal explanation cannot threaten the freedom of *any* agents, human or divine, even though it may be made com-

patible with it at one level of understanding.) This freedom ingredient in every act will prove to be the basis for the irremovable
mystery that any true doctrine of God must defend because it is at
the heart of our *experience* of God. And finally, action is the ultimate vehicle for establishing and maintaining relationships. Therefore, if God is in relationship to something other than Godself, the
basic and most satisfactory concept for articulating that relationship will have to be that of action and, therefore, of God as divine
Agent acting upon other agents and non-agents in an ongoing context of intentional mutuality.

What I intend to show is that God can be partially but truly
understood straightforwardly ('literally') as an Agent whose intentional action brings other agents and non-agents into being, sustains
them, affects them in their situations, and redeems them. (I say
'partially' because there may be many things about God that are
not capable of being 'literally' understood, including some aspects
of *how* God acts. But I also say 'truly' because there is a real, literal, basic sense in which God *is* an Agent, and not just symbol-
ized metaphorically as one.)

God's actions can have many different forms (from overarching,
e.g., sustaining the world according to its present causal laws, to
specific, e.g., interrupting the otherwise natural sequence of events
in order to bring about a particular effect, as in the parting of the
waters of the Red Sea; from direct, e.g., the act itself is the intended
effect, as in the resurrection of Jesus, to indirect, e.g., the act helps
to bring about the intended effect, as in the parting of the waters;
and from basic, e.g., wherein God's intention is sufficient to bring
about the intended effect without relying on intermediate means,
(as in God wills that the waters part and they do [the notion of a
divine basic act will need some further modification later on], to
instrumental, e.g., wherein God brings about the desired result by
utilizing intermediary beings, as in God causes the wind to blow
in order to part the waters). These forms of action, as well as varia-
tions on them, can all be employed by a divine agent and require
somewhat different specific forms of explanation, although all remain dependent upon the basic principles of understanding ingredient in the underlying notion of act/agency.

If God can be understood straightforwardly as an Agent, then
the interesting theological questions become, not whether God can
act, but *what* God's actions are, what intentions they reveal, what
kind of relationship God intends, what that relationship demands
of the partners who are engaged in it, and what explanation and

response are justified regarding those occurrences that seem fundamentally opposed to God's intentions and capable of being prevented
by God's power (i.e., the problem of evil)? Simply put, the relevant
religious issue shifts from *whether* God can be understood as Agent
to what *kind* of Agent God is. What are God's intentions and how
does God act to further them? What kind of relationship with us
does God want, what does God do about creating and sustaining it,
and what does God expect us to do in reponse?

As we work our way through the notion of act/agency in more
detail and show its application to God, one of the most basic hurdles
we have to face is how to reconcile explanations of the world that
employ the notion of free, intentional action with explanations that
attempt to reduce all occurrences, exhaustively without remainder,
to causal law explanation as understood by the disciplines of natural science. It has often been said that the fundamental objection
to retaining any notion of God as Agent is that it contradicts our
scientific understanding that all 'events' fall under the laws of finite
cause and effect and that those laws have no place for 'actions' that
are both freely originated (at least in part) and not reducible *solely*
to causal explanation. (It has not usually been observed that in
rejecting the notion of divine agency because it conflicts with the
deterministic and reductionistic explanations of causal law, one is
also rejecting any notion of *human* agency as free and nonreduc-
tionistic).

The Limitations Intrinsic to Relationship

The difficulty most theologians face in utilizing models for God
drawn from the 'finite' ontological context is that they seem necessarily limiting of God's freedom and power. If we are to use the
agent model to understand God straightforwardly, it will be necessary to show that it does not limit either God's freedom of action,
or God's range and depth of power. Of course, we are predicating
the use of the agent model on the basis of a *relationship* in which
God is together bound with us. This predication is important to keep
in mind because, as such, it presupposes some limits from the very
outset.

Relationships between two or more entities are necessarily limiting in the sense that each of the partners in relation (no matter
what enormous differences might exist with respect to their respective *degrees* of power and freedom vis-a-vis each other) limits all
the others. At one level this limitation occurs simply by virtue of

each entity's very *being* itself. It cannot *be* unless its being is in some real sense distinct from, over against, and therefore, not identical to the being of the other(s). (Recognition of this fact is what impels the monistic model ultimately to *deny* any distinctions between God and 'other' beings.) Even the most powerful 'other' is limited in the sense that it cannot *be* the other being(s). (Recognition of this fact is what ultimately drives the dualist model toward monism.) This ontological limitation does not, of course, imply that the most powerful entity has no role in sustaining the other entities in their being, but it does entail that as long as these other entities exist as such, they *are* (by virtue of their being) ontological limits in a fundamental sense on the sustaining being.

Limits on the most powerful being will also exist insofar as the other entities have (or are given) some degree of freedom vis-à-vis the sustaining being. If their freedom is genuine, even the most powerful, sustaining being is limited in not fully knowing all the decisions they will make and in not overriding them. (See the previous section on notions of divine omniscience and omnipotence.)

The real question, then, is not putting limits *per se* upon God but in determining what *kinds* of limits are appropriate to God's nature as a loving person in intimate and decisive relationship with other beings. (We would not, of course, even be raising the issue of limitation had we not *first* experienced God as a personal Other bound with us in a life-transforming moment or series of moments.) Our own experience of agency provides us with a model that both acknowledges the kinds of limits entailed by relationship with others and affirms the widest possible arena of freedom in which to fulfill those relationships.

Causal Law and Free Agency

Given the hegemony often attributed to the causal explanations of modern physical science, we need to begin our analysis by examining the way in which our freedom to act is compatible with but transcends the limitations inherent in causal explanations of bodily operations. If we can show that causal law (a shorthand reference to the laws of cause and effect *within* the 'natural' or 'finite' universe bounded by space-time, which physical science believes describe all physical, and even mental, operations) is compatible with the operation of free agency, then we will have established the basis, in human action, for understanding divine action as compatible with causal law. At the heart of this compatibility is the claim that free agency transcends and supervenes that realm of nature with respect to its *initiation* of free acts, and utilizes it as an infrastructure for the execution of those acts.

We can begin our analysis by claiming that the fundamental unit to be understood is the agent. This may seem trivial but it is not. It has been a hallmark of science that the fundamental units of reality are its smallest, most minute, least complex elements. This conviction has driven science to identify such elemental entities as the atom, the quark, and the meson, as the 'building blocks' of the universe. If one follows this line of thinking, anything more complex than one such basic 'element' will not be basic and will, therefore, be capable in principle of being broken down into its more basic constituent parts. Thus, neither an agent nor the agent's action is a fundamental unit. They are considered to be complex arrangements of more basic parts and the explanation of an agent's action is therefore necessarily reducible to these more basic entities that are less complex than either act or agent. Full and satisfactory explanation will be in terms of atomistic causes that only through complexification emerge as apparently free acts and agents. But the real causes are themselves nonintentional and subject only to the strict laws of cause and effect in the physical realm. This kind of explanation is inherently *reductionistic*, meaning that it reduces apparently complex entities down into their more basic, elemental parts and builds an explanation of their behavior upon those parts.

One obvious consequence of reductionism has been the tendency to deny the basic reality of such things as freedom to choose some courses of action, and even action itself. If we are to preserve the freedom of the agent, we need to question the assumption of reductionism, namely that the fundamental unit of reality is more basic and elemental than the agent herself. This is not easy to do given the hold reductionism has upon modern science and the obvious fact that agents do seem to consist of 'parts'. It is not adequate simply to deny the force of reductionism and to assert that one will believe in the irreducible, basic fact of freedom. Nor is it adequate to assert the 'two angles' view, which holds that reductionistic determinism is quite real from one point of view and that freedom is quite real from another. This way of dealing with the problem simply provides for obscurity, confusion, and, ultimately, dualism. Rather, what we need is a way to accept the genuine observations that underlie reductionistic determinism, but to place them within a larger context that includes freedom to choose but that is, itself, a fundamental, basic unit of reality.

"Systems" Philosophy

One of the most important advances in the philosophy of biology has been the development of the notion of the "systems," or hierarchy, approach to entities. This notion holds that as reality becomes more complex, the higher-level complex entities include but go beyond (transcend) the lower levels.[2] The systems approach holds that higher-level entities are units, not reducible to their lower-level parts precisely because they hold those 'parts' together at a higher level of integration. A higher-level being, such as an animal, is a hierarchically organized unity, holding together a series of levels of reality such as the physiological and the organic, but transcending them in the sense that the 'laws' describing the operation of the animal itself cannot be accounted for solely by reference to the laws operative at the lower levels. The whole entity is subject to principles of explanation unique to itself (though dependent upon and not in contradiction to the principles explaining the lower levels that it integrates), and is not reducible through analysis to principles that apply exhaustively at the lower levels. The higher-level being, for example, can be self-directing in a way that is simply not possible for the lower levels, and its capacity for self-direction cannot be explained simply by 'adding up' the principles applicable to the lower levels. As Ervin Laszlo has put it, "Organisms of all kinds are built by the integration of systems into superordinate systems, and these again into still higher level systems, until we encounter the organism as a whole. Each subsystem finds constraints imposed on its behavior by the higher system, with the result that the total organism's functional behavior dominates the behavior of all its parts, through successive hierarchically organized steps."[3] And Paul Weiss, a biologist, has expressed this hierarchical notion in the following terms:

> An organism as a system reveals itself as encompassing and operating through the agency of subsystems, each of which, in turn, contains and operates through groups of systems of still lower order, and so on down through molecules into the atomic and sub-atomic range. The fact that the top level operations of the organism thus are neither structurally nor functionally referable to direct liaison with the processes on the molecular level in a steady continuous gradation, but

are relayed step-wise from higher levels of determinacy ... through intermediate layers of greater freedom or variance ... to next lower levels of again more rigorously ascertainable determinacy, constitutes the *principle of hierarchical organization.*[4]

Although much of systems philosophy developed in order to clarify the work of the biological sciences, it can be applied to an understanding of agents because it provides a basis for challenging the dominance of the reductionistic assumption. In particular, it opens up the possibility of considering the agent as a 'systems' unit, one that is hierarchically organized but, as a unit, not analyzable reductively and without remainder into its constituent parts without eliminating some of the essential traits that characterize its higher-level unity. A contemporary philosopher of science, Hilde Hein, notes that traditional scientific thinking has been "indoctrinated with the geometric principle that complicated things are built out of simple ones, and that fruitful analysis is the result of careful separation of the simple elements which together produce a complex synthesis."[5] An alternative way of looking at things, according to Hein, and one that is completely compatible with the systems approach and therefore with the fundamental unity of the agent, rejects the 'sacrosanct' pattern of reductionism and starts instead with a "fresh set of categories," a 'reverse reductionism' which begins with the complex unity of an entity as a way of understanding its individual and constituent parts.

Edward Pols and a 'Fresh Set of Categories'

The work of the contemporary American philosopher Edward Pols provides precisely the kind of reflection on the unity of the agent that exemplifies the 'fresh set of categories' to which Hilde Hein points. His work on the 'system' of the agent as a unifying hierarchy both distinguishes the agent as a unique unity and reconciles and integrates that uniqueness with the 'lower' levels of nature normally explained by the reductionistic causal laws of physical science. I want to mine the work of Pols in order to establish a notion of the agent (and of action/agency) that, with respect to some of its basic elements, can be applied straightforwardly to a notion of God as agent. (Pols himself does not utilize his own analysis in exactly this way, it should be immediately confessed). If Pols' analysis is correct, then the explanation of both human and divine agents will have the necessary metaphysical room for freedom and power of action, irreducibility to lower levels of reality, nondualistic transcendence over those levels, and integral relation to them. Thus, a basis for understanding God's *relationship* with other beings will have been created that neither reduces God to a less-than-personal level of reality, nor limits God's freedom and power of action over an infinite range, nor requires an apparent 'higher' conception of God as something other than 'a' being. At the same time, however, it will establish an ontological link between God's being and the being of other entities, a link that undergirds our straightforward knowledge of God and reflects the necessary foundation for any relationship with God.

The heart of Pols' argument is that the agent is a 'basic' unified whole who utilizes in the execution of his or her freely chosen intentions subwholes or 'infrastructures' that are, taken by themselves in isolation from their integration into the unity of the agent, quite capable of being understood in nonintentional, traditionally reductionistic ways. Ultimately, the explanation of an agent's action must include the agent's own intention, and not be simply an analysis of the parts of the biological or physical infrastructure through which the act was carried out. An explanation that "comes back to [the agent] himself is final, satisfactory, and not to be set aside by any other. This means that it is also not to be set aside by scientific explanations that avoid the category of action entirely, and are couched instead in terms of entities, processes, functions, states, or events related under the laws of nature."[6]

For Pols, each act in a hierarchy of acts has an 'ontological authenticity'.[7] It is a basic unity explicable only by reference to itself. It is the work of a rational agent, the exercise of "the most fundamental and concrete sense of power accessible to our intelligence."[8] It is important to note that Pols suggests that any exercise of power is power exercised by *an* agent, *an* entity, *a* being. This suggestion will make a powerful undergirding to our argument that if we want a notion of God as powerful, that is, able to exercise efficient power, then that notion must be one of *a* being, not of something more abstract like Being-itself, or the ground of being. Action is, as Pols puts it, opaque to complete explanation by any other mode of explanation than action itself:

> Whatever functions in explanation in a way not reducible to or replaceable by other explanatory categories is an explanatory ultimate, and what is thus ultimate cannot itself be explained. . . . [S]omething in the development and activity of the agent should be inexplicable except by calling attention to the fact that the agent indeed did thus and so. . . . [T]here must remain some features of the agent-in-act that

are inexplicable in the sense that no explanatory technique can further illuminate what is expressed in the statement that the agent indeed acted in just that way. Otherwise agency is inauthentic in the sense that it is not what it purports to be."[9]

A 'radical pluralism of acts' is, according to Pols, "as good a model for explanatory ultimacy as one could wish for."[10] This means that metaphysically one has reached the north pole of explanatory capacity when one has reached the act of an agent, or, more precisely, when one has reached the initiation of an act in the intention of its agent.

It simply will not do to try to tease apart 'segments' of the act or its agent in order to discover the 'underlying' explanation for it. This is the kind of fresh insight to which Hein points us.[11] Analysis has traditionally assumed that ultimate explanation resides in getting down to ever finer, more discrete, more basic units inside or underneath what appear to us as assemblages of elements. But Pols is suggesting that the unity of the act *is* the ultimate explanation of what the act unifies. To separate that unity by reductive analysis is to lose the act, and the agent whose act it is, in the process. We get off on the wrong foot, as it were, if we start by asking what causes the agent's intention because that question already presupposes the explanatory ultimacy of a reductionistic cause-effect explanation. What Pols is suggesting is that explanation in terms of the unity of the agent and his or her act is an explanation *sui generis*. It is not piggybacked onto or fitted into a causal explanation. In fact, Pols argues, causal explanation takes on its real significance only *within* the more basic, inclusive, overarching explanatory power of explanation in terms of agent-act.

The Originative Act

The act of an agent is 'originative'. It initiates and unifies (holds together as an irreducible unit) a series of subacts and an infrastructure through which the act manifests itself. This series of subacts or infrastructure "includes all the functions and processes that take place within the persistent physical structure of the body. . . ."[12] and includes the firing of neural cells, the contraction of muscles, the movement of bones, the circulation of blood, and all the other biological and physiological functions that are necessary to the existence of the biological body of the agent. This entire infrastructure can be understood in itself in a thorough, precise, and reductionistic way through the explanatory categories of the natural sciences without any reference to the unity it acquires in and through the agent's action *provided that this understanding abstracts it theoretically from the more inclusive context of action in which it serves as the infrastructure of the act.*

When the agent acts, however, her act overarches and unifies this infrastructure hierarchically without separating it into a discrete series of independent atomic parts that seem to be held together only artificially. The originative act remains throughout "an absolutely seamless unity."[13] "However fine-grained your analysis of the infrastructure may be, extending even to the details of its mediation between the world outside an agent and the agent himself, you will find there the full story of the act itself."[14] The act, in other words, cannot be divided up into parts (except for purposes of abstraction and theory). Its unity extends throughout the whole temporal sequence necessary for the carrying out of the act. (And Pols argues that different acts have different temporal reach. My act of writing this text may extend over a year or more. The act of typing one letter on my keyboard may take less than 1 second.) Each act may include subacts, subwholes, or a multiplicity of complex infrastructural mechanisms, but the act itself is a seamless whole and not to be understood solely by picking apart its constitutive elements.

The act must be understood as a whole because the act is what it is precisely through its unifying of a multiplicity of elements in its infrastructure. Pols suggests the richness of this notion of the act's capacity to unify its infrastructure by listing a series of synonymous terms conveying its meaning: the power of the originative act "orders, disposes, uses, deploys, shapes, binds together, [and] wields the multiplicity of the spatiotemporal elements that make up its infrastructure."[15]

For example, when I as an agent choose (intend) to wink at someone, my intention originates the act that then "deploys, shapes, and wields the multiplicity" of things that are needed physiologically and biologically by my bodily infrastructure, especially my eyelid, if the wink is to be *enacted*. A physiologist or biologist would be able to dissect the mechanisms utilized in the wink itself according to the canons of strict causal law. At no point in her analysis would she 'find' an intention lurking alongside or buried underneath one of the neurons or muscles used in the wink. But *if* the wink was intentional, then its explanation is incomplete and inauthentic until and unless reference is made to the intention that initiated it. But the intention is not to be understood as simply the first temporal stage of the act. Rather, as Pols insists, the intention ramifies and unifies the whole of the act (which takes both time and space). The intention is present throughout the whole of the act. The act of the agent is "everywhere and at every time in the manifold of an infrastructure understood in other terms."[16]

The act is a basic unit (not to be further reduced) just because it *is* the unification of less basic elements that, apart from their ordering and deployment within the act, are nonoriginative and dependent upon a more inclusive unifying power. (This fact can, of course, ground the claim that God is the Agent who, through a creative originative act, unifies reality as a whole and gives it the enduring order it possesses and that we, as human agents, depend upon when we act in less extensive ways.) That inclusive unifying power is, ultimately, the agent who stands to the act as the act stands to its infrastructure. The category of the agent "is more fundamental than that of action, although obviously inextricably mixed up with it."[17] The agent is "an entity with an ontological status more fundamental than the acts themselves."[18]

Drawing upon 'systems' or 'hierarchic' analysis in the work of Paul A. Weiss, Pols suggests that the agent presides over the hierarchy of lower levels of reality (e.g., organism, organ, cell, organelle, and molecule) through which the act is carried out. A unit at any level exercises power over the units below it but is itself a subsystem under the control of the units above it.[19] When we reach the agent as an entity, we reach that reality unifying all the sublevels, or infrastructures, through which the agent acts. The agent is the 'real causality' through which the causality of the lower levels is initiated and unified.[20] The agent is the entity through whom subacts originate (and in this sense the agent 'transcends' his or her acts).[21] The agent's self-identity is not simply the aggregate of these subacts or atomic units—it is *sui generis*, authentic, and basic in itself precisely because it is the source of the unity of the elements traditionally identified as basic by reductionistic causal analysis. Pols likes to use the word 'asymmetrical' to describe the relation of the agent to his or her infrastructure. It is the ontological source of the complex, unified cause-and-effect relations within the infrastructure but it is not exhaustively caused by them, even though it is obviously limited in what it can do by them. (The agent would not be able to enact her intention unless the infrastructure through which she must carry it out is capable of that enactment, and in this sense the infrastructure limits the capacity of the agent both to act and to intend. It would be hard—some have said impossible—to intend, not to say imagine, something that is literally impossible to achieve, such as willing myself to be on Mars 5 seconds from now, because the infrastructure is not there to enable the intention to be enacted successfully.) This would seem to suggest that the one difference, a crucial difference perhaps, between a divine and a human agent is that a divine agent's infrastructure (e.g., the cosmos) permits an infinite (or at least infinitely greater) capability for successful action while a human agent's infrastructure is comparatively far more limited. Despite the restriction placed upon the 'reach' of the agent's action by the infrastructure, the agent, nevertheless, transcends his or her infrastructure simply by virtue of being able to utilize it for the carrying out of his or her intentions while 'it' does not have the power to utilize the agent for the carrying out of its intentions, because it has none.

However, the transcendence of the agent over his or her acts, as Pols writes,

> does not require us to locate the act 'above' the infrastructure as an ontological item thoroughly distinct from it. The act endures through and completes itself in its own time unit, and its self-completion is the giving of a pattern to that infrastructure, but when that pattern is completed the act is 'gone': it does not endure after the pattern, nor is it elsewhere than in the pattern. Its transcendence consists solely in its being, qua power, distinguishable from the mere multiplicity of the context it pervades and unifies.[22]

But the transcendence of the agent cannot cut off the being of the agent from his or her acts. "He becomes in his acts: but his becoming is the unifying power in each of his acts and the unification of all them. . . . An act wells up out of an entity . . . [and] . . . over against the potential multiplicity of his acts his unity is absolute."[23] The causal 'necessity' that may prevail at lower levels of the agent's infrastructure does not obtain exhaustively at the level of the agent himself or herself, taken as a unity: his or her acts are not predetermined by the causal laws to which the agent is asymmetrically related and which the agent utilizes in carrying out his or her intentions. In this way, both reductionism and dualism are avoided.

The brilliance of Pols' analysis is that it provides us with a concept of agent and act that integrates without dualism the authenticity of free (intentional) action (the supervening and superordinate power of the originative and unifying act) and the reality of causal law (the subordinate power of the derivative and unified infrastructure) through which the intention is *enacted*. By forcing us to think from the point of view of the basic unity of the agent, Pols leads us to understand the agent as the ontologically fundamental reality *from which* we can derive, by a process of conceptual abstraction (eliminating for the moment consideration of its ultimate source and unifying power), the meaning and application of causal law. The agent *needs* causality and its structuring of physiological, biological, and chemical reality, in order to carry out his or her intentions in the world. In this sense the agent is dependent upon causal law and cannot act in such a way as to disregard its reality. Nevertheless, the origination and ultimate explanation of the agent's acts that utilize causal law transcends and cannot be reduced to causal description.

Causality and Agent Interference

This point reminds us that the notion of cause is, in fact, derived from an ontologically prior and more basic notion of action from which the element of intention has been conceptually removed. John Macmurray made this point over 30 years ago in his Gifford Lectures, in which he noted that the conception of 'cause' "is the conception of an agent that is not an agent, the negation of agency."[24] A causal explanation is, therefore, not really an explanation at all, but a *description* of what takes place within an action. A cause cannot explain itself except through a prior cause, which then forces us into an infinite regress. If we begin with the explanatory ultimacy of causal law we are necessarily driven 'backward' to the cause of the cause of the cause, and so on. There can, in principle, be no stopping point in this regress unless we simply assert that at some point we reach a uncaused first cause (Aquinas' God). But Aquinas' argument only provided us with a single self-caused entity precisely because he assumed, for the sake of the argument, the explanatory ultimacy in the finite realm of causal law. What Aquinas left out is what Pols and Macmurray point to—the initiating activity (their analogue to the notion of the uncaused cause) of *each and every agent who acts*. And these actions, and the agents who initiate (cause) them can only be grasped by an explanation that includes reference to something 'more' than one more cause in a sequence of causes. The laws of nature are simply descriptions of what Macmurray calls 'natural constants', that is, those things in nature that will continue to occur in some regular sequence provided that no agency interferes with them. They describe the world as its exists without agents.

But it is precisely interference into that world by agents that makes all the difference. Every time an agent acts intentionally she 'interferes' with the natural constants that would have remained the same following the 'natural' sequence of events had she not interfered. "All our physical predictions depend upon an abstraction from the presence of agents"[25] because agents have the capacity, within limits, to upset predictions that presume only the continuation of natural laws obtaining within the scope of the agent's anticipated action. We know, for example, that there is a natural law or constant regarding the biological need for the eye to be watered regularly by the closing of the eyelid over it. As long as 'nature takes its course', the laws of nature can predict, with a reasonable degree of accuracy, just how often the eye will be watered in a given period of time and under clearly defined conditions.

But suppose the agent whose eye is under consideration decides deliberately to lower the eyelid over the eye as a wink at someone. If we assume that agents have both the freedom and the power to do this from time to time, we have a case of an agent 'interfering' with the laws of nature. Her intentional (originative) act of winking now 'causes' the eyelid to close at a time not predicted (unless purely by coincidence) and definitely not caused by the natural causal laws. And her act now unifies and deploys the *very same mechanisms* 'used by' (notice the unavoidable but misleading agential reference here) the body in watering the eye according to the natural constants covered by causal law. *Descriptively*, the operation of the infrastructure will appear the same whether what is being referred to is an act or an event (Macmurray's term for an occurrence that is not an act). But if there is a genuine difference between the two occurrences, only reference to an intention that initiates, precedes, unifies, ramifies within, and pervades the occurrence can ultimately explain it if it is an act.

The agent has, from the point of view of the natural constants, 'interfered' with them. From the point of view of the agent, she has 'employed' them. Both points of view are correct provided that we don't understand 'interference' as a *violation* or *contradiction* of natural, causal law. Traditional reductionistic explanations do, of course, charge that interference is unacceptable precisely because it is violative of and contrary to natural law. But if Pols and Macmurray are correct, 'interference' is what happens every time agents act. But interference does not mean violation: it means *utilization* of causal law. It is not contrary to the natural constants; it simply subordinates them and unifies them under the overarching-ness of an originative act. It would be a violation of natural law if

natural law alone *exhaustively* explained *everything* that occurs in
the world. By definition, anything that purports to bring something
about through something other than a natural constant or cause
would have to be an exception to or a violation of explanation
through causal law. But if explanatory ultimacy, at least for some
occurrences, is found only in reference to the originative acts of
agents, then causal law cannot be explanatorily ultimate for *all*
occurrences, even though it will still be for those that are *not* the
acts of agents. The interference question, therefore, is a problem
only on the assumption that causal law is monolithic and exhaustive—an assumption that Pols and Macmurray are at pains to reject.

But just how can one fit an intention into a causal chain at the
level of the infrastructure? Aren't the elements of the infrastructure causally 'determined' from the distant past? If the infrastructure is merely 'used' by the intention, how does the intention
interrupt the causal chain?

The answer lies in the nature of interruption: an intention in-
terrupts a deterministic chain by inserting into it a causal factor
that it would not otherwise have had, a factor that exploits the
chain toward an end different from (though it might look the same
as) the end toward which the chain was tending 'naturally'. But the
intention is a causal factor in one sense[26] and not in another. It does
'cause' to happen something that might not have happened in its
absence, but it is not a cause in the sense of being predetermined
in an exhaustive way by preceding causes (intentional and nonintentional).

Intentions and Causes

This is not to say that the intention is totally *sui generis*, without
any prior influences shaping it. But the whole point of appealing to
an intention is precisely to distinguish it as cause from other causes
that do not seem rooted in the free choice of the agent.

There is something self-referential or tautologous about appealing to intentions: there is no absolutely convincing argument against
the determinist who insists that even intentions are merely the
result of prior nonintentional causes linked deterministically in a
causal chain stretching back to the beginning of time. In fact,
determinism is, in this sense, nonfalsifiable: it cannot, in principle,
recognize any occurrence as refuting its fundamental assumption
that all occurrences are the result of nonintentional causes (or that
intentional causes are simply caused by nonintentional causes). At

a certain level, therefore, as nonfalsifiable, determinism cannot refute (and cannot be refuted by) the claim that as human agents we 'know' that some of our actions are brought about freely by us in conjunction with (and limited to some important degree by) causal chains.

This is not to deny that there is a logical consistency to the argument that claims complete, exhaustive explanation by causal law, including the implication of complete, exhaustive determination of literally everything that happens by prior natural constants. One can, in theory, cut through the problem of reconciling free action with causal law by simply ruling out the possibility of the former. Determinism and materialism are cogent theories, provided we are willing to dispense with our commonsense experience of at least feeling free in some instances.

Often, however, the debate between determinists and free will defenders revolves around the construal of the word 'cause'. In one very real sense a freely initiated action 'causes' something to happen. It could even be said that intentions 'cause' actions. Thus my actions 'determine' a particular sequence of events. Whether causality therefore is necessarily coincident with determinism depends upon whether or not we take causality to rule out free will as a cause of those occurrences we have called actions. Causality as a concept needs either to be restricted to what causes something apart from free will, or free will must be understood to be one cause among others in bringing something about.

We also need to note the important distinction between the conditions for a cause and the cause of the cause. A free will cause can be conditioned by previous factors (age, experience, desire, motivation, etc.), but these conditions do not determine or cause the free will decision necessarily, which, as such, must in some sense escape from complete causal determinism. The question is how. Since we apparently think in causal terms about the natural world (as Kant insisted, in developing his notion of the synthetic a priori, the forms of sensuous intuition), it is virtually impossible to conceive of a cause (free will, intention) that is, while conditioned, not completely conditioned and thus is able to insert itself into the causal flow (nexus, chain) as one more additional cause helping to alter what would otherwise have been the deterministic outcome of that chain.

In other words, we cannot get away from some notion such as the intervention into or interruption of a causal chain that, apart from the intervention/interruption, would have produced one result according to one description (i.e., as determined by prior causes) and another result according to a different description (i.e., as the outcome of a free decision to act in a certain way).

The whole point of the Pols-Macmurray construal of action is that there is determination in nature but *some* (not all) of those determinations are by the will or intention of the agent. The agent, by initiating an action, determines what takes place at levels below (and incorporated under) his action. As Pols puts it,

> considered in abstraction from the action in question, the complex multiplicity of the infrastructure should be indeterminate. But, in the circumstances of precisely that action, the infrastructure is unifed by the action that is thus 'related' to it. And this means that what was indeterminate and determinable in the infrastructure is now determinate. . . . The action determines what was determinable; its absence would be the presence of some other action or else the presence (in passivity) of multiple units proper to some level below that of action. And in either of *those* cases a C–E [cause-effect] analysis after the event would yield a perfectly determinate physical system. . . . On this interpretation of the determination exercised by the power of an originative act, any given infrastructure level will be indeterminate in relation to the one above.[27]

The presence of statistical laws at some level is a prima facie indicator of the possibility of the "supervention of determinations consisting of the unifying presence of higher levels in 'relation' to those lower ones."[28]

Georg Henrik von Wright has expressed this crucial point in somewhat different language. "When a person raises his arm he sets in motion . . . a 'closed system'. . . . Any claim that there is a closed system with initial state p or a closed system with initial state q can only be substantiated provided there is some agent, outside these systems, who can operate them, put them in motion, by initiating their initial states in situations when he feels sure that they would not originate if it were not for his intervention. . . . In the 'race' between causation and agency, the latter will always win. It is a contradiction in terms to think that agency could be completely caught in the nets of causality."[29] When we act we put in motion the initial state of a closed system. When we observe we watch what takes place within the closed system without disturbing it. Causal relations, in the strict sense, are what we observe: they *are* the world without interference by agents. And we need to have knowledge of these causal continuants if we are to act successfully. "Our knowledge that we can do things . . . rests on our assurance that certain states of affairs will stay unchanged (or will change in a certain way), unless we interfere, productively or preventively, with the course of nature."[30]

This view of free interference into otherwise closed causal systems needs to be carefully distinguished from a popular version of determinism, which holds that causal coercion does not impair the autonomy of the agent.[31] Lawrence Davis, defending determinism, argues that "the whole course of [a] person's development, may be fully explainable deterministically, inevitable in the light of laws of nature and prior events. Being autonomous is compatible with having been *caused* to become autonomous; autonomy is compatible with determinism."[32] However intelligible the sequence of an agent's volitions, if they are not determined, they may on occasion or often be contrary to his motivation. This would impair his autonomy, not improve it!

The problem with Davis' argument is that, while affirming a kind of stoic acceptance of our determined state, it eschews any notion of our freedom to contribute to that state by freely choosing certain courses of action (however conditioned they may have been by other factors, provided only that they were not entirely determined by them). The position I have taken in this argument is that determinism is true only *under* the actions of an agent (when those actions 'determine' a sequence of events in a closed system) and only *in* those parts of nature that are (temporarily or necessarily) beyond an agent's reach.

The problem of freedom and determinism is too complex to be resolved completely here. Nevertheless, an explanation that explains away something that seems so basic to our experience as that of (at least some) free choices is not an explanation that can carry much existential weight. (It is not even clear how determinists explain to themselves the acts of reflection, argument, and debate through which they reach their conclusion—and hope to change their philosophical opponents' minds—that everything is determined and nothing is really an act.) And if we have a way to bring together an explanation that has room for deterministic causality with an explanation that requires a free act to exercise such causality along the way, then we may have found a way around this perennial thorny problem. At the same time we may have found a way not just to preserve the freedom of human agents to act without having their actions reduced to deterministic events, but also to establish the freedom and power of a divine agent to act without having to contradict or be diminished by the ontological context of other agents nondualistically relating to each other through mutual action.

Notes

1. Paul Tillich, *The Courage to Be* (New Haven: Yale University Press, 1952), pp. 184–85.

2. This concept of transcendence, as we shall see, is different from that employed in the dualist frame of understanding insofar as it does not assume a radical, ontological gap or change of ontological context between the transcending and the transcended entities.

3. Ervin Laszlo, *Introduction to Systems Philosophy: Toward a New Paradigm of Contemporary Thought* (New York: Gordon and Breach, 1972), p. 97.

4. Paul Weiss, "The Living System: Determinism Stratified," in Arthur Koestler and J. R. Smythies, eds., *Beyond Reductionism*, The Alpbach Symposium 1968 (Boston: Beacon Press, 1969), p. 33.

5. Hilde Hein, *On the Nature and Origin of Life* (New York: McGraw-Hill, 1971), pp. 172–73.

6. Edward Pols, *Meditation on a Prisoner: Towards Understanding Action and Mind* (Carbondale: Southern Illinois University Press, 1975), p. 11.

7. Edward Pols, "The Ontology of the Rational Agent," *Review of Metaphysics*, 33, no. 4 (June 1980): 690.

8. Edward Pols, "Power and Agency," *International Philosophical Quarterly*, 11, no. 3 (September 1971): 295.

9. Edward Pols, *The Acts of Our Being: A Reflection on Agency and Responsibility* (Amherst: University of Massachusetts Press, 1982), pp. 36–38.

10. Ibid., p. 36.

11. It may not, however, be one that she herself would identify as such.

12. Pols, *Meditation on a Prisoner*, p. 103.

13. Ibid., p. 99.

14. Edward Pols, "Human Agents as Actual Beings," *Process Studies*, 8, no. 2 (1978): 111.

15. Pols, *Meditation on a Prisoner*, p. 105.

16. Ibid., p. 110.

17. Ibid., p. 72.

18. Ibid., p. 309.

19. Ibid., p. 42.

20. Ibid., p. 65.

21. Ibid., p. 310.

22. Ibid., p. 311.

23. Ibid., p. 315.

24. John Macmurray, *The Self as Agent* (London: Faber and Faber, 1957), p. 52.

25. Ibid., p. 159.

26. See Donald Davidson, "Actions, Reasons, and Causes," in Alan R. White, ed., *The Philosophy of Action* (Oxford: Oxford University Press, 1968), pp. 79–94.

27. Pols, *Meditation on a Prisoner*, p. 304.

28. Ibid., p. 306.

29. Georg Henrik von Wright, *Explanation and Understanding* (Ithaca, N.Y.: Cornell University Press, 1971), pp. 78–81.

30. Ibid., pp. 190–91, n. 41.

31. See Lawrence Davis, *Theory of Action* (Englewood Cilffs, N.J.: Prentice-Hall, 1979), pp. 112ff.

32. Ibid., p. 122.

6

God: The Supreme Historical Agent

With Pols' explication of agent-act as our foundation, we can now begin to develop its application to a concept of God as the supreme Agent who acts decisively in history. The notion of personal agency as a model for divine action is not new in Christian theology.[1] Our task is to show how a 'literal' application of agency is appropriate to God as the Agent who is together bound with us in the deepest possible kind of mutual relationship. In particular we want to show that this relationship must include the possibility of divine action at particular times and places, in addition to an overarching divine act through which everything created is sustained in existence. At the same time, however, we need to identify those elements in the concept of God as Agent that distinguish it from the concept of the human being as agent. We will have to walk a rather narrow tightrope between reducing God to the status of being simply a very powerful human-type agent and extending God to a transcendent realm so utterly different from that in which we human agents act that God's being becomes absolutely unintelligible to us.

The 'Hard Literal Core' of Our Talk About Divine Action

William P. Alston has recently used the phrase 'partial univocity' (i.e., partially literal application of finitely derived terms to God) to describe the kind of attribution to God of the categories of personal agency that we can legitimately make. While differing with some of the things Alston thinks require univocal attribution to be only partial (e.g., he believes God has no body and I am not sure God cannot have a body), I think the notion of partial univocity is a good one because it makes the crucial assumption that if God is to be intelligible at all (and God's *real relationship* with us, the experiential fact of being together bound with God, requires some degree of intelligibility), God must share at least partially in what we have called our finite ontological context. This partial univocity provides us with what Alston calls "a hard literal core to our talk about divine action."[2]

At the most basic level, or minimally, God must be able to *intend* and to *enact* intentions within and with respect to the world. And any divine intention and enaction must have at least partial univocity with what we as agents do when we intend and enact our intentions. As Alston says, "unless our understanding of divine purpose, intention, and will had at least as much commonality with human motiviational concepts as I have been alleging, we would, justifiably, doubt that the divine states in question deserve to be called 'purpose,' 'intention,' and so on."[3] For Christians, in fact for all within the biblical tradition, it is mandatory to retain the concepts of divine purpose and intention because they are the core of the biblical description of God. The question is not whether Christians can or should think of God as a loving Agent with whom they are together bound in mutual love through God's gracious acts, but *how* that thinking can best be articulated intelligibly and in accord with the most rational concepts possible.

If we can provide that 'hard literal core' to our thinking about God, including what is often left out of such discussions, namely God's performance of *particular, specific, historical acts* that are distinguishable from God's overarching sustaining acts, two major challenges will then emerge. The first is to find a way to protect our concept of God from being reduced to something not worthy of worship or of metaphysical ultimacy. In particular, we will have to take on the problem of whether God's ultimacy as supreme Agent requires that God also be timeless, bodiless, and immutable, as well as omnipotent and omniscient in all respects. At what precise points is the univocity of our language about God truly partial and not wholly literal? The second challenge will be to find a way to protect our belief in God from being rendered religiously unacceptable by the existence of evil actions and occurrences, the cumulative effect of which might overwhelm the conviction that God is at work in the world for good.

As we pursue these questions, we need to be aware of the almost monolithic view among contemporary Christian theologians that any attempt to talk intelligibly about God's action in the world must avoid speaking of God's specific acts in relation to particular historical and/or physical occurrences. The notion of an 'interventionist' God is dismissed as unintelligible to a modern intellect, shaped as it is by the prevailing scientific view of a 'closed causal nexus,' in which only finite causes and effects obtain. Any divine intervention into this nexus is assumed to be 'supra' historical, and therefore beyond explanation in historical, scientific terms. Any attempt to speak of God as an agent *in* history (as distinguished from the notion of a God for whom all of history is a single master act) must be regarded as scientifically and rationally unintelligible and literally incredible.

Divine Action and Causal Law

A common thread running through many of the traditional attempts to limit the use of agent language with respect to God is the conviction that causal law is explanatorily exhaustive of *all* that happens *in* the world. Consequently, divine action cannot be understood as a violation of that law without falling into incoherence or unintelligibility. If it is to be understood at all it will have to be as something other than action *within* the world of cause and effect. Langdon Gilkey put it well for a generation of theologians when he said in an article nearly 30 years ago that the analogy of the mighty acts of God in history is "empty, . . . void since the denial of the miraculous."[4] For the allegedly more primitive mentality represented in the Bible the language of God acting was univocal (albeit not metaphysically sophisticated): God acted as we did though on a far grander scale. But for us, as Bultmann argued, univocity is dead. No one expects to see an act of God 'alongside' or 'among' the other acts that constitute the history of the cosmos because causal law rules out any occurrences that do not conform completely to the finite cause-effect paradigm developed by modern science. "I need to see the worldly events as linked by cause and effect. . . . In doing so there remains no room for God's working. This is the paradox of faith, that faith 'nevertheless' understands as God's action here and now an event which is completely intelligible in the natural or historical connection of events."[5] Gilkey challenged theologians to find "an ontology of events specifying what God's relation to ordinary events is like,"[6] but did not really think such an ontology would or could be forthcoming precisely because he accepted, as did most twentieth-century theologians, the monolithic sway of causal law explanation of events in nature and history. Contemporary theology simply accepted without question the essential premises of metaphysical dualism, namely, that God (whatever God really was in Godself) was 'in' a radically other ontological context and could not be made to connect (as a direct causal force) with our ontological context without violation of the very principles of scientific understanding and historical explanation by which our context was metaphysically represented.

Kaufman on an Act of God

In 1968 Gordon Kaufman tried to provide a more coherent explanation of an act of God, but assumed, as had Gilkey and Bultmann, that the notion of a God "who continuously performs deliberate acts in and upon his world . . . has become very problematic for most moderns."[7] It is, he proclaimed, "precisely by *excluding* reference to such a transcendent agent that we gain genuine knowledge of the order that obtains in nature. . . ."[8] In other words, Kaufman accepts without question or qualification the explanatory ultimacy of causal law for the 'natural' order and the radical dualism separating that order from the divine reality. His way around that dualism was to assert that *the whole course of history*, and not particular acts within it, is the 'master' act of God. For Kaufman, this master act

> is not a new event that suddenly and without adequate prior conditions rips inexplicably into the fabric of experience, a notion consistent neither with itself nor with the regularity and order which experience must have if it is to be cognizable. Rather, here God's act is viewed as the course of precisely that overarching order itself: it is God's master act that gives the world the structure which it has and gives natural and historical processes their direction. Speaking of God's act in this sense in no way threatens the unity and order of the world as a whole.[9]

For Kaufman, God is not a 'being' or agent standing in relationship with the other agents in the world, but is rather the 'wholly other', the 'limit' of our reality or ontological context. Kaufman's claim is that the notion of God's transcendence can be understood as analogous to the transcendence of the human agent over his or her acts. Kaufman seems to draw heavily on a residual Cartesian-ism[10] in distinguishing between the 'real' or 'true' agent, hidden behind her acts, and the acts themselves, which are external and observable to others. As is the case with human agents, God can be known only when God acts in and through those acts and 'reveals' Godself.

But Kaufman's dualism remains unmodified throughout his development of the model of 'interpersonal transcendence'. As McLain has pointed out, for the 'residual Cartesianist' "the essence of the self consists of inaccessible, 'private' attitudes and feelings and states which are known to others only when disclosed."[11] But, as P. F. Strawson has argued, the Cartesianist cannot justify *any* claim to know the 'real' agent if there is an ontological gap sepa-rating the agent from her external acts since no commonality or univocity has been shown to exist between (the inner, true) her and her external acts.[12] The dualist assumption necessarily voids any justified inferential link between what we see and what Kaufman claims is the hidden reality 'behind' what we see. We have, in other words, no meaningful analysis or explication of the relationship he has labeled 'behind', or 'transcendent of'. In that case, the analogy of interpersonal relationship through action really gets us nowhere.

Like Kant, Kaufman winds up with a concept of God as an ultimate limit of experience and knowledge. As a limiting concept, it is not itself capable of being understood as we understand other things by means of the principles of knowledge *within* the world of experience. We only 'know' that God is not one of 'those things'. But just as Kant was therefore unable to provide us with any con-crete concept of God as a being who acts, so Kaufman preserves God's transcendence only at the price of rendering our knowledge of God completely equivocal. There remains no 'hard literal core' in that knowledge. The unity of God with God's act is shattered, propelling God out beyond the ontological context in which we, human agents, act and experience the actions of others.

Wiles on Divine Action

A more current approach to God's action in the world, which draws on Kaufman's attempt to link God's relation to the world only to a 'master' act, is Maurice Wiles' development of the notion of divine action as "God's relation to the world as a whole rather than to particular occurrences within it."[13] Wiles is concerned with both the conceptual intelligibility of divine action as well as its religious adequacy. He is well aware of the fact that religiously it is necessary to say something about God's activity in relation to the world. Quoting Walter Kasper, he acknowledges that deism is tantamount to atheism: "'The God who no longer plays an active role in the world is in the final analysis a dead God'."[14] Despite this acknowledgement, Wiles ultimately cannot avoid a form of deism himself. He confesses that his own view is "deistic in so far as it refrains from claiming any efficient causation on the part of God in relation to particular occurrences."[15] But Wiles is convinced, as are countless other contemporary theologians, that notions of divine intervention *into* the course of human history or natural processes are simply not intellectually convincing or religiously salutary. Wiles, like Kaufman and most other contemporary theologians, sees divine causation of specific events (which they almost always identify with 'acts') as entailing the view that God then becomes "just one more causal agent alongside others in the world."[16] Being "just one more agent" obviously threatens, from their point of view, God's uniqueness and transcendence. This implicitly dualistic orientation ultimately undergirds their rejection of any attempt to understand God as literally an agent like other agents, no matter what qualitative or quantitative differences set God's agency apart from human agency within the same ontological context. To involve God in any way directly in the causation of some specific acts (Wiles even rejects Kaufman's allusions to divine sub-acts within God's overarching 'master act'), is to enmesh God in all the nasty questions, such as "Why did God act here and not there?," "Why is God seemingly arbitrary in choosing to act only on some occasions and not others?," and so forth. Wiles explicitly rejects even my own earlier attempt to build a case for God's action along the lines of human action's transcendence of strict causal determination because it would then force us to acknowledge that God's action has "been sparingly and strangely used."[17] I will deal with that 'religious' (as distinct from conceptual) difficulty later on. But the underlying objection to specific divine action is that it forces the believer to develop a presumably retrograde argument inserting divine action incongruently and inexplicably into an otherwise coherent and seamless web of intramundane cause and effect. Like Kaufman, Wiles offers an alternative view of divine action as the single, overarching act of creation. The "gradual emergence" of the world should be seen as "a single divine act,"[18] and no further, specific, historical acts of God *within* the world are necessary. The world as a totality, with all its processes and characteristics, constitutes a single divine action rather than an arena for particular or discrete divine acts *in addition to* the original creative and ongoing sustaining act. God is the ultimate source of the conditions within which all *other* acts take place, but, as Creator, God does not act alongside those other agents or in the causal order itself.

Farrer on the 'Causal Joint' Between Human and Divine Action

An argument similar to Wiles', and one that has formed the basis of a number of recent attempts to articulate God's relation to the world, is found in the work of Austin Farrer. Farrer also is suspicious of the intelligibility of speaking about specific acts of God in history that would distinguish them from other, ostensibly non-divinely initiated occurrences. Like Wiles, he wants to say that God works in and through the whole cosmic order, in and through each and every situation, without violating or interfering with any of the particular causal processes or regularities. At the same time, he wants to talk about *some* occurrences as being especially revelatory of God's overarching intentions for the world. But these occurrences are revelatory not because God has caused them (and not others) to be so, but because we have *taken* them, or interpreted them to be so. It is our subjective judgment or discernment that yields the claim that a certain occurrence is a divine act. It is not, by necessity, that an occurrence is a particular divine act objectively. Farrer relies on a concept that he calls the 'causal joint' between divine and human action, but acknowledges that ultimately that concept is inscrutable to human understanding, precisely because God's action cannot be understood literally. Strictly speaking, for Farrer there is no place in the world for God to act specifically because "the pattern of physical forces fills all the time all the space there is, and allows no irruption from the divine."[19] Even the word 'irruption' suggests a kind of violence being done to a closed system of causes and effects in which, apparently, not even human acts can occur unless they, too, are the results of and subsumable under causal law. Farrer does appeal to a notion of 'double agency' to explain how an event caused completely by natural forces can be taken as a divine act. He points out that because we don't really know *how* the human will brings about efficient causation in the world, we can admit our fundamental ignorance of how God can be both the author of a finite act which is completely caused by finite factors. A single event has two distinct meanings, one for the creature acting and the other for God as its supporter. "Subjectively considered, there are two doings; physically, there is but one event."[20] But this solution is radically incoherent and trades unjustifiably upon an 'ignorance' that is particular to the finite context (how an intention brings about an effect) in order to justify a very different kind of ignorance (how a divine being can bring about an effect that has already been brought about by finite agents). In fact, it is not even clear how Farrer would be able to explain a human act that is free from causal determination and thus is some kind of 'irruption' or 'intervention' into the otherwise closed causal nexus. This incoherence makes it impossible to give any meaningful account of specific divine actions in history. As Vincent Brummer has put it, in summarizing both Wiles' and Farrer's views, "the claim that God brings about *all* events excludes the possibility of identifying particular events as acts of God distinct from the rest which we ascribe to other agents. . . . [This claim] would seem in the end to make all talk of divine agency vacuous."[21]

Tracy on God as Agent

The most recent, and by far the best, attempt to talk of God as an Agent is Thomas F. Tracy's *God, Action, and Embodiment.*[22] Tracy, as I am, is committed to the claim that "the concept of God as an agent whose actions engage humankind in a decisively important way is unquestionably a fundamental strand in Western theistic traditions."[23] He then sets out to show the rational and theological utility of applying the concepts of agency and action to God. I believe Tracy goes a long way toward realizing the full potential of these concepts, but his analysis needs to be supplemented by the work of Pols and Macmurray in order to provide a fuller and more satisfying explanation of God's *specific* historical acts.

Like most theologians who want to think of God as an Agent, Tracy begins his analysis by developing what we mean by the human agent. At the heart of our understanding of human agents is the ascription to them of 'character traits' (i.e., traits of moral character, personality traits, and qualities of the intellect). Obviously we distinguish and know persons by their particular character traits, such as, Mary is a promise-keeping but impulsive person with an enormously keen wit, or John is a liar with fairly regular habits, and somewhat slow of mind. To describe any person by his or her traits requires that that person be characterized as an agent whose intentional actions are at the core of our description. This means that if God is to be described as loving, just, and forgiving, there must be some intentional acts performed by God on the basis of which we ground our ascription of these divine character traits. Thus, if Tracy is correct, knowledge of God requires both that God acts in a way that is accessible to us directly and that such direct accessibility provides at least a minimal ontological context common to both God and human agents within which we can develop a core of literally true assertions about God's character.

Tracy says at the end of his analysis that "as with other agents, we will be able to give an account of *who* God is on the basis of what he does . . . [and] . . . insofar as God's actions fall under the informal criteria that govern the use of terms like 'loving,' 'just,' and 'wise,' these character trait predicates can be applied to him just as 'literally' as they are applied to persons. None of the rules . . . for the use of these predicates need be modified in order to ascribe them to a divine agent on the basis of his intentional actions."[24] At the heart of the unmodified application of these predicates is the fact that God does things in order to realize God's intentions and that those things are done in and upon the same world in which we do things (even though one of the things God does is to create and sustain the very conditions of that world itself). The philosophical issue is whether God can be conceived literally as an Agent. And, provided that one does not assume at the outset that God's nature is such that it cannot be so conceived, one can make a solid metaphysical argument that *only* agents can exercise the range and degree of power that entitles them (though perhaps only one of them) to our worship and to our trust that they are entities decisive and essential to the fulfillment of our being. Tracy's argument links the dualistic halves that Cartesianism and Kantianism traditionally have kept separate and that have made it impossible for the model of agency-action to transcend the finite ontological context in order to be straightforwardly applicable to God.

But now the issue that must be faced is the *difference* between God's agency and ours, and ultimately, the ontological difference between God the Agent and the human person as agent. If those differences can be construed in such a way that God remains both worthy of worship and decisive on the one hand and accessible and knowable on the other, then in the notion of agency-action we will have found the rational concept that can most adequately give expression to our primary experience of being together bound with God. Until those differences can be both articulated and reconciled with the common ontological context out of which our 'literal' knowledge of God arises, we are left only with a metaphysical possibility. The theological reality is our relationship with God. But we still need to find a way in which the metaphysical representation of that relationship preserves what is unique and distinctive about God without undermining the mutual reality through which God is known by us.

How Does God's Agency Differ From Ours?

If God *is* an Agent, what kind of Agent is God? In what ways does God's agency differ from ours? In what does *partial* univocity consist? We need to begin this analysis with a closer look at the relation between God and God's *specific, particular* acts in history. This relationship has traditionally been one of the stumbling blocks toward accepting a literal understanding of God as Agent because a divine action *within* the world seems to embed God too much *within* the very matrix that God is fundamentally supposed to create and sustain *as a whole* from *without*.

But the world itself (understood in this context as the totality of all beings and relationships in the complex of 'space-time') is usually accepted as a closed set, closed, that is, to individual, specific interventions from without. The world is exhaustively understood in terms of 'finite' causal law: for every occurrence in the world there is (only and without remainder) a complex of finite, intraworldly or natural causes behind it. Naturally, no divine cause (coming from a radically other transcendent ontological context) could ever be *understood* as operative within this closed set because we have no conceptual categories for grasping it. The Kantian legacy of a world of phenomena subject to the laws of the understanding (i.e., the laws of natural cause and effect) has remained to this day part of most theologians' outlook.

But the significance of the work of Kaufman, McLain, and, more recently, Tracy, lies exactly here: while none of them draw the inference as thoroughly as they could, they all seem to deny the Kantian legacy at just that point where they try to leave room for the freedom and mystery ingredient in the actions of *human* agents. The problem with the Kaufman approach is that the attempt to preserve this residue of human freedom requires a dualism between the premise that the world is completely explainable through causal law and the assumption that human agents do sometimes act and that those acts must be, in some real sense, free from *complete and exhaustive* causal explanation. Kaufman's insistence on the 'closed' nature of the space-time continuum has the ironic, and unintentional, consequence, if his argument were to remain completely self-consistent, that it virtually eliminates the possibility of free *human* action as well as divine action. If the continuum or set is truly closed to 'interventions' from above the realm of reality exhaustively described by causal law, then it is equally closed to human interventions as well as divine if they presuppose some degree of freedom on the part of the agent to act, a freedom that complete and exhaustive causal determination would eliminate.

What we need in order to rescue the 'world' for action is a conceptual analysis that will rescue it for both divine and human action simultaneously, if God's action is the basis for understanding God 'literally' as an Agent. And the rescue operation can be performed by nothing more than the distinction already elaborated between those occurrences that are events and those that are actions. As Pols and Macmurray have argued, an event is an occurrence brought about by a nonagential cause, that is, a cause which is not an agent. An act is an occurrence freely initiated (caused) by an agent utilizing causal infrastructures. If the world described by causal law is the world as it is *'provided nothing interferes'*, and if interference is what any agent does when she acts by employing that 'portion' or 'level' of the world as it is hierarchically structured 'under' her initiating action, then all action at least partially transcends the closed world of causal law.

We have seen, of course, that such transcendence is not a 'violation' of causal law but rather its employment in the carrying out of the agent's intention, an employment that 'shapes, wields, and deploys' it to that end.

The Problem of Divine 'Interference'

Virtually all theologians who reject the possibility of specific divine acts in the world do so, in part, because of their rejection of the notion of 'interference' by a divine Agent in the regular, lawfully ordered causal processes of the world. In order to move forward, we need to remind ourselves of the appropriate context for understanding 'interference' in the world by agents, human or divine. The 'bad' kind of divine interference seems to mean that God is a kind of "demiurge, struggling to make the best of recalcitrant brute matter . . . [working] against the grain of the natural law that he himself has ordained."[25] This suggests that interference is taken to mean a violation, overturning, irruption, or disrupting of the very causal laws that God has created and sustains continually. Sometimes this kind of interference is rejected because it leads to the notion of a capricious God, a deus ex machina performing divine tours de force.[26] Religiously, such divine arbitrariness is, of course, unacceptable. But metaphysically, it is not at all clear that interference, per se, entails anything other than the notion of a being *capable* of utilizing the causal order for his own purposes. We have argued, however, that *every* agent utilizes the causal order in some sense. Every act is the initiation of a sequence of causal effects that carry out the agent's intention. And every initiation is an interference into a causal order *that in the absence of such freely initiated interference would have remained the same, subject to the laws of the causal order*. As Mats Hansson has put it, in a very recent, comprehensive analysis of divine action, "had an agent not interfered with the world . . . the change would not have taken place."[27] We can recall that Macmurray and Pols both have validated the insight that causal law obtains *provided that nothing interferes* with its regularities. But my act does, in fact, interfere with the natural order in order to bring about an occurrence that would not otherwise have taken place. When I choose to blink my eye, I interfere with the otherwise predicted course of events (in which my eyelid will close over my eye in a regular, repeatable fashion a certain number of times every minute), in order to bring about a specific, particular closing of the eyelid (a wink at my wife across the room signaling that it is time to leave the party).

Hansson has even suggested, consistent I believe with my argument, that as creator and sustainer of the causal order, God's *noninterference* with that order is necessary for every event that happens (i.e., by not interfering, God permits events to happen according to the regularities of the causal order. Equally, by not interfering with the biologically determined sequence of eye blinks, I 'permit' that sequence to occur as predicted by causal law). It is only when God interferes with God's own causal order that we have a specific divine act as distinguished from the overarching divine act of continual maintenance of the natural world. The metaphysical issue is not interference versus noninterference, but rather the *character* of the intentions that guide and structure the interference. What we need is a 'good' interference, the kind that permits agents to initiate new causal chains for purposes that are benevolent, loving, and so on. The noninterventionist account of divine action inevitably winds up with some version of the double-agent theory, which we have concluded is incoherent because it requires us to view one and the same occurrence as both a causally determined event and the act of an agent. This is conceptual dualism and it fails to account adequately for the experience of God as the agent directly responsible for some occurrences and not others.

God must, of course, permit some events to occur in the sense that without God's sustaining power they would not exist at all. This kind of permission is what might be referred to as God's contributing efficacy: it is necessary for the existence of all occurrences in the world but not sufficient *in those cases where the occurrences are acts performed by agents other than God.* The noninterventionist account seems to entail a divine determinism (God as the underlying cause of the whole natural order), whereas the interventionist account allows us to maintain both that God permits all occurrences (by not intervening to annul them or eliminate their causes) and is directly responsible for some (by intervening at discrete, particular points in the causal order). If we wish to uphold both human freedom of action (given the appropriate limits) and genuine interaction between God and human persons, such as in divine response to human prayer, the interventionist account is clearly necessary.

If one is looking for 'room' for divine acts, one will find it in exactly the same way as one finds room for human acts, namely as the transcendent source and unifying power through which the causal infrastructure is used in the enactment of *an* agent's intentions. (Transcendent does not mean, of course, located in an totally other ontological context, but rather presiding over dimensions or levels of reality that are less inclusive than the transcendent level.) This means that there need be nothing 'unique' about the relation of divine actions to the infrastructures of the world that is not also 'unique' about the relation of human acts to their infrastructures. The link between divine action and the world is identical *in this respect* to the link between human action and the world. God would have to be understood as the Agent whose acts unify and ramify throughout a complex of infrastructural mechanisms to achieve their intended purposes. God's relation to those acts would be the same as a human agent's relation to her acts, namely as the one who presides over and utilizes a causal infrastructure in the accomplishment of a (free) intention.

The Mystery of Intentions

What is brought about in the world can generally be observed empirically. In many cases the mechanisms through which it is brought about can be analyzed scientifically. But what 'holds together' this empirical complex is not itself observable or analyzable in the same way, for it is the intention of the agent ramifying throughout the whole of its enactment. As Georg Henrik von Wright puts it, "It is a contradiction in terms both to let and to make the same thing happen on the same occasion. Therefore no man *can* observe the causes of the results of his own basic actions."[28] And, as an act, its initiation lies in the intention of the agent (which is not to be reduced to or identified with one more empirical cause in a sequence of causes and effects if that means that the intention is *nothing more* than the effect solely of preceding nonfree nonintentional causes).

From the point of view of causal law per se, the origination of an act is always mysterious (that is, beyond complete or exhaustive analysis or explanation). Thus the origination of something that is a *divine* act is neither more nor less mysterious, in this respect, than the origination of something that is a human act. Simply by virtue of being an act, it transcends causal reduction and explanation. The link between an intention and the causal infrastructure that it deploys is never fully explainable if the terms of explanation assume (as does the causal law model) the explanatory ultimacy and adequacy of causal law, which has no place for intentions.

But a divine act may be mysterious in other ways without thereby falling into the incoherence or unintelligibility of dualism. It is clear that most human acts require an empirical infrastructure to be enacted. I cannot write these words without the use of the neuronic structure of my brain, the physiological structure of my fingers, and the mechanical hardware of a computer keyboard. These instruments are essential to the carrying out of my intention to communicate in written words what I am thinking. But it is not clear that a divine Agent needs to utilize the same mechanisms in the same way to achieve the divine intention. It may well be the case that the complete 'how' of divine action is hidden from human understanding. The mechanisms and operative principles by which the divine Agent deploys the infrastructures of the world may not be as accessible to human investigation as are those that are present in human action. The essential reason for this hiddenness is the infinite range and power of divine action. It simply may be the case that quite apart from the 'mystery' of how *any* agent utilizes the causal infrastructure, the infinite complexity of divine action will always remain beyond human understanding. This divine mysteriousness, however, does not nullify the literalness of understanding God as an Agent. Rather it is due precisely to that understanding given the inherent mysteriousness (though not irrationality), from the point of view of causal explanation, of the relation between an agent's act and its infrastructure.

Divine Basic Acts

One important concept that has been used to explain divine action has been the 'basic act', which the philosopher Arthur Danto introduced.[29] (Danto has changed his mind in some regards respecting his original formulation of this notion.) He intended to refer to those acts that do not require an intermediate instrument through which they are enacted, or as he put it, acts that the Agent does not cause to happen by doing something else but that he simply does. When I choose to blink my eyelid, I do this without first causing something else to happen, which in turn causes the eyelid to descend. A basic act still requires an agent to perform it, but it is performed, as it were, directly, without doing one thing in order to do something else. Not surprisingly some theologians (e.g., Tracy) have suggested that most, if not all, of God's acts are basic in this sense. The reason for calling in the notion of a basic act to explain divine action seems to be that it permits God to work in and upon the world without being dependent upon worldly, causal infrastructures that could be taken to limit the range of God's actions. William P. Alston has established the logical possibility of God performing basic acts (those that God does simply by doing them, as distinct from doing something else first in order to do them). A basic action "is one that is performed *not* by or in (simultaneously) performing some other action" and "every nonbasic action is done *by* performing a basic action".[30] God can simply bring something about without having to utilize an instrumental substructure. If God decides to have rain fall, it will fall. Presumably, God does not need first to cause rain clouds to form as a causal precursor to rain falling, and thus God is freed from dependence upon the causal conditions that normally precede rain falling.

Does appeal to God as performing only basic acts constitute one of the significant differences between divine and human action? The answer will depend upon whether God really can bring it about that the rain will fall regardless of whether there are clouds in the sky at that particular time and place. If we say that God cannot cause it to rain, in a basic way, if clouds are not present (since rain, according to the laws of physics, requires the presence of clouds), are we not saying that God *does* need the infrastructures of the physical world to accomplish God's intentions even if those intentions do not require a prior cause (other than God's simply having them)? And if we are saying this are we not denying that God can act basically?

Or is it, perhaps, better to say that the notion of a basic act is not particularly helpful simply because all acts require some kind of causal structure through which they are enacted? God may well need the infrastructures in order to accomplish God's intention (rain without the infrastructure that makes rain rain in the first place is not rain). It is almost tautologous to say that I need the infrastructure of the eyelid and eyeball if I intend successfully to wink since winking *is* the closing of the eyelid over the eyeball. But do I need to do something over and above and prior to my blinking of the eye in order to bring it about that the blink occurs? If the answer is 'no' because this is what it means to be a basic act, then God's acts can all be basic without denying the necessity of their utilization of an infrastructure. But to imply that God can act without *any* infrastructure may be to imply what is literally inconceivable.

God may have so much control over the entire space-time complex of infrastructures that it requires only God's intention for something to happen within and by means of those infrastructures. In this sense, everything that God does could well be a basic act if God chooses, assuming that God's control over the world is in principle as decisive as my control over those parts of my body that I can affect directly without doing something else to cause the result I want.

But this may not require us to admit the possibility that God can do some things completely independent of any and all infrastructure. If a miracle is defined as the occurrence of something completely without a causal infrastructure, does this mean that God *cannot* cause miracles? Could God, for example, bring it about that rain begins falling from a cloudless sky? Suddenly, while the sky remains cloudless, drops of water begin appearing literally out of thin air. Could such an occurrence happen and if so could it be attributed to an act of God? This is a difficult question but it at least puts this concept of 'miracle' where it belongs, namely as an occurrence that does in fact *violate* the principles of the causal infrastructure as it exists in the absence of actions. Acts, remember, only *interfere or intervene* in the causal infrastructure. The question is whether God can act so as to bring something about that overturns or simply bypasses causal mechanisms instead of utilizing or deploying them. Most theists would probably want to say 'yes' because to say 'no' implies an unacceptable limitation on divine power. That God can bring about the falling of rain in the complete absence of clouds whenever and wherever God wants would seem to be essential to both the pro-miracle and anti-miracle arguments. But those who want to shy away from miracles as *violations* of the causal order would then have to argue that in order for God to bring it about that it rains now in the arid southwest where no rain clouds have formed for months, God would first have to bring it about that those causes that produce rain clouds come into existence. And that would mean that God's intention, while capable of freely initiating the process by which rain will fall (bringing about by an intervention the beginning of a new causal chain that will result in rain), is subject with respect to its enactment to that process, which may or may not take a considerable period of time to produce the rain. Even though it might be argued that God could 'speed up' the process, it would have to be conceded that if what is ultimately going to happen is rain falling, *what it means for rain to fall* involves a formation process culminating in condensation falling from its physically immediate source, namely the rain cloud. And it is, therefore, to and by this process that the enactment of God's intention must conform.

Miracles

Those who would argue that God can peform genuine miracles are committed to the view that God can bypass the formation process and literally cause raindrops to appear in a cloudless sky without any prior causal preconditions. They might have to accept the point that what is falling is not literally rain (if we define rain in terms of the causal process by which it normally occurs), but they would insist that what is falling is, in fact, watering the earth exactly as rain does and that it is, after all, this result that is the intention of the divine miracle. One could, of course, define rain as the moisture that waters the earth without tying one's definition to a prior causal sequence necessary to the production of rain. This stipulative definition would enable one to then claim a divine intention as the cause of the rain without having to link that intention to a finite causal sequence or infrastructure. But is it even coherent to think the occurrence of something with literally no preceding or conditioning casual antecedents?

My argument for the concept of God as Agent does not stand or fall on the justification of the argument that God can perform genuine miracles. I do think that such miracles fall into a different category from those divine acts that, like human acts, *initiate* processes within the causal infrastructure but do not *violate* or overturn those processes. Those defending miracles have, of course, an additional burden of explanation: they cannot appeal simply to the transcendence that all agents have in relation to the causal order, because that transcendence is quite compatible with the limitation of acts to a utilization of the causal order (the more powerful the agent the more power he or she has over the causal order). The additional burden is explaining how an act can, as it were, *fail* to utilize the natural infrastructure. I do not think such a possibility can be ruled out, especially given that an agent (God) has created that infrastructure in the first place, but I do not underestimate the difficulty in comprehending it. I don't know what an explanation would consist of. The initiation of the act in and through an intention is not problematic, but what would it mean for an intention to fail to utilize infrastructures? Somehow the intention would have to result directly, without infrastructures, in its enactment. This is, of course, the import of the concept of a basic act. It suggests that some enactments occur directly as a result of the intention alone. But, as I have suggested, even Danto's original conception of a basic act never contemplated the possibility of my blinking my eye without utilizing an eyelid. Maybe a better analogy would be if my intention was to make my eyeball moist, a basic act could accomplish that without the causal intermediary of the eyelid closing over it. Obviously, the *how* of that accomplishment would be fundamentally mysterious to causal explanation since the normal causal process had been bypassed. But precisely because it is mysterious we tend to dismiss such a possibility even while upholding the authenticity of explanation by reference to human intention. If we want to defend the notion of miracles, God's relation to God's world would, correspondingly, have to be even more mysterious than our relation to our own bodies, since none of our basic acts require a violation of the causal mechanisms through which we perform them. And that second level of mystery simply may not be necessary to explain those things that we have experienced God as doing in our lives.

The core issue should be whether there are any causal structures in the world that God has created that stand as an impediment to the accomplishment of God's purposes. As long as God has complete control over those structures, and can utilize them at will to carry out God's intentions, we will have the full complement necessary for understanding God as omnipotent in every relevant respect. It may well be enough that God can condense or speed up the causal mechanisms of the world by means of God's infinite power and through God's intentions, in order to bring about the results God wants to accomplish in the world. Just where in the causal order God would have to intervene may be part of the divine *how* that is beyond our grasp, but it need not require an overturning of the causal order. Human beings have learned a great deal through science about how to alter the causal structures, without violating them, in order to bring about results that those structures on their own would not have produced in the same way or at the same time had agents not interfered. The history of medical technology and its interventions into the human biological processes is ample testimony to the power of intervention. One need only consider the extraordinary range and power of God's capacity to intervene to accept the possibility of God's speeding up and altering the causal infrastructures without violating them. In this case, we would not necessarily have provided room for genuine miracles, but if the *results* of miracles (e.g., healing, communication, avoidance of disaster, etc.) are what is of primary concern, then those results can be achieved without recourse to miracles *per se*. And if we understand God's relation to the causal infrastructures as analogous to our relation to our own bodies, then each divine intervention could be understood as a basic act.

It may, however, also be the case that while God could bring everything about through basic acts even while conforming them to the infrastructures of the world (which are in turn the result of an original divine creative act), God may *choose* to bring some things about more indirectly. Suppose God is an Agent who intends to have persons respond lovingly but freely to God's concern for them. God may perform some basic acts, such as causing the rain to fall to water their crops (but without failing to utilize the appropriate infrastructures), intending that that basic act will indirectly cause those who are grateful for this benefit to worship God. Their worship, while perhaps the chief end God had in mind in acting, is not directly caused by God even though God has directly caused some things that God hopes will inspire such worship. Thus, God could certainly have the same capacity to employ a variety of kinds of acts in God's relationship with others just as we do.

If God did utilize the causal mechanisms of the world in order to produce an intended result, does it really matter whether God did this immediately as a basic act or mediately, through a series of events that were initiated by a basic act? In other words, as long as the initiation of at least one act falls within the meaning of the concept 'basic act', is it necessary (for religious as well as philosophical reasons) to insist that *all* of God's acts are basic, as Alston seems inclined to say. "It is a live possibility that all God's actions are basic."[31]

If the parting of the waters at the Red Sea (a controversial but explicit example of a divine act) was a basic act (no prior causal conditions issuing in the parting) then it would fall into the category of miracle: namely something that occurs without the utilization of causal mechanisms as we have come to know them through scientific analysis. Absent the blowing of wind or other climatic factors, the waters would simply (had one been an observer) have been seen to have parted. An observer might have been looking at the still waters when suddenly they parted without the presence of wind or any other natural cause being seen to contribute to their parting.

But would it be any less of a miracle for God to have begun a sequence of events, each of which was in conformity with normal causal conditions, that culminated in a strong wind blowing the waters apart? The parting would no longer be a miracle (since winds parting waters is perfectly consistent with causal law) but would the initiation of the sequence now have to be seen as a miracle (and as a basic act?) Certainly human basic acts are not miracles. I do not violate causal law in raising my arm even though the initiation of the raising is not *caused* by anything other than my intention to raise it. However, causal law as such cannot *predict* or *exhaustively explain* (without remainder or reductively) the initiation of the sequence of causal events which permits (but does not cause in this instance) the arm to rise. Absent my intention to raise my arm, it will not go up (in this instance). By definition, an intention is not causally predictable if I am a free agent (though it may be anticipated for other reasons, such as being in keeping with my character as this particular type of agent, etc.). And if the initiation of the sequence of events is not itself solely the result of prior causal sequences (absent an agent's intention), then its explanation cannot be complete or adequate solely in causal terms.

This view implies that all acts are, in a sense, an agent's interference in the causal order that, in the absence of that interference, would not have produced the result that the act intends (or, more precisely put, that the agent intends by means of the act). The intention behind the act initiates a causal sequence in order to accomplish that intention. It enters the causal infrastructure, as it were, in order to deploy it toward a particular end. That end may be simply the act itself. (I raise the arm for the sheer delight of raising it.) But the entry of the act into the infrastructure, or, again more precisely, the act's utilization of the infrastructure beginning at a certain point in time and space, is not itself capable of being fully explained in terms that are exhaustively reducible to the causal factors of the infrastructure taken in and of themselves. The initiation of the causal sequences, if it is the beginning of an act, is explained only in agent-causation terms that refuse to be reduced to causal language alone (though causal language is appropriate to describing its execution following its initiation). I intend the rising of my arm, the intention initiates a sequence of occurrences that then take shape over a period of time and by means of the material infrastructure of nature, the whole sequence (except its initiation) taking place in accordance with natural, causal law.

Now it may be helpful to describe the initiation of any sequence of causal events as a basic act in the sense that the agent needs to do nothing else first before initiating the sequence. The intention of the agent at that time and place are sufficient for act deployment or utilization of the causal infrastructure.

But this fact seems to suggest that the real issue here is whether God can initiate a sequence of events that culminates in what God intends. That which is intended may or may not, as Alston points out, be a basic act (in the way that my arm rising is a basic act and the signaling of someone by means of the risen arm is not). "It is equally possible that God chooses to influence some situations *indirectly*. . . . I am quite willing to leave the decision on this one up to God."[32]

We have only just begun to learn something about the intricate, complex, mysterious worlds of the subatomic and the cosmic. The 'simple' laws of the old Newtonian block-universe have proven not to be so simple after all. The kind of events taking place at the subatomic level as well as at the origins of the universe (in the microseconds after the initial 'big-bang') are so far beyond the older 'laws' determining how causal structures work, that we would be well advised not to claim too much for what is or is not possible ontologically in the empirical world. If this is so, then we cannot rule out that even a 'resurrection' from the dead is a utilization of causal structures (though one that we presently have no way of understanding given the limits of contemporary empirical knowledge).

The point is that it may not be possible or necessary to reserve space for divine basic acts that override or bypass causal mechanisms. Apart then from the necessity for each divine act to have a beginning that does not depend upon anything other than God's intention to begin it (a necessity for *all* acts, divine or human), not all divine acts need be basic.

The difference between God's and our capacity to act, of course, would ultimately have to reside in the range, power, and moral integrity of what God does. Can we justify a claim that God's range, power and integrity are so much greater than ours that God is worthy of our worship, devotion, and absolute commitment? Or is the notion of God as Agent inherently too limiting on God, rendering *this* God incompatible with the only God genuine theists believe we should both worship and rationally understand?

Notes

1. See the Appendix for a listing of sources on the concept of God as Agent and God's acts in history.

2. William P. Alston, "Divine and Human Action," in Thomas V. Morris, ed., *Divine and Human Action: Essays in the Metaphysics of Theism* (Ithaca, N.Y.: Cornell University Press, 1988), p. 280.

3. Ibid., p. 275.

4. Langdon Gilkey, "Cosmology, Ontology, and the Travail of Biblical Language," *Journal of Religion* 41 (1961): 200.

5. Rudolph Bultmann, *Jesus Christ and Mythology* (New York: Charles Scribner's Sons, 1958), p. 65.

6. Gilkey, "Cosmology," p. 200.

7. Gordon Kaufman, "On the Meaning of 'Act of God'," *Harvard Theological Review* 61 (1968): 175.

8. Ibid., p. 176.

9. Ibid., p. 192.

10. See F. Michael McLain, "On Theological Models," *Harvard Theological Review* 62 (1969): 162.

11. Ibid., p. 163.

12. See P. F. Strawson, *Individuals: An Essay in Descriptive Metaphysics* (Garden City, N.Y.: Doubleday-Anchor, 1963).

13. Maurice Wiles, *God's Action in the World* (London: SCM Press, 1986), p. 29.

14. Ibid., p. 2.

15. Maurice Wiles, *Working Papers in Doctrine* (London: SCM Press,

1976), p. 140, as quoted in Mats Hansson, *Understanding an Act of God: An Essay in Philosophical Theology* (Uppsala, Sweden: University of Uppsala Press, 1991), p. 63. See also, for example, the criticism by John Polkinghorne, *Science and Providence: God's Intervention with the World* (Boston: New Science Library, 1989), p. 6: "Wiles' view, swallowed whole, has all the detachment of deism."

16. Ibid., p. 56.

17. Ibid., p. 66.

18. Ibid., p. 54.

19. Austin Farrer, *The Freedom of the Will* (London: Adam and Charles Black, 1958), p. 313.

20. Austin Farrer, *Faith and Speculation* (London: Adam and Charles Black, 1967), p. 159.

21. Vincent Brummer, "Farrer, Wiles and the Causal Joint," *Modern Theology* 8, no. 1 (January 1992): 7.

22. Thomas F. Tracy, *God, Action, and Embodiment* (Grand Rapids, Mich.: William B. Eerdmans, 1984).

23. Ibid., p. 4.

24. Ibid., p. 152.

25. Polkinghorne, *Science and Providence*, p. 46.

26. John Polkinghorne, *One World: The Interaction of Science and Theology* (Princeton: Princeton University Press, 1986), p. 75.

27. Mats Hansson, *Understanding an Act of God*, p. 51.

28. Georg Henrik von Wright, *Explanation and Understanding* (Ithaca, N.Y.: Cornell Univerfsity Press, 1971), p. 130.

29. Arthur Danto, "Basic Actions," *American Philosophical Quarterly* 2 (1965): 141–48.

30. William P. Alston, "Can We Speak Literally of God," *Divine Nature and Human Language* (Ithaca, N.Y.: Cornell University Press, 1989), p. 55.

31. Ibid., p. 57–58, n. 22.

32. Ibid., p. 61–62.

7

Refining the Concept of God as Agent

What would a notion of God as supreme Agent, literally understood, and as conformable to what a community of faith would want to say, based on its experience of God, look like? Let's sketch out such a notion and then see in what respects it fails to conform to classical theistic notions and in what ways it compensates for these alleged 'failures'.

I would not be bold enough to suggest that my development of the concept of God as supreme Agent will be sufficient to persuade those who are convinced that God, to be God, must be transcendent (in a dualist sense) of time, space, and matter, *per se*, as well as omnipotent and omniscient in all respects. And if someone is committed to the view that these characteristics are essential to the very meaning of the notion of God for Christians, then my alternative concept of God simply will not satisfy. Two things need to be remembered, however. First, early Christians simply did not think in terms of dualistic transcendence, omnipotence, and omniscience. Those terms are the result of a later metaphysical scheme inherited by western Christians from the philosophies of Greece, especially those of Plato and Aristotle. Therefore, they cannot claim the same kind of ultimacy and authority that the biblical community's experience of God has. Second, an alternative understanding of God as Agent, while revisionary of traditional dualist understanding, does seek to preserve those elements in the *experience* of

God that have been common to all Christians (e.g., power, grace, redemption, etc.) and to provide a coherent and metaphysically satisfying *concept* of God, just as the dualist understanding has sought to do. The real question, therefore, is whether the notion of God as Agent *omits* or *undervalues* anything in either the experience or understanding of God that is authoritatively part of the community's heritage and self-understanding. I would argue that it does not. What, then, are the elements in the agential concept of God that speak to traditional Christian religious and metaphysical concerns?

The Divine Creative Act

First, the relation of God to the cosmos could be articulated through the notion of a genuine divine creative act—a basic act in the sense that God brings the cosmos into being without causal intermediaries. (This basic act is quite different from God's subsequent basic acts as discussed in the preceding chapter, assuming as we have already done, that God will (normally) act *through* causal structures, even if God does so by altering, condensing, compacting, speeding them up, etc.) The original basic act would be, therefore, beyond literal comprehension (insofar as the comprehension of acts assumes the existence of a causal infrastructure). It would, in this sense, be the first (and only?) instance of a genuine miracle. That creation is the result of a divine intention can be affirmed as logically coherent (requiring only the acceptance of the notion of a divine Agent), but the 'mechanics' of the operative relation between that intention and what it produces without causal infrastructures would have to be fundamentally, perhaps irremediably, mysterious. It might even be the primordial mystery behind which we cannot go. All subsequent divine acts may involve the infrastructure in some way or another and thus be subject to the authenticity of agent-explanation without being themselves involved in this primordial mystery.

But if we insist that God must have created the infrastructures for action, that creative act is in some irreducible way mysterious to human consciousness, not only because it is ontologically unique, but because it is an *act*. If the mechanics of a human act are in some sense inexplicable, (i.e., the exact link between the agent's intention and the subsequent or simultaneous enactment of it is incapable, in principle, of being understood in the explanatory categories of causal law whose meaning and application always lie only *within* the structures of the enactment), how much more inexplicable must be the mechanics of a divine act (but not because it is divine, per se) that brings those structures into existence in the first place and continues to sustain them?

If our grasp of causal production already presupposes the causal infrastructure itself, can we ever grasp the 'production' of that infrastructure in the first place? But if we admit that we cannot grasp how it is produced, are we thereby committed to confessing that we simply don't know what we mean when we affirm that God is its 'producer' or agent-cause? Can we affirm intelligibly that something is a cause without having any understanding of the means by which it is a cause? Is this ignorance a fatal defect?

Once again we need to revert to our understanding of human causality. We know, both foundationally (i.e., without having to observe ourselves empirically) and with corroboration from observation, that we 'cause' things to happen without knowing fully 'how' we do so. As long as the explication of the 'how' is left to scientific analysis of the causal infrastructure, it will never completely capture the link between that infrastructure and the intention that utilizes it since it transcends the infrastructure in that specific respect. It is therefore intelligible, provided there is other compelling evidence to support it, to claim that an agent can link his or her intention to a concrete result without having full knowledge as to how that result was brought about. Now in most cases of human action we can know a great deal about the infrastructure despite our inability to know, in *its* terms, how it is utilized by intentions. In the case of divine action, we can know literally nothing about how God brings the cosmic infrastructure into existence in the first place precisely because God does not utilize an infrastructure to create that infrastructure. God's act of creation is sui generis, but not, for all that, *not* an act.

Invoking Analogy

This may be the appropriate place to invoke analogy or metaphor. As long as we are committed to the notion of God as an Agent who utilizes infrastructural means for carrying out intentions in the cosmic order, it may not be irrational to claim that God's creation of that order is itself, at least analogously, an act. We would not be conceiving God as an Agent in one context and covertly denying God's agency in another, which is what normally happens in most dualistic attempts to employ the analogy of God as Agent. Instead, we would affirm the authenticity of the notion of God as Agent in the cosmic context (i.e., as capable of acting within it) while at the same time admitting that we cannot know *how* God brings that context into existence in the first place or sustains it in existence. In this sense, we would have to confess that our use of the concept of action as the ground of the existence of the cosmic order may not be literally correct but that it bears a far greater conceptual resemblance to intraworldly action than to any other type of relationship between beings within the cosmic order. We cannot say that God is literally the Agent who creates the cosmic order because we cannot employ the concept of an infrastructure in that affirmation since it is the existence of that infrastructure that is in question. But we can say that God stands to the cosmic order in an analogous relation to how we stand to our creative acts. The use of analogy allows us the necessary conceptual latitude to stretch the relation of agent to act to include God's relation to the initial creation of the cosmic order itself.

God and the 'Big Bang'

It might seem as if this is the appropriate place to employ recent speculation on the possibility of a divine being as the initiator of the 'big bang', that 'event' out of which the universe as we know it seems to have come. There seems to be strong scientific evidence that the universe (the complex of space/time) is expanding. If so, then it follows that its expansion (including space/time itself) must have originated in a single 'moment' or 'singularity' (an edge or boundary of space/time at which matter and influences can enter or leave the physical universe in a totally unpredictable fashion).[1] According to Milton Munitz a singularity "marks the point at which some law for describing the pattern among quantitatively expressed terms reaches a breakdown in its application,"[2] or the horizon of the intelligible universe, from which everything else, including the current 'laws of nature', derived (though not necessarily in a totally predetermined fashion). It is certainly tempting to infer from this that the big bang had to have an author, namely God. Lending support to this view is the claim that many scientists make that the universe was at the outset highly unlikely to be ordered. If the big bang was random (as opposed to intentional), then it was overwhelmingly probable that the universe would now be in thermodynamic equilibrium at maximum entropy with zero order.[3] For example, had the initial explosion differed in strength by only one part in 10^{60}, the universe as we now perceive it would not exist.[4]

Recently, however, the work of people such as Stephen Hawking, Milton Munitz, and Paul Davies has made us more cautious about utilizing the big bang theory to 'prove' the existence of a God who stands in some sense 'outside' that singularity as its creator. Hawking has argued that there is more than one singularity in the universe and that space and time together might form a finite, four-dimensional space without boundaries, and be completely describable by a unified scientific theory.[5] What this leaves open is not a God who created the whole complex of space/time but instead, and at most, a being who operates *within* it, which is consistent with the notion of an acting God for which we have been arguing. Paul Davies, for example, says that it is "perfectly possible for much, if not all of what we encounter in the universe to be the product of intelligent manipulation of a purely natural kind: within the laws of physics. For example, our galaxy *could* have been made by a powerful mind who rearranged the primeval gases using carefully placed gravitating bodies, controlled explosions and all the other paraphernalia of a space age astro-engineer."[6] God could be the fashioner and organizer of matter:

> God could be eternal, infinite and the most powerful being in the universe, . . . the creator of everything we see, having made matter from preexisting energy, organized it appropriately, set up the conditions necessary for life to develop, and so on, but he [sic] would not be capable of creation out of nothing. . . . We might call this being a natural rather than a supernatural God . . . a supermind existing since the 'creation', encompassing all the fundamental fields of nature, and taking upon itself the task of converting an incoherent big bang into the complex and orderly cosmos we now observe; all accomplished entirely within the framework of the laws of physics. This would not be a God who created everything by supernatural means, *but a directing, controlling, universal mind pervading the cosmos and operating the laws of nature to achieve some specific purpose.*[7]

Hawking also seems to suggest, though much more obliquely, that it is possible to think of a God who could choose *how* the universe began (but no freedom to choose the initial conditions themselves). In other words, God could control the order that emerged from the big bang, that is, the natural/causal laws that the universe now obeys in fact, without being credited with the big bang singularity itself or with creating the very energy/matter that now obeys causal law.

Milton Munitz also reminds us that the universe is "a maximally comprehensive ordered domain of processes and objects, to the extent that this can be made intelligible by means of physical theory." In other words, it is that reality that is made intelligible by our models of understanding.[8] We cannot transcend those models in order to ask intelligibly how the universe came into being in the first place. "The horizons of intelligibility [for understanding the universe] are determined by [the rules of language]."[9] If a singularity marks the point at which the rules of understanding break down, then one cannot utilize the notion of God as a singularity in explaining why and how the universe came into existence. "The initial cosmological singularity is a property of a cosmological model, a sign of the model's breakdown in making the universe intelligible, not a property of the universe it would describe."[10] Thus, reference to a God 'outside' or transcendent of the universe is simply not intelligible. It would be, in our terms, trying to put something whose existence and meaning are defined within one ontological context into a radically and totally other ontological context (i.e., dualism). We simply have no conceptual bridge or intelligible transition by which such a move could be made.

The problem, of course, with thinking of God as somehow supernaturally 'external' to the big bang is that God's act is presumed to be the *origin* of space/time, and acts (including the 'act' of creation) presuppose the condition of space/time. We are thus thrown back on the problem that we cannot employ a concept of action that *presupposes* space/time in order to justify a claim that an act brought space/time into existence in the first place. Either we say, by analogy, that the creation was a not fully intelligible 'act', and/or we say that the truly operative concept of God is that of the most powerful being *in* the universe who has all the power necessary to affect decisively its infrastructures as well as the course of the events that constitute its natural evolution and its human history.

It may not, however, necessarily be fatal to Christian belief if one should concede the impossibility of an act *ex nihilo*, on the grounds that such an act is literally incomprehensible. (To assert the reality of what is literally inconceivable is not metaphysically credible.) Even if, as some process theologies seem to suggest, God and the world are coterminous, the primary issue for Christians would be the operative degree of God's control over the world. As long as God's control was sufficient to enable the achievement of divine purposes (always allowing for the human freedom to thwart those purposes to some extent), one could accept the eternity of the world. While this was not exactly what Aquinas had in mind in accepting through reason the philosophical coherence of the world's eternity (and rejecting it through revelation), it does not completely undermine his more fundamental point, namely that the world is radically dependent upon God for what happens within and to it. As long as God retains the power to interfere in and to deploy the infrastructures of the world in the enactment of God's intentions, the world's dependence on God seems firmly enough grounded to satisfy the Christian experience of trust and hope in the power of God to fulfill God's purposes.

God as Intervening Agent

The second thing that could be said about God would be that God (whether coterminous with or creator of the world), is able to intervene decisively and universally in its structures in order to carry out specific purposes. It is, in fact, easier to apply the concept of action literally to God's actions *within* the world than to God's creation *of* the world. We have already argued that it is no diminution of God's power nor a reduction of God to anthropomorphic dimensions to permit God to act concretely and specifically *in* the world. As an Agent God can intervene in the cosmic order that God created at any time or place God so desires. The interesting questions would be why God *in fact chooses* to act concretely in some times and places more particularly than in others, and how we can discern *which* occurrences in the world *are* divine acts.

Related to these issues is the traditional claim that God is 'necessary' in a way that nothing else is. In one sense the claim of divine necessity is simply a way of asserting that God depends on nothing over which God has control. This means, as Swinburne has argued, that God "does not depend for his existence on himself or on anything else. No other agent or natural law or principle of necessity is responsible for the existence of God. His existence is an ultimate brute fact."[11] God could not cause himself to exist because that would require that He exists (in order to cause anything) before He exists, which is plainly self-contradictory. But as 'the' ultimate brute fact, God's powers as agent explain the existence of everything else. This notion leads to the claim that God creates *ex nihilo*, a claim we had reason to be sceptical about above. The only alternative to this is that God is the fashioner or shaper of something that is *also* a brute fact, namely the constituents of the universe as they emerge in the first milliseconds of the big bang. But if one rejects this alternative view as diminishing too much God's abso-

lute necessity, one is back into the problem of providing intelligibility to a notion that transcends the boundaries of sense and meaning, namely a notion of an act (creation *ex nihilo*) by an Agent prior
to the existence of an infrastructure in which acts 'normally' are
understood to take place. If we stay with the notion of necessity as
entailing creation *ex nihilo*, then we are committed to invoking
some kind of very stretched analogy of the concept of 'action' to
refer to God's creative act.

No matter how these problems are resolved, we do need a way
of articulating God's continuous perservation of the cosmic order
itself. It cannot be the case that God, having created (or fashioned)
the cosmic order, then withdraws from it except in those moments
when God chooses to intervene. Intervention by God within the
order presupposes God's ongoing maintainence of the order. The
order is not sui generis, it does not explain itself (this is the force
of the principle of sufficient reason), nor does it seem able to sustain itself. Thus, God must at all times act to keep the order in
being. But this divine act, the sustaining act (which is conceptually distinct from the creative act and may consist of an infinite
continuous series of preservative sub-acts), does not eliminate the
possibility of God's acting in unique moments within and upon the
order that the divine sustaining acts preserve. It is, rather, the condition for those intervening acts. Using analogy, we might think
of our relation to our own bodies (which is only analogous to God's
relation to the world inasmuch as we did not create our bodies, but
God did, let us assume, create the world, or at least gave it its order).
We can intervene in the working of our bodies without contradicting the ongoing act by which we (metaphorically speaking) keep
our bodies in existence. In this regard, one might say that God's
overarching act of sustaining the world is the literal meaning of
'sustaining' the field of action, whereas our relation to our bodies
is the analogous or derived meaning.

Once again, we would have to admit that we do not know *how*
(i.e., the mechanics by which) God sustains the world (keeps it
existing in some order), but the force of the traditional cosmological arguments can be appreciated precisely here. They had the merit,
despite their unfortunate dualist assumptions, of reminding us that
God's being is logically demanded by the ongoing existence of beings
who cannot account for their own endurance. The logic of action
permits us to affirm that God's act explains their endurance without requiring us to understand *how* it does so. Most theisms are in
agreement up to this point. Where they abandon the logic of action

is in their reluctance to affirm the possibility of God's acts *within* the very order God's sustaining act preserves. But as we have seen, there are solid metaphysical grounds for affirming that very possibility without incoherence or unintelligibility.

This view of divine intervention is not far from Peter Van Inwagen's argument (in defense of the place of chance in a providential world) that God can supply some of the basic particles that constitute the universe with "causal powers different from their normal powers".[12] Van Inwagen holds that God decrees a certain initial structure or state for the number of basic particles that constitute the universe. God also decrees that these particles have the same causal powers (specific to each and with the same causal effects, more or less) throughout time. As long as God issues no different decrees, these particles will interact and cause, over time, a whole series of different effects, many of which are unpredictable given some element of indeterminism in nature and the fact of human freedom. God's issuing of these decrees constitutes God's sustaining of the universe through the continuance of its natural laws (which simply reflect the full instantiation of God's decrees). But from time to time God can supply some particles with sufficiently different causal powers so that "a certain part of the natural world [will] diverge from the course that part of the world would have taken if He had continued to supply the particles in that part of the world with the usual complement of causal powers."[13] Van Inwagen says this account of divine action (or miracles) is better than the interventionist approach that I am defending. He objects to intervention because he believes it implies that nature has some sort of power independent of God that God has to *overcome*, presumably meaning that God and the causal order are *rival* powers. I have argued, however, that one power (the causal) is deployed under the superior power of the other (the agent). But since I am using 'intervention' in connection with Pols' notion that *all* agents intervene in the sense of utilizing or employing a causal chain that would otherwise, absent the intervention, have produced a different outcome, I don't think my interventionist account really differs from Inwagen's in any significant respect. Agents don't have to overcome causal sequences; they merely have to utilize them. My account is perfectly compatible with the notion that God sustains the natural elements of the world without completely determining the course they take under the power of other agents. Whether agents exercise their power by exploiting the natural powers of non-agent entities or by causing them to diverge from the course which their natural powers would lead them into is more a matter of semantics than a substantive disagreement. Van Inwagen's approach does have the merit of stressing God's *permission* of certain things without entailing God's direct production of those things, a merit particularly useful in dealing with the problem of evil (as we shall see in chapter 8). God may, by supplying causal powers to elementary particles, permit their eventual production of an event inimical to God's intentions, provided that God does not directly control each moment of the future course of each of those particles either singly or collectively, in all their complex and infinite permutations. God could, of course, choose, in Van Inwagen's words, "to decree different causal powers for certain particles from the ones He normally decrees."[14] But unless he does so, the event that results from his sustaining of the initial decree regarding those particles would occur by his permission, not by his direct intention. God's decision not to intervene each and every time an event inimical to his plan occurs does not need a specific explanation unique to each of those times since, on Van Inwagen's argument, those times are the result of chance. God may have reasons for permitting chance in general but not for permitting (or failing to override) each and every instance of chance. And, as Van Inwagen concludes, instead of attempting to explain every particular evil, "concentrate instead on the problem of what sort of reasons a loving and providential God might have for allowing His creatures to live in a world in which many of the evils that happen to them happen to them for no reason at all."[15]

From a deist perspective, of course, God does not *need* to intervene in the cosmic order. Like a perfect watchmaker, God can create an instrument so perfect that its infrastructural mechanisms need no further tinkering or adjustment. If there occur less than perfect acts within the world, they can be blamed on the ignorance or maliciousness of less than perfectly wise free (human) agents. But a Christian, Islamic, or Jewish theist wants to say more than this. She is an inheritor of a tradition that proclaims the 'mighty acts' of God in history. And she can, of course, point to the scriptural basis of her tradition for narratives presuming to tell the story of the divine acts. We will return to this issue shortly.

God as Agent and the Classical View of God

Having established the metaphysical foundation for the possibility of God's action within the world, we now have to face the question of whether this possibility contradicts, bypasses, or complements the traditional theistic claims that God, to be God, must be eternal (nontemporal), omniscient, omnipotent, immutable, and without material body. On dualist assumptions, of course, these attributes are necessary for God because they demarcate the radical otherness of God's ontological nature. They set God off from the entire ontological context within which finite being exists. But do these assumptions have the same meaning or force in a pluralist framework wherein God and the world are in continuous dynamic interaction?

God as Temporal

Certainly, the claim that God is not 'in' time is not credible on pluralist grounds. Any act 'takes time' to enact and as long as the agent must 'be there' throughout the act (deploying, wielding, overarching it), the agent must endure throughout the course of the act (unless, of course, the agent ceases to exist once the act has been initiated). Even if it could be argued that the agent is not literally 'in' the act once it has been initiated, as long as there are subsequent acts by the same agent, that agent must in some real sense be in time from one act to another. And so an acting God is in time.

But doesn't this make time 'superior' to God? Or, to put it differently, isn't God subject to time, a prisoner of time, as it were? It would certainly be true that God is not completely transcendent of time. It may also be the case that either God is coterminous with time or that God's 'creation' of time is beyond all knowledge or comprehension. But what is at stake in God's relation to time? The answer, I think, is, once again, God's control over those events and acts that occur in time. Time is, after all, only the condition for action. It is not, in itself, a 'thing' that stands in opposition to or as a countervailing force against agents. It does not have the same metaphysical status as agents. It is, along with space, simply the 'arena' within which agents act. It is *per se* impossible to achieve one's intentions 'outside of' or beyond time. Therefore, it does not enhance God's power as Agent to insist that God must be outside time since all that God does (from Creation to the everlasting Kingdom) is time-bound.

If the issue is construed to be one of the noneternal endurance of finite agents through all time (given the empirical fact that finite entities decay or wear out over time), then the divine Agent could be affirmed as the eternally enduring Agent. Eternal in this sense would mean literally without end, that is, there would be no time at which God has not been and will not be. If that affirmation is made, and if God's power is undiminished throughout eternity, then, it seems to me, that nothing either metaphysically or religiously is lost by conceding that God exists 'in' time, although, unlike all other agents, God exists throughout *all* time and is coterminous with time.

God as Omnipotent

The issue of God's omnipotence is not, in itself, particularly difficult. Almost all commentators have acknowledged that the only power (potence) of God worth considering is the power to *do* what God intends, or, to put it differently, there can be no countervailing power in the universe sufficient to frustrate God's intentions ultimately (unless God permits that to happen). God must have the power to control every single part of the universe (though whether God exercises that power, except to sustain the universe, is another question and one related to what God's overarching and specific intentions actually are). No one would seriously suggest that God must also have the power to do what is logically or metaphysically impossible, such as making two plus two equal seven, or squaring the circle, or creating a weight so heavy that God cannot lift it, and so forth. It may be agreed that the notion of divine omnipotence means that "God can perform any action the performance of which is logically consistent, and consistent with God's own nature."[16] The whole concept of God's omnipotence actually rests on the metaphysically prior and more ultimate concept of God's agency since power is the means of action. As long as God has the power to do everything God intends to do, God is, in the relevant sense, omnipotent. As omnipotent in this sense, God can also be affirmed as 'Infinite', provided we mean by that term 'without meaningful limits on one's capacity to accomplish what one intends'. We do not have to shift the notion of 'infinite' to a totally other ontological context in order to believe in God's infinity. 'The Infinite' is not usefully understood as the ontological alternative 'Other' to 'the Finite'. Rather, it is better understood as the capacity to do what one intends without meaningful limits. Human agents do not have that capacity (and thus are finite), but God does, (and thus is infinite). Richard Swinburne has captured the sense of omnipotence I am supporting when he proposes what he calls a 'modified' account of it. If theism "wants the power of God to be compatible with his being perfectly free, it can in any case say no more of him than that he is omnipotent in the following sense [E]: a person P is omnipotent at a time t if and only if he is able to bring about the existence of any logically contingent state of affairs x after t, the description of the occurrence of which does not entail that P did not bring it about at t, given that he does not believe that he has overriding reason for refraining from bringing about x."[17] This sense of omnipotence entails that God cannot do evil, or anything logically impossible (such as create a round square or predetermine a free action).

God as Omniscient

The question of God's omnipotence is tied up with the issue of God's omniscience, or knowledge of everything. If the issue were simply one of whether God knows everything that there is to know now and in the past, no one would object to the claim that God has such knowledge. The more controversial question is whether God knows the future. According to one version of the classical view, God is 'outside' time and therefore knows all that happens 'in' time from God's own timeless perspective. The claim of God's omniscience is meant to protect God from the possibility that things in the future might happen that God did not know beforehand from God's eternal standpoint. The problem that this raises, of course, is that if God knows (and therefore knows infallibly, since knowledge by a perfect being must be without error), for example, that tomorrow I will take a bus to work, then my belief that I have some degree of free choice in deciding whether to take a bus, my car, walk, or stay home is false or illusory since God cannot be wrong about what God knows. I may think I have a choice in taking the bus but if God knows I will take a bus, then I will take a bus regardless of how much freedom I think I have in choosing another option. Such a view of God's omniscience seems to rule out human freedom except as a belief that is not supported by 'the facts'. It is better, as Swinburne has shown, to adopt a notion of omniscience that accepts the fact that if there are free human actions God cannot know their outcome before they happen. Such actions, before they happen, are neither true nor false, since their truth or falsity has not yet been determined. It will be determined by the free decision formed by the agent at the time of the act itself. Being neither true nor false *ahead of time*, therefore, it is impossible for any being to know it as true or false before it happens. "An omniscient person knows of every true proposition that it is true. But if propositions about the future actions of agents are neither true nor false until the agents do the actions, then to be omniscient a person will not have to know them. ... [A being] is omniscient if he knows about everything except those future states and their consequences which are not physically necessitated by anything in the past."[18] (For a fuller discussion of the problems entailed by notions of omniscience, see chapter 4, "Refining Dualism" pp. 48–52.)

Another consequence of the traditional or classical view of omniscience is that God is unable to *respond* to human actions. Response presupposes waiting (a temporal, not a timeless act) for the other person to act. But if God knows omnisciently what my action will be and has programmed his own 'response' to it before time began (since God surely knows what God will do), it hardly makes sense to say that God genuinely waits upon my response. And it makes even less sense, therefore, to ask God to do certain things in response to prayer since whatever God does has been determined beforehand by God, including my own request for help. God's involvement with as well as our actions in the world would seem to be predetermined by God in all respects (otherwise God could not know God's and our actions omnisciently).

God's Knowledge of Me

Another implication of the omniscience/timeless character of God is that God cannot know me in my temporality. God's way of knowing is entirely conceptual (being timeless). God cannot know time in God's eternal ontological context. The only realities in that divine context must themselves be timeless, namely concepts or ideas. But I am not a concept. I am a temporal, spatial being. And God would seem unable to know me in my historicity since God cannot experience time or space *as* time or space. As William Hasker has put it, "that God in very truth knows us, and relates to us, only as the eternal representations in his own essence—this is a hard doctrine. ... And if ... in order to have immediate awareness of temporal facts, God must himself be temporal, then so be it. To make the other choice [that God is timeless] leaves too great a distance between the God who is affirmed theologically and the God who is known through Scripture and experience."[19] Hasker also quotes Nicholas Wolterstorff on this point: "It is not because he is outside of time—eternal, immutable, impassive—that we are to worship and obey God. It is because of what he can and does bring about

within time that we mortals are to render him praise and obedi-
ence."[20]

God and the Matter of the Body

The issue of God's immateriality, or whether God has a body, is
somewhat more difficult. Bodies, as we know them empirically, are
not just a condition of action but more importantly they do wear
out. The matter that constitutes them erodes and eventually every
finite agent's body dies (achieves maximum entropy). Bodies are also
limiting and restricting with respect to the agent's range and
capacity for effective action. My body limits my 'reach' in carrying
out my intentions. There are simply some things I cannot intend
to do realistically because I am limited by the spatiality of my body.

At one level, therefore, one would have to ask whether God has
the power to overcome the empirical limitations of matter. An
omnipotent God would certainly have to have such power. It is
certainly conceivable that if God had a body (i.e., some material
structure out of which or from which God issued God's power), God
could ensure that the matter that constituted that body was continually replenished for all eternity.

At the same time, it needs to be said that what we know of
matter is itself extremely limited and that matter may well take a
variety of forms, some well beyond our present scientific understandings. As the world of subatomic physics begins to approach
the near-mystical realms of the literally unimaginable, it would be
shortsighted to say that God's material body (if God has one) is just
like our material bodies and subject to the same physical laws.
Those laws are now in the process of being radically revised and
elaborated to take account of the mysterious new worlds of subatomic physics. Who is to say that the older, bulkier, Newtonian
laws must apply to God's body in the way they apply to our bodies, at least at the macro level? Jonathan Harrison, in an important
analysis of embodiment, has said that "there might be more ways
in which a person can be embodied than by having a body of the
common or garden sort. Embodiment . . . might admit of degrees."[21]

This level of analysis, however, does not get us to the heart of
the matter (as it were). The real question is whether having a body
in any way contravenes God's power to act effectively in the pur-
suit of God's intentions. It may well be the case that God's action
is not dependent upon a body, *nor necessarily restricted by* having
a body of some material kind. God's power depends upon God's

ability to be present in, to, and upon the world. Such presence, as
Grace M. Dyck has argued, does not entail that God have a body
or not have a body. What is crucial to presence is the ability to affect
what one is present to.[22] It therefore requires us only to conceive
of the possibility of effect without physical contact between one
body and another. The concept of telekinesis might supply the foundation of that conception. Telekinesis is not yet a proven fact but
its concept is within the realm of scientific possibility. It is the effect
upon an entity by another entity not utilizing physical intermediaries (as we know them at present) and separated by physical distance. Most commonly, it is understood to refer to the possibility
of affecting something by means of one's mind alone. (We can ig-
nore for the moment the various and complex relations that might
exist between the mind of the mover and its bodily infrastructure
—relations that seem necessary if we are to avoid Cartesian dualism, but that are not directly involved in the relation between the
mover and what she moves at a distance.) So-called 'psychics' are
reported to have the ability to alter physical structures at a distance
'merely' by mental action. Assuming that such acts are not *per se*
impossible, it might well be the case that God can act upon bodies
with which God has no physical contact primarily or even exclusively through telekinesis. Such action would not, therefore, require
God to have a body as the vehicle of action upon another. God could
be present to and have an effect upon other beings without having
bodily contact with them. God could be omnipresent in the universe without being bodily present everywhere. Incorporeality, as
Dyck has argued, is not the only way to ensure God's omnipresence.

But this does not show that God does or does not have a body.
The issue of the body, I believe, is essentially the issue of the *source
from which* proceed a series of acts and intentions so unified and
consistent with each other as to reveal a single enduring personality. As long as the effects attributed to God are unified in such a
way that they can be seen as issuing from the intentions of a single,
consistent, purposeful agent, we have adequate grounds for affirming the existence of a personal source responsible for those effects,
even if we cannot locate that source in a particular body similar to
our own. *How* God exercises divine power to bring about those
effects if they issue from no body would remain a mystery, not
because God must have no body but simply because we have no
empirical experience of nonbodily sources issuing effects. But as we
suggested earlier, the nonbodily source for God's effects could be
due to the fact that God's body is constituted of matter in such

radically other kinds of configurations that our coarse-grained optics are incapable of perceiving it in principle. It might also be the case that God acts in such a way as to keep the divine body (in whatever material form it takes) from being perceived by us in fact (though it might be so perceived in principle). Or it could be the case that it is only a contingent and not a necessary principle that all acts proceed from material bodies, even though our experience is limited only to those that do so proceed.

It has been suggested by some, for example process theologians, that the matter of God's body can be resolved by postulating the world as God's body. This notion certainly links God and the world in the most intimate way, thus rejecting the dualistic separation of God and world. The only difficulty with this view is that it makes individual human persons *parts of* God's body, rather than distinct entities capable of *relating to* God in mutuality and interdependence. The analogy for our relation to God would have to be one based on our relationship to the parts of our own body. In process theology this analogy can be successfully sustained because of its underlying metaphysical claim that the ultimate real things of which the world is made up are actual occasions, events, or entities, none of which can be identified nonreductively with human persons. Persons are complex societies of occasions and thus are what they are solely through the occasions that constitute them. At one level, then, persons are less basic and more abstract than are their constitutive elements, the occasions. But the position taken in this book is that persons, as agents, are irreducible entities presiding over the occasions, events, and infrastructures that they deploy or utilize. Thus, the basis for the analogy of the world as God's body is not available. On that analogy, human persons are less ontologically distinct and irreducible than is the God who contains them. If we can find a view of God that permits both God and human persons genuine mutual interaction without making one a part of the body of the other, we can avoid the negative implications of this particular analogy.

But the underlying question is whether having a body of some sort in any significant way limits God's power over the cosmos. Certainly, from a religiously experiential standpoint it does not, since our lives are still decisively affected by God's power, no matter from what it issues or how it is carried out. But even from a metaphysical standpoint, it is not clear that anything essential has been denigrated by admitting the possibility of a divine body, provided only that we do not limit our understanding of bodies to the configurations of matter that constitute the Newtonian view of matter. Matter is much more subtle and complex than the traditional Newtonian understanding has led us to believe. As long as God can utilize all the dimensions of matter (only some of which we are now beginning to appreciate) to carry out God's purposes and to be present to us, and to do both forever without the threat of bodily decay, the issue of matter and body for God are not metaphysically significant.

God as Immutable

Traditionally related to the issue of matter has been the claim that God is immutable, meaning that God undergoes no change whatsoever. Historically, change was associated with the decay intrinsic to all material bodies. Thus, to avoid such degradation, God was believed to be completely incapable of change since God had no body. In one sense, as we have just seen, even if God does have a body there is no reason that God could not, with the immense powers available, keep renewing the divine body forever, and thus be immutable in something like the traditional sense. But in another sense, immutability is better understood as referring to God's unchangeable purpose. It is far more appropriate to the religious experience we have of being together bound with God to speak of God's immutable love, commitment, and fidelity to the divine intentions. *These* are what are truly immutable, not some more abstract element in God's 'being'.

Transcendence

Finally, a word about transcendence. It should be apparent that the traditional notion of transcendence as a 'going beyond' all forms of time, space, and plurality, is not applicable to God as Agent. Transcendence in the traditional sense is more appropriately understood within the dualist framework. However, there is a form of transcendence in the pluralist view. But it is rooted squarely in the notion of agent, agency, and act. As we have seen, all agents 'transcend' their acts precisely insofar as they are the unifying source of the acts they perform. They, as agents, cannot be reduced to or strictly identified with their acts because they transcend them even while manifesting themselves in them. In this way agents have the quality of transcendence while non-agents do not. Agents always transcend the knowledge others have of them since their future actions, and even the *how* of the relation between their intentions and their acts, are not knowable either reductionistically or in principle. Agents with genuine power also transcend others in the sense that through their power they can overturn or surprise whatever predictions we make about their future acts. And agents with the greatest power of all are truly transcendent because their power alone can determine their own as well as others' futures (provided they are willing to override the freedom of those others). Agents, in short, are, at least to some degree relative to their respective powers, beyond (transcendent of) the power, control, and complete knowledge of all other beings, notwithstanding the fact that whenever they act they reveal their intentions and embody their power in determinate ways.

Faith

Transcendence and revelation, openness and determinateness, are two sides of the same coin. We could not know that there is a transcendent God *with specific attributes* unless God had first manifested something determinate and fixed in specific acts through which God revealed Godself. What God *has done* is fixed, determinate, and no longer transcendent. What God *will do* is open, indeterminate (subject only to God's intentions), and transcendent. The meaning of our lives depends upon both: we cannot be grounded in the present unless God has already 'come down' from God's transcendence—and we cannot be open to the future unless God remains transcendent, unbounded by the fixities of the past. Revelation of who God is and what God is up to is therefore an indispensable ingredient in God's communication to us. But this revelation is not different in kind from the revelations all agents make to each other in and through their acts. It does not require a special, distinct faculty of apprehension to grasp it, a sacrifice of the intellect as such. It does require a willingness to subject the intellect to the painstaking reading of historical acts, including the risky and less than certain conclusions that are drawn from historical inferences. This, however, is the heart of what faith really is.

Faith is really trust in a twofold sense. It is trust *that* one has read the historical evidence correctly *as* revelations (that reading, by the nature of the case never being absolutely certain), and trust *in* the One whose acts are the basis of those historical revelations. As one comes to infer a historical pattern, revealing an overarching, unifying, loving intention being woven throughout the histories of particular peoples and persons, one comes to trust in the trust-worthiness of the One who is enacting that intention. And this entire process of faith, in its twofold sense, is based on God's self-revelation in and through divine historical actions. Revelation, therefore, is essential in God's self-communication and in God's establishment of a relationship with us.

It now becomes necessary to examine the specific claims about God that have been based on what those who call themselves Jews and Christians have inferred from their experiences, both now and in the past. This is the question of the historical credibility of claims that God has acted in history. It is the question, not only of God's overarching intention, but more specifically (and more problemati-cally and controversially) of God's direct, unique, and particular acts in history.

Are Divine Acts Arbitrary?

But before we begin that examination, there is one further issue relating to the metaphysical underpinning of God's action that needs to be addressed. One of the persistent reasons given for denying that God acts in particular ways in history is that such divine action would, apparently necessarily according to its critics, make God *arbitrary*. Discrete, particular actions are ones done here, not there, and now, not then. In this sense all specific actions discriminate one moment and location from others in that they interfere with the causal infrastructure not everywhere at all times but at specific times and places; otherwise they would not be specific acts. Now we have conceded that God's underlying action is one that sustains and maintains the structures of the universe as a whole. But doesn't God's decision to do particular acts over and above God's underyling one make those acts arbitrary?

The answer to this objection must take the following form. If by 'arbitrary' one means simply that a particular act is done here and not there, now and not then, then *all* acts, human *and* divine, are arbitrary in that sense and the objection is trivial. The only nonarbitrary acts would be ones with universal, comprehensive effects. But as long as agents act historically, not all their acts can be of this kind. If, however, one means by 'arbitrary', capricious, random, without forethought, or whimsical, then God's acts are never arbitrary (at least as far as we can infer). God, as most agents, acts according to intentions that constitute a unified whole. God's character is one that perfectly integrates all God's intentions into a harmonious, unified pattern. Thus, all of God's acts are purposeful according to God's overarching intentions. No act is, in that sense, arbitrary. Now, as we shall see, there are enormous difficulties involved in determining *which* historically recorded or personally experienced events *are* God's acts, but if we can legitimately infer them to be such, then, emanating as they do from a single, integrated, harmonious, and intentional agent, they cannot be random in the sense of capricious.

There are also enormous difficulties, even assuming we can trust that some particular acts *are* God's, in knowing *why* God performed that one and not another. This is at the heart of the problem of evil, which I will take up in Chapter 8. But the problem of evil is a problem distinct to itself. It should not be used, *a priori*, to decide that *all* specific acts of God are *ipso facto* so arbitrary (i.e., capricious) as to be religiously as well as metaphysically incredible.

Ironically, the religious feeling that God, to be God, must ultimately be mysterious combines with the metaphysical claim that all agents necessarily act in a way that cannot be entirely explained by causal law (and thus, in the first sense of the term, act arbitrarily). If we really want to affirm God's mystery, the logically most secure place to locate it is in God's will. All agents, to the extent that their wills are free from casual determination, are mysterious to those who want to know beforehand exactly what they will do. At the same time, all agents, to the extent that their actions reveal their will, lose some of their mysteriousness, though never entirely. If the opposite of arbitrary is completely predictable, then the only beings that are not arbitrary are causal forces without intentionality. If the opposite of arbitrary is purposeful, then agents are neither arbitrary nor completely predictable. And in the space between their revealed (and thus known) character and the intentions (and actions) they may form and enact in the future, lies their mysteriousness. God, therefore, is ultimately mysterious in the sense that God alone chose, for reasons 'of God's own', to create the forms that the structure of the universe presently has, and in the sense that God has the power to choose, also for reasons of God's own, to alter or eliminate those forms, as well as to perform specific acts at unpredictable times and places according to intentions God may or may not have previously revealed. This 'mystery of God' is the chief exemplification of the ultimate mystery of personal beings in relation to each other.

At the same time, however, the mystery of God is diminished or opened up by the very fact that God *does act* and, at least according to the inferences drawn by Jews and Christians, acts according to a coherent, unifying, loving intention in specific times and places in history. God's mystery is not eliminated by God's acting but it does not remain absolute, either. It may be a mystery *why* God loves those whom God creates (unless love is its own explanation) and *why* God continues to actively seek their reconciliation even after they have spurned God's love, but through God's creation and acts of liberation and reconciliation, God allows us to know God more intimately and more truly. God's actions remove the charge of arbitrariness just as they provide a counterbalance to divine mysteriousness.

Inferring God's Nature From Divine Action

Only through God's actions do we have any basis for inferring the character of God. Those who have objected to the notion of a 'finite' God, or a God who acts powerfully in history, have often charged that such actions turn God into either a tyrant or a 'big brother', a 'buddy-in-the-sky'. In either case, God becomes the personification (the anthropomorphization) of loathsome or infantile human traits. But again, the issue is not what God *could be* if God has the capacity to act, but what God *has revealed* Godself to be in fact. As an acting being, God *could*, in principle, act capriciously, tyrannically, mean-spiritedly, or in any other way God chooses. (Though, it could be argued, an all-powerful being who did act tyrannically could not be regarded as morally good and would thus be unworthy of worship. But the traditional ascription to God of moral perfection is based upon (and does not precede) a reading of God's character from God's acts in history). And, as free human beings who must infer God's character from God's acts, we could choose to think of God any way we wanted (provided we were willing to dispense with the historical obligation to remain as faithful to the warranted evidence as possible). But if God *has acted*, and has acted in specific ways in accordance with God's overarching intention, then God's character will have to be understood as being whatever God has truly revealed it to be. If God has not chosen to act as a tyrant, or as a 'buddy', or capriciously, then there will be no basis (other than our own fears and imaginings) for thinking of God in any of those ways. If God has chosen to act instead as liberator, nurturer, lover, friend, and redeemer, then *those* acts become the authentic revelation of God's true character. Those in the biblical tradition stake the meaning of their ultimate trust upon their belief that through

God's actions, God invites us into a closer, deeper, more personal relationship, one in which we become together bound with God and God with us in the fulfillment of God's purposes and our nature.

Notes

1. Paul Davies, *God and the New Physics* (New York: Touchstone Books, 1983), p. 56.

2. Milton Munitz, *Cosmic Understanding* (Princeton: Princeton University Press, 1986), p. 170.

3. Davies, *God and the New Physics*, p. 168.

4. Ibid., p. 179.

5. Stephen W. Hawking, *A Brief History of Time* (New York: Bantam Books, 1988), p. 173.

6. Davies, *God and the New Physics*, p. 208.

7. Ibid., pp. 208–10 (emphasis added).

8. Munitz, *Cosmic Understanding*, p. 54.

9. Ibid., p. 170.

10. Ibid., p. 175.

11. Richard Swinburne, *The Coherence of Theism* (Oxford: Clarendon Press, 1977), p. 267.

12. Peter Van Inwagen, "The Place of Chance in a World Sustained by God," in Thomas V. Morris, ed., *Divine and Human Action: Essays in the Metaphysics of Theism* (Ithaca, N.Y.: Cornell University Press, 1988), p. 214.

13. Ibid., p. 214.

14. Ibid., p. 218.

15. Ibid., p. 235.

16. Michael Peterson, William Hasker, Bruce Reichenbach, and David Basinger, *Reason and Religious Belief: An Introduction to the Philosophy of Religion* (New York: Oxford University Press, 1991), p. 56.

17. Swinburne, *The Coherence of Theism*, p. 160.

18. Ibid., pp. 174–75.

19. William Hasker, *God, Time, and Knowledge* (Ithaca, N.Y.: Cornell University Press, 1989), p. 184.

20. Nicholas Wolterstorff, "God Everlasting," in Clifton J. Orlebeke and Lewis B. Smedes, eds., *God and the Good* (Grand Rapids, Mich.: William B. Eerdmans, 1975), p. 203, quoted in Hasker, *God, Time, and Knowledge*, p. 185.

21. Jonathan Harrison, "The Embodiment of Mind or What Use Is Having a Body?," *Proceedings of the Aristotelian Society* n.s. 74 (1973–74): 44.

22. Grace M. Dyck, "Omnipresence and Incorporeality," *Religious Studies* 13 (1977): 85–91.

8

The Credibility of Biblical Claims That God Has Acted Historically and the Problem of Evil

The Credibility of Biblical Claims for Divine Action

What I have tried to do to this point is establish the metaphysical credibility, *in principle*, of divine acts in the world. What now needs attention is the question of whether there is *historical* credibility to the claim that there have been, in fact, some divine acts in the world. Without denying that such acts could have occurred (and probably did) in the historical experience of many different peoples and persons, I will focus my attention upon the record of what Jews and Christians have traditionally believed to be such acts, namely the Bible.

The Status of Biblical Narratives

The biblical narratives of the 'mighty acts of God' have come to be seen as something less or other than straightforward 'objective' reportorial accounts by religiously indifferent observers of occurrences that took place, as it were, before the public eye. We now know that the scriptural accounts are at the very least a combination of mythology, communal faith, and secondhand explanation. The question is whether they are also at least partially credible accounts of some occurrences that can legitimately be understood as divine acts. Is it possible, in short, that the scriptural 'record' of divine acts has a hard literal historical core? What I wish to explore needs to be carefully stated in order to avoid confusion: I am not going to 'validate' the specific biblical claims that God did, in fact, act here and there as the narratives report. Rather, I am interested in exploring the *possibility* that many (if not all) of these claims *could be* true; that they fall into the category of acts in history that by their nature are historically possible (i.e., do not violate any known metaphysical laws of historical possibility nor what we know of the historical record, apart from the biblical claims).

In order to get at the question of the possibility of divine acts in history as recorded in scriptural narratives, we need to go back to our starting point—the experiences of persons who feel that their lives have been touched, even transformed, by the power of a force far greater than their own. There is no doubt that the biblical narratives, for example, are written out of or from the dramatic experiences of persons and communities who felt that they lived in the presence of, and as a result of, the graceful acts of a living, acting God. The biblical narrative is an attempt to tell the story of what God was up to in those actions and what the recipients of those acts learned from them about God and the divine intentions. But as we have already seen, the manifestation of an agent is always and irreducibly through specific actions. Thus, it would seem to follow, that through the overlay of mythology and faith, the biblical narrative might well disclose an underlying reality of divine acts in history.

We have to sort out that underlay from both its mythological covering and its fanciful embroidery. We also need to distinguish between the credibility of a claim that a *particular* occurrence was a divine act and the coherence of the claim that a pattern of divine intention is manifest in a *series* of occurrences, one or more of which might be shown to be noncredible without the whole series being so. One need not be a biblical fundamentalist (believing that *every* occurrence attributed to God in the Bible did literally happen and was literally God's act), in order to draw a reasonable inference that there is an overarching pattern of acts recorded in Scripture that reveals a consistent and coherent divine authorship and intention.

We have to steer carefully between three extremes: the liberal insistence that every finite occurrence is only metaphorically a divine act; the fundamentalist insistence that every biblically recorded divine occurrence is, literally, an act of God; and the scientific insistence that nothing is an act of God. Actually the liberal and the scientific extremes collapse into a single denial that God can perform specific acts in history. But we also have to avoid the fundamentalist claim that anything recorded in Scripture as an act of God *is* an act of God if for no other reasons than that many of these 'alleged' acts are in contradiction with each other, and that fundamentalism generally is out of touch with the most reliable work of contemporary biblical scholarship.

The Overarching Divine Intention

What are the parameters within which we can discuss the biblical view of divine acts? First, the occurrence in question must be related in a coherent way to an overarching divine intention that is itself consistent with the fullest possible picture of God's overall purposes in history. In other words, any specific act of God, to be believed as such, should form part of a coherent, consistent pattern of actions manifesting a coherent, consistent pattern of divine intention(s). (There is an inherent circularity, hopefully not vicious, in this way of proceeding. We need a pattern of actions in order to locate a specific act as the act of the agent whose pattern it is, and we need the specific acts in order to determine the pattern. This circularity is not vicious primarily because it is part of the way in which we know any actions of any agent, and this kind of knowledge is not normally problematical, though it can be in particular instances.) We know something about this way of interpreting alleged acts from our knowledge of other human persons. We know, for example, that Liz is a person of compassion who listens well to other people and always acts in a way that intends to support them. We know this about Liz because we have a record of her acts (some of which we have witnessed, many of which have been told to us by others) in which compassion and support have been consistently manifested over a long period of time in our mutual experience of her. Over this period of time we form a coherent picture of Liz's underlying (or overarching) intentions and, consequently, of her personality or character. We even venture to predict in a rough sort of way what kinds of things Liz will do in the future provided she remains characterologically consistent with her past actions. (These predictions are not based on causal necessity, always assuming a relevant degree of freedom on Liz's part as an agent, but on our experience that persons tend to act in ways that are relatively consistent with their 'character'.) Then someone claims that he has heard that Liz struck and killed a young child. Under the circumstances, we are

prepared not to countenance this claim because it does not immediately fit into the coherent, consistent pattern of actions that have
manifested a coherent, consistent pattern of Liz's intentions in the
past. In other words, this particular claim simply doesn't fit our
picture of her character or her past pattern of actions. (It may, of
course, turn out that the claim is true, leading us to revise our picture of Liz's personality, or to decide that Liz has now altered her
intentions dramatically, or to find some extenuating explanation,
or even, in extremis, to revise our interpretation of all her past acts.)
But the mere fact of having to consider both specific acts as constituting a pattern and utilizing the pattern thus inferred to determine
whether a later act is consistent with that pattern is not a 'problem' unique to interpreting divine action.

It may also be the case that, after a very long period of acting
consistently and coherently, Liz produces a kind of awe among some
people, who, believing they are celebrating her, add fanciful details
to acts she performed or even make up a series of stories about some
acts that are then falsely, but in the spirit of praise rightly given
her for her other, well-validated acts, attributed to her. These imagi-
native additions to her repertoire of acts are, in fact, not strictly true,
but they appear consistent with what she has done and do not,
ultimately, falsify the truth of our reading of her core personality
or her overarching intentions as revealed in what she *has*, in fact
done.

It is also possible that Liz has done many other things, consistent with everything else she has done, that are never recorded or
even observed, simply because they were not done before witnesses
or because they occurred in contexts in which prior knowledge of
her was missing and thus no background pattern was available into
which to fit an interpretation of occurrences *as* her acts. (She may
have entered another country and performed compassionate acts
that, because she was a stranger to its inhabitants, either went
unnoticed or uninterpreted because there was no prior pattern of
such action and thus no interpretive framework into which to put
her actions. Something similar to this may explain how the God of
the Jewish and Christian traditions could have acted in the lives of
Buddhists and Hindus but without being recognized.) These acts
do not appear in the central recorded history of her deeds but may,
nonetheless, have been essential to the fulfillment of her purposes,
especially those not directly affecting the community of persons that
has been compiling what is to it the 'central' record of her acts.

And, finally, it is possible that Liz performs some acts that are
simply incidental or unrelated to her basic, dominating intentions.

She may, for example, drive her car around the block every evening 'just for fun'. This act neither supports nor undermines her over-arching intention to be a compassionate person. It is just something she has chosen to do and it would not, unless observed directly, normally be attributed to her.

Now there is nothing in the way in which we depict Liz's acts that cannot, in principle, be applied to God's acts. What is important is that the entire context and pattern of divine action be taken into account in trying to ajudicate the claims of any single divine act. The context and pattern, as well as the single act, mutually implicate each other. No single act can stand alone, outside the pattern, and no pattern can be discerned without a series of single acts linked by a unifying intention.

Six Possibilities for Interpreting Claims of Divine Action

About any claim regarding a specific divine act there are at least six possibilities: it *did not occur* (or at least there is no evidence that it ever occurred); it *occurred* but was not done by God since it is inconsistent with the overall pattern of God's acts and with God's character as revealed in that pattern; it *may have occurred* and is consistent with that pattern *but*, at a deeper level, *is* either trivial or irrelevant to it; it *did not occur but* had it occurred it *would have been consistent* with the overall pattern; it *did occur and is not consistent* with the overall pattern; it *did occur, is consistent* with the overall pattern, *and is a decisive event* in furthering and/or revealing God's overarching intention.

Personal Experience of God's Action

How can we approach these possibilities? First, we would have to touch base with our own experience. It is hardly possible to give much credence to the biblical claims about God's acts unless our own experience provides a point of contact with them. This is not to say that a person ungraced by God's presence could not read Scripture and discern a pattern of acts performed by a self-consistent being. But such a person could only admit the theoretical possibility of such a series of divine acts: she would have no basis for claiming that the narrative is true. (Or at the very least she might have to make the same claim for every narrative in which a self-consistent being is reported to have acted consistently, leaving her in the uncomfortable position of claiming truth for the sacred narratives of Islam, Christianity, Judaism, Mormonism, varieties of African religions, etc., uncomfortable precisely because these narratives cannot *all* be true in *every* respect since they make *some* conflicting claims about God—though it is not impossible that somehow these claims, with suitable modification, might be made reconcilable in some way.)

But if someone has felt touched by the power of God (presumably over a period of time and in different moments), the narrative of other people's experiences of what appears on the surface to be the same kind of power, experienced similarly, can be approached as more than a theoretical possibility. If, as Christians often claim, they have experienced a new birth, a transformation in their lives from being paralyzed by fear to being freed by a loving, gracious force that convinced them that they had nothing ultimately to fear because this force's love was stronger even than death itself, then they become open to a text in which similar experiences are rehearsed. This openness is more than the receptivity of the dispassionate observer who can admit theoretical plausibility: it is an openness to the possibility that the narrative is not only true, but decisive for her own life in the sense that it reveals the *will* or intention of the Being whom she has come to believe has acted in her life. Her knowledge of that divine intention then becomes the source of direction and sustenance for all her future actions and beliefs. She finds a confirmation that her initial experience (in itself at first uninterpreted because it has no initial interpretive framework) does fit into a larger perspective consistent with many other persons' experiences. Her experience gives vitality to the biblical narrative and the biblical narrative gives meaning to her experience. (Of course, both she and the biblical narrative may still be wrong in their interpretation of the acts that they reflect.)

While personal experience of divine empowerment is necessary for a complete acceptance of a biblical narrative it is not sufficient. The faithful person will still have to confront the historical context and conditions in which the alleged divine act has taken place. Our metaphysical basis for divine acts only establishes the possibility of their occurrence. By itself, it does not permit us to know which claims about them are true and which are false. Acts that violate traditional understandings of causal law are not impossible but they stretch credulity more than acts that utilize and intervene in causal law.

The Causal Context of Specific Divine Acts

If we take, for example, the allegation that God parted the waters of the Red Sea in order to permit the Hebrew people to cross over, we would have to determine whether such 'parting' is a violation or a utilization of the natural forces of the universe. It might be argued that God, whose control over the forces of nature is analogous to our control over (some) of the biological forces within our body, utilized the forces of wind in order to blow what some scholars believe were the very shallow waters of a 'reed' sea hard enough to clear a path for a crossing by foot by the Hebrew people and then God ceased causing the winds to blow so that the waters returned to their original state and drowned the Egyptians crossing by horse. Whether this account in any way corresponds to what actually happened (if anything at all did) we have no way of knowing for certain. But if our explication of the notion of an agent's utilization of the infrastructures over which he or she has control is credible, then the credibility of God's utlization of the forces of the wind can be established.

In this context it is fascinating to note a new study by two scientists, one in oceanography and the other in atmospheric sciences, that addresses the question of whether there are oceanographic explanations for the crossing of the Red Sea.[1] While taking no position on the question of whether there was an agent (God or any other) bringing about the 'parting' of the waters, Nof and Paldor argue that the occurrence as described by the biblical narrative could well have happened. They argue that "a relatively simple oceanographic process related to a northwesterly wind pushing the water offshore and the water returning as a fast high-amplitude nonlinear wave (once the wind relaxes) can explain the 'parting of the sea'."[2] The description of the wind blowing in the Exodus account corresponds nicely to their account of the blowing of moderate winds in the Gulf of Suez for about ten hours, followed by several hours of strong winds. Once again, this scientific explanation of the occurrence in no way proves it to be an act of God, but if acts are the result of a chain of causal forces initiated by an agent who intervenes in the causal process to change what would otherwise have been the case, there is no reason in principle to rule out the possibility that the parting of the waters was a divine act.

In some ways, the more important question for interpreting an occurrence as a divine act is the one of pattern. Did this alleged act contribute to or fit consistently within a pattern of uniform divine intentions? The biblical narrative insists that it did. Out of compassion for God's human creation, God chose to utilize an oppressed people as a way of demonstrating God's compassion and lordship over God's creation. God's covenant with this people would seal God's care for them but the rescue of that people from their bondage, and their creation as a people, was forwarded by the intermediate step of bringing them safely out of slavery. Thus the allegation that God 'parted the waters of the Red Sea' can be made historically credible if not provable.

But what about the possibility that any sequence of alleged divine acts can be given credibility simply by providing some (any) interpretive schema to it? Would we not wind up with a whole host of competing interpretive schemas, all of which are historically plausible, but none of which can be historically proven? And if this is the case, what advantage have we gained by establishing only the historical possibility of divine acts?

Faith as Credible Trust

This is the point at which the element of risk, faith, or trust enters the picture. The historian can assemble the evidence (or lack of it, or counter-evidence) for or against an alleged occurrence. The historian, qua historian, is in no position to decide whether the evidence points to a *divine* agent behind it, but she can tell us whether there is evidence that something like the occurrence (the spatio-temporal event) narrated in the text probably, most certainly, or most certainly did not occur, given the historical evidence as we now have it. There may be, for example, historical evidence for a migration of an enslaved people out of Egypt at roughly the time described in the biblical narrative. There may be evidence that in order to get to what was then called the land of Canaan this people would have had to pass over a shallow, marshy area. There may even be evidence that some Egyptian troops were lost during this period. There is unlikely to be evidence (other than that which reflects the experience of the participants as recorded only in Scripture) that a 'miraculous' passage over this marshy area occurred, though there is probably no decisive evidence that it did *not* occur. At this point, the one who believes the narratives must take a risk of belief: she must accept the truth (in its general form) of the narrative on the basis of trust because it makes sense according to the pattern of divine action that she has inferred from a multitude of other alleged divine acts and from her own experience of being herself a recipient of what she takes to be God's acts. This act of trust is neither blind nor certain. It is a trust that the narrative faithfully records a divine act consistent with her picture of the kind of acts God performs, is not inconsistent with historical possibility, is metaphysically credible, and forms a coherent part of a larger overarching pattern of divine acts culled from the narrative as a whole.

Ultimately, of course, her act of trust will be validated by whether, in the long run, it leads her to act in ways that are sustained or supported by reality. If she is right, she has inferred an intention undergirding and shaping the structures of reality and the movement of history. If she acts according to that inferred intention, she will trust that her actions will ultimately be 'rewarded'. She will be acting with the grain of history, rather than against it. Unfortunately, there may be no short-run, let alone decisive, confirmation of her trust. This fact may well be the single most important impediment to belief in a loving, personal God. It is the impediment of evil and it is an impediment precisely because it presupposes the metaphysical credibility of the notion of God as an Agent who can act in history.

The Problem of Evil

There are many concepts of God that ultimately escape the problem of evil. The monist view, for example, can simply deny the reality of evil as any kind of 'other' or alien entity or set of occurrences apart from God, since God is, after all, the *only* reality. What we view as evil is ultimately a problem in the viewing—an illusion, not ultimately a problem of being. In monism, nothing exists apart from the single reality of God and, therefore, evil cannot exist as a problem 'for' God since it has no status apart from God. And since God is not evil, evil does not exist.

Likewise, the dualist view of God, especially when it pushes the logical implications of God's omnipotence, virtually has to deny the reality of evil as any kind of 'other' that is ultimately outside of God's control or intention. If God is truly omnipotent and omniscient, then literally nothing can occur which is not either caused by God or permitted by God (and in either case, foreseen by God). Evil can be explained away as that which we do not yet fully understand but which from God's point of view (which, as transcendent, is beyond our cognition) is both necessary and 'good', and therefore not *really* evil since it is, after all, compatible with God's infinite goodness, which cannot coexist with anything *truly* evil.

In both monism and dualism, God is in no sense an agent who can act against evil. If evil is the experience of actions (or events) that bring pointless suffering, then God, not being an agent at all, can hardly be held responsible for not acting *against* or preventing evil. These 'actions' for which God cannot be held responsible since God cannot perform them, would also include intending, conceiving, and creating the world in which the alleged evil occurs. The irony is that only a being capable of acting can be held accountable for acting or failing to act so as to bring about or prevent evil from happening.

Only the view of God as a personal Agent has to confront the true horrors and feel the full weight of the problem of evil. If evil is understood to be the existence of pain, suffering, and wickedness that seem to have no ultimate benefit to human beings (and perhaps to the ecological order as well), then the existence of evil must be reconciled with the *character* of a loving God who has the power to eliminate those things that cause evil (or to eliminate their actually causing evil without necessarily eliminating *them*). If God *can* act in history, and if action in history is necessary in order to keep some things from happening or cause others to happen instead, then an Agent God not only can but must bear some responsibility for the evil things that do, in fact, happen in history.

Have we, then, painstakingly developed a defense of the notion of God as Agent only to have it wrecked upon the rock of evil? It is certainly true that the problem of evil is felt with full force by the notion of God as Agent, especially if as a result of the risky inference from history one trusts that God acts lovingly, not wickedly. And one cannot give with one hand and take away with the other. The heavy weight of the problem of evil cannot be removed simply by honestly acknowledging its peculiarly difficult application to the notion of God as Agent. So what is said about the problem should not be understood to have eliminated or 'solved' it. Nevertheless, a few things need to be said about it.

Human Freedom

First, it would be the case that an acting God could permit the actions of other agents with whom God is interacting to be free from (complete) divine determination. (All interaction determines to some extent the actions of the agents with whom one is interacting and thus, if God does act, God's actions will 'determine', limit, or condition to some extent the range of counter-actions open to the beings upon whom God acts, just as human actions in some sense limit God's range of actions.) But an interacting God need not be understood as absolutely omnipotent if that concept is taken to imply complete and exhaustive determination of everything that happens in the universe. God could be the *decisive* agent, the agent whose actions are pivotal and indispensable in shaping the course of history, without being the *only* agent. This fact could leave open the freedom of other agents (with less power) to act contrary to God's intentions and thus to act evilly. The existence of human freedom from complete divine determination and for some degree of self-determination has often been affirmed by supporters of the dualist view of God but not usually with metaphysical consistency since they do not usually abandon their assumption that nothing happens without God's foreknowledge and foreordination.

The pluralist view need not hedge on the concept of divine omnipotence because in this respect it denies that the concept applies. In fact, the entire biblical picture of God reaffirms the reality of the human freedom to respond to God's initiatives. That freedom seems to be respected in almost every instance by God as well. There are some biblical scholars who insist that God only 'guides' human will, never suppresses it. As Ludwig Kohler puts it, "God's guidance in the Old Testament does not imply the complete subjugation of man [sic] nor the suppression of his will. In fact, as the prophets show, it effects a conscription of all the human, all the individual powers and gifts of the person being guided."[3]

I am not convinced that God, even in the biblical record, *never* coerces human beings (God is said, for example, to have hardened Pharoah's heart). Nevertheless, it certainly seems to be a consistent claim throughout that record that human beings do have freedom vis-à-vis God. That freedom is almost an absolute value for God, since God seems to respect it even on those occasions when overriding it would produce apparently less immediate suffering and calamity. But if God will not override human freedom, then one explanation of evil that neither explains it away nor forces God to be its author is that evil is what results from the *misuse* of human freedom.

The notion of misuse must itself, of course, be carefully articulated. If God is inferred to be a consistently loving agent whose overarching intentions are to bring fulfillment to God's human partners, then the divine intentions will be such that if they are fully enacted with no opposition they will achieve their end, namely a world in which pointless harm does not occur. Now it would follow that if human agents successfully align or conform their intentions with God's, then they will be using their freedom 'correctly'. That is, they will use their freedom in such a way as to enhance, advance, supplement, support, or codevelop God's intentions. And if God's intentions are to realize a world in which evil does not occur, then supportive human intentions (even though freely chosen) will not introduce evil into that world. The misuse of freedom, consequently, would be to enact those intentions that would impede, retard, divert, or counter God's intentions. If God does not choose to override the consequences of those human acts (by intervening in the course of their enactment and the chain of consequences that ensue), they will necessarily introduce some (greater or lesser) degree of evil into the world.

And, it would also follow that if God is to respect human freedom, God could not consistently or always override even terrible human choices. If freedom is to mean anything at all, it must mean the realization in fact as well as in theory of what one has chosen. To cut the link between the intention and its enactment or between the act and its consequences is to cut the heart out of responsibility for our freely enacted choices. Someone who is told he is free to use a handgun and yet who is prohibited from ever firing it or who finds that upon firing it the bullet simply vanishes before striking anything, is hardly free in any real or genuine sense to *use* the gun. Thus if God permits human freedom, God must permit us to experience the full exercise of that freedom, meaning the complete realization of our intentions in the actual warp and woof of history. If we choose to misuse our freedom and fire the handgun at an innocent person, God cannot intervene in the course that links the intention with the final impact of the bullet without in some sense undercutting the very essence of what it means for God to permit us to be free and accountable for that freedom in that instance.

The Historical/Social Context of Human Freedom

On this basis, it could be argued that much (but not all) evil in the world is the result of not only individual instances of the misuse of human freedom, but also of the social accumulation of those instances, including the failure to make other choices that, had we made them and had the results of those choices accumulated in and through both personal and social contexts over a sufficiently long period of time, might have resulted in the elimination of things that we now regard as 'natural' and not simply as 'chosen' evil. For example, it might have been the case that evil choices by numbers of individuals in the distant past (say, choices that intended solely the protection of themselves at the expense of others) accumulated socially in such a way that after a period of time whole cultures and institutions became dedicated to providing barriers of protection for some at the expense of others. These individual *and* social decisions led to further choices as to the personal and social expenditure of time and resources, for example, for armaments and weapons of protection instead of for medical cures or techniques of conflict resolution. Over time the social conditions made it harder and harder for single individuals freely to decide to cure cancer since social resources were already disproportionately devoted to military expenditures and even the psychological option of devoting energy to curing cancer could not be seriously considered. As cancer continues to strike down innocent individuals (a clear case of evil), no single individual's free choice, or failure to choose correctly, can be held responsible. But the accumulated social effect of generations of human choices in other directions might conceivably be regarded as one of the tragic results of the earlier misuse of human freedom and the cause of continuing evil in the world now.

It still might be argued, of course, that the trade-off for us between exercising our freedom to the fullest and having that exercise short-circuited by an occasional divine intervention is not self-evidently justified in all instances. Might there not be some occasions in which we would be willing to accept an override of human freedom in order to eliminate evils of such magnitude that our loss of freedom would seem a small price to pay to avoid them? The classic example is God's intervention in the conception of Hitler. All God would have had to do is to have intervened in the causal processes to abort the fetus that became Hitler or even to frustrate the act of Hitler's conception itself. A small divine intervention with extraordinary benefits for the human race!

Of course, if God could eliminate a Hitler even before he was born, God surely ought to have done the same with every Stalin, Idi Amin, Pol Pot, Nero, Caligula—the list becomes almost endless—who have afflicted the world with their tyranny. And is it self-evident that with the elimination of each of these proven tyrants, no new tyrants would have emerged to take their place? Is it even self-evident that it is only the tyrants who cause the evil for which they are held accountable? Are they not equally dependent on thousands, even millions of persons, who passively accept their tyranny, even become complicit with it, or do not actively oppose it? Should not God, therefore, at least alter the genetic cells or the wiring in the brains of each of us who tacitly supports the tyranny of monsters?

The point is that in hindsight each of us can draw up a better sequence of events than the ones that have actually transpired, and give God a set of retrospective directions that would have apparently resulted in less evil in history. But if we do this, are we not in effect pretending that all the consequences of one act are somehow completely predetermined by that act and that evil can be avoided simply by eliminating that one act? If only Hitler had not been born, no Holocaust would have occurred? But surely Hitler alone could not have caused the Holocaust! Thus, each act ramifies in a thousand directions, each one opening up new possibilities that then branch off again and again into ever newer, equally free (as well as conditioned) options for the future. To ask God, from our present historical vantage point, to have done a few things in the past in order to make things work out better in the present ignores the extraordinary complexity and ramifications of free acts performed by millions of free agents in (direct and indirect) relation to millions of other free agents. It is simplistic in the extreme to assume that only a few divine interventions could have or would have brought about far less evil in history. Evil occurs within and as a result of the whole of the vast complex of all interrelated decisions made throughout history. We do not solve the problem of evil, therefore, simply by having God perform a few, isolated surgical interventions. If evil is in part the result of the human misuse of freedom, it could only be avoided if God intervened in every single act at every single moment of human history. And this, of course, violates the principle with which we began, namely that God respects human freedom and its right to experience the full consequences of its individual and collective choices.

Natural Evil

But have these considerations disposed of the problem of *natural* evil—those events which happen without any human intervention and therefore are not attributable to human freedom? Surely hurricanes and earthquakes and cancer, which kill millions of persons, are not to be explained as the result of the complexification of networks of human acts or failures to act. In one sense, of course, this is a fair point. Human beings have had nothing to do with the natural disasters that have struck them since the beginnings of the human race. But unlike the evil that results from the misuse of human freedom, natural evil may be the result of the structures of physical reality that are necessary to human existence as such. If, as much recent speculation on the origin of the universe would have us believe, only certain highly specific (and cosmically improbable) empirical conditions will support human life, it might be the case that God's freedom to 'create' human life was limited by the kind of 'infrastructure' such life requires. This infrastructure might, in turn, be such as to require the possibility (and therefore the likelihood) of hurricanes, earthquakes, and other 'natural disasters'. Perhaps what we know as 'human' life is not possible in any other kind of cosmic or natural environment (just as rain is not possible unless it occurs within the specific environment of clouds and moisture). This is not to say that God did not create the infrastructure as well, but it is to say that in order to get human life God might have had to create this particular infrastructure, which carried with it the possibility of natural events such as hurricanes. In other words, human life may be compatible only with some physical infrastructures (boundary conditions) and that, therefore, God had to bring those particular infrastructures into being in order to provide the conditions for human life (and, concomitantly, human freedom). (See the earlier discussion in chapter 7 about God's relation to the 'big bang' and God's possible role in determining the laws of this particular cosmic arena.)

This concession, however, does not require that human beings go on forever being the victims of these natural disasters—with enough creativity and attention it is at least conceivable that human beings could use their freedom to predict and build protections against, or even modify, the natural occurrences that currently wreck such havoc. Thus human freedom becomes a factor in combatting these 'evils'.

This consideration would clearly imply a limit on God's omnipotence (and we have already conceded such limits). But would it not also imply a trivializing of what acts God does in fact perform? If God will not override human freedom and cannot eliminate natural evils (since they are part of the infrastructure that 'comes with the package' of earthly and human reality), is there anything significant left for God to do? Have we not, in effect, stripped God of the last vestige of anything that constitutes worthiness of worship? In principle, this is a very serious problem. If the meaning of God resides in God's capacity to be the decisive cosmic agent, and if God's agency is subject to the limitations of human freedom and the natural infrastructure, are there any acts left for God to perform that would constitute 'decisiveness' and worship-inspiring responses from us?

This question leads us directly into the heart of the Christian faith. That faith is ultimately based on the experience of some particular divine acts that Christians take as revealing the overarching intention behind God's involvement in the created order. These divine acts do not 'solve' the problem of evil but they provide a foundation of meaning from which that problem can be integrated into a set of convictions about the purpose of human life and its redemption. What the Christian offers to the discussion of the problem of evil is not an explanation that 'accounts for' all evil acts or 'reconciles' them with God's goodness. Instead, the Christian offers an interpretation of a series of acts, which she takes to be those of God, which reveal a divine intention to confront and overcome (but not explain away) the reality of evil.

Notes

1. Doron Hof and Nathan Paldor, "Are There Oceanographic Explanations for the Israelites' Crossing of the Red Sea?," *Bulletin of the American Meteorological Society* 73, no. 3 (March 1992): 305–14.

2. Ibid., p. 307.

3. Ludwig Kohler, *Old Testament Theology*, trans. A. S. Todd (Philadelphia: Westminster Press, 1957), p. 97.

9

Refining the Biblical Picture of God's Actions in History

Interpreting the Book of the Acts of God

At the heart of the Christian faith and its Scriptures is the conviction that God is together bound with God's creation in the struggle to achieve justice and peace, for humanity as well as for the natural order as a whole. The Scriptures have been called the book of the acts of God. And those acts have been understood by countless generations of Jews and Christians as constituting God's attempt to steer the course of nature and history toward the building up of an inclusive community in which all have become reconciled with all—in which the bonds of love have bound together all of creation and in which God is to be the focus and the source of the mutual celebration of loving communion, ultimately triumphing over the counterforces of evil.

The biblical picture of God has God acting all the time, both in creating and sustaining the world, as well as in specific ways for the realization of particular divine intentions in history. Most biblical scholarship supports the claim that the Bible is the record of a consistent and coherent interpretation of divine acts as emanating from God's intention to restore the world to peace and community from the disordered, fractional state into which the human refusal to trust God has led it. The Bible is a narrative of the acts of God as God seeks to embody (and for Christians ultimately to incarnate) God's intention that the world be at peace with itself and with God. This narrative is, in effect, the biblical response to the reality of evil: to tell the story of God's work, along with the cooperative work of those who love and follow God, in combating the recalcitrance, obstruction, indifference, fear, hate, and evil of those forces that use their freedom either to promote or, as a natural part of the infrastructure, work blindly against the fulfillment of God's intention of love.

This is not to deny that within the biblical narrative there are many 'traditions', each one focusing upon some particular aspect of God's actions or of human response to divine initiatives. The wisdom 'tradition' and the prophetic 'tradition' are not identical in emphasis or focus. But this is not to say that the multiplicity of scriptural traditions should lead us to the conclusion that there are many divine agents revealed in Scripture. While one must be extremely careful in drawing general conclusions, there does seem to be support from biblical scholars for the view that the text as a whole discerns an overarching unity and coherence in divine action from creation to the (promised) end of time. Biblical scholar Paul Hanson's recent *The People Called: The Growth of Community in the Bible*, for example, carefully and thoroughly exegetes the text as a compilation of a variety of "responses to a God experienced within the struggles of life, struggles accordingly interpreted as manifestations of God's efforts to release humans from bondage to all that diminishes life, and to free them for the life of shared blessing in communion with God and in human fellowship."[1] At the heart of this biblical story is the conviction that there is a purposeful movement, a "transcendent dynamic".[2] The story would be simply incoherent unless one accepts its underlying conviction that history is a mutual engagement between the acts of God and the acts of human beings.

Any reading of Scripture must take account of a number of things: the variety of texts that constitute it; the variety of writers, historical settings, communal and personal experiences, speculative reflections, and specific intentions guiding each text; the interpretive overlay on the 'real' (objective) historical substratum; and the historical claims that constitute its narrative core. It is also essential that a contemporary interpreter of the interpretive text understand that its narrative reveals the character of the agents whose actions comprise its underlying meaning. At the heart of this narrative is the agent God whose character is known precisely through the deeds that God performs. At the same time, from the community's interpretation of those deeds emerges an *inference* regarding the underlying (or overarching) unifying intention that each of God's acts embodies and carries forward. When that inference is internalized within the believer, it becomes the basis of faith (i.e., trust) that in responding appropriately to God's acts one is aligning oneself with a purpose (and a purposer) that will ultimately bring fulfillment to all those who adopt it as their own.

Now, how are all these things brought together into a coherent understanding that can give guidance to contemporary Christian communities seeking to be faithful to God? The first question is whether the biblical narrative is sufficient to establish a historical basis for belief in a historically active divine being (provided that one is willing to credit the intelligibility of the notion of an acting God). There is virtually no question that for the writers and users of Scripture its record of historical events warranted or justified their belief that a divine Agent had encountered them and worked historically on their behalf. The historical events that constituted the Exodus from slavery to freedom, the reception of a covenant of laws (Torah) at Mount Sinai, and the eventual settlement of the 'promised' land had been sufficiently real and embedded in the memory of the community that wrote the story down that they formed the core of the historical experience of the people of Israel. There is no doubt that those who formed this account believed that God was, despite the contributions of many others, the decisive agent who brought these events about.

The question that is often asked, of course, is whether the 'objective' or 'secular' historian can credit these accounts. How could a historian ever certify that it was God who empowered Moses to lead his people, or who enabled the fleeing slaves to cross safely over a body of water that then drowned their pursuers? If the historian is committed to crediting only those acts whose agents are in some sense visibly connected to their acts, she cannot warrant the claim that God 'parted the waters of the Red Sea'. But if our argument developed earlier regarding the plausibility of divine acts is sound, then there is nothing, *in principle*, to rule out divine responsibility for this specific action. Our argument, however, only established plausibility. The historian demands more than that. She demands *evidence* or reasonable grounds for the inference that this particular occurrence, provided it can first be established that it happened, is an act to be attributed to God and not just an event caused by a concatenation of natural forces, such as 'fortuitous' winds drying up shallow marshy areas just as the Hebrew slaves approach. How can the historian move from a reading of events as 'fortuitous' to a reading of them as 'intentionally enacted by God'?

Pannenberg and the 'Historical Foundation' of Biblical Claims

Wolfhart Pannenberg has, perhaps, among contemporary scholars, made the strongest claim that reported acts of God (especially the resurrection of Jesus) have "good historical foundation."[3] Pannenberg is absolutely convinced that the Christian faith stands or falls on the historicity of that act as credited by historians faithful to the principles of their craft. Neither its truth nor its meaning can be secured by faith if it does not first possess historical credibility. "Whether or not a particular event happened two thousand years ago is not made certain by faith but only by historical research, to the extent that certainty can be attained at all about questions of this kind. . . . If historical study declares itself unable to establish what 'really' happened on Easter, then all the more, faith is not able to do so; for faith cannot ascertain anything certain about events of the past that would perhaps be inaccessible to the historian."[4] At the same time, Pannenberg reminds us, natural science cannot rule out the occurrence of an event simply because it does not conform to natural law.

> Conformity to law embraces only one aspect of what happens. From another perspective, everything that happens is contingent, and the validity of the laws of nature is itself contingent. Therefore, natural science expresses the general validity of the laws of nature but must at the same time declare its own inability to make definitive judgments about the possibility or impossibility of an individual event. . . . The judgment about whether an event, however unfamiliar, has happened or not is in the final analysis a matter for the historian and cannot be prejudged by the knowledge of natural science.[5]

Pannenberg is arguing essentially that the rules of judgment to which *any* historian commits herself (whether Christian, atheist, or agnostic) cannot be suspended at the time of making a decision whether a certain occurrence was an act and an act of this particular agent. This is particularly true for Christian historians who, by the nature of their religious beliefs, are committed to the notion that God does in fact act in history and therefore leaves evidence of the divine intentions (and character) in the historical deposit of those acts.

Fortunately for the Christian, Pannenberg maintains (after an exhaustive analysis of the texts), the reality of Jesus' resurrection,

which he considers, as would most Christians, *the* decisive historical claim of Christianity, appears "as historically very probable, and
that always means in historical inquiry that it is to be presupposed
until contrary evidence appears."[6]

Pannenberg's claim is similar to that of William Abraham, who
has said that biblical examples "of direct divine action provide significant warrants for claims about God's acts in history, for his
intentions and purposes in acting, and for his love for mankind. . . .
[These] claims can legitimately be interpreted as factual."[7] But their
facticity is a "judgment of probability arrived at after a series of considerations have been weighed together."[8] Abraham means that any
judgment that a particular claim refers truly to a divine act in history must be put into a "wider conceptual scheme that gives point
and intelligibility to their occurrence."[9] Ultimately, the argument
for God's acts is both inferential, cumulative, and, at best, probable, not certain. But so it is with almost all historical claims about
previous acts not observed directly by the historian.

There is, for the Christian believer in a God who acts, no
escaping the necessity for inferential belief regarding those acts.
Faith cannot provide a historical certainty that inference is unable
to supply. In fact, it seems far more appropriate and true to the original meaning of the word 'faith' to understand it as a 'trust' or 'confidence' that we have read the record correctly and that on the basis
of that reading we are willing to trust our lives to the God whose
loving purpose we have inferred from the record. This is not to deny
that individual persons can and do have experiences of immediate
certainty, a kind of direct experiential knowledge of God. But even
these experiences have to be put into the context of the record of
divine acts on other persons at other times and places. The knowledge of that record simply is unable to secure the kind of immediate certainty that direct, personal experiences often provide. Putting our own experiences, therefore, into the context of a larger,
more comprehensive, historical train of actions, necessarily entails
a level of risk, inference, and trust.

Harvey and the Autonomy of the Historian

Van Harvey's assessment of the principles that should guide historical judgment are still, I believe, relevant to the faithful Jew or
Christian who wants to make sense of the biblical claims that God
has acted in history. First, the historian must be autonomous in
the sense that she has a right to "be free from any authority that

would circumscribe research and inquiry."[10] It is the historian, after all, who decides which witnesses are to be given credibility or authority. She "reserves the right to judge who or what will be called an authority, and [s]he makes this judgment only after [s]he has subjected the so-called witnesses to a rigorous cross-examination."[11] Second, the arguments and claims to knowledge by the historian must "achieve whatever cogency or well-foundedness can relevantly be asked for in that field."[12] While Harvey himself is far more inclined to grant scientific explanation a virtual veto over historical claims than I believe is warranted (given my argument to this point), he is right in asserting that there must be some justification or warrant for any such claims. This leads to the third principle, which is that the believer must accept a claim only on the basis of an argument from the evidence. To move from the data to a conclusion requires an "inference-license" or warrant.[13] Warrants "not only legitimize the step from data to conclusion but also confer *differing degrees of force on a conclusion*. They permit us not merely to assent to a claim but they justify a certain texture of assent"[14] (i.e., as certain, probable, barely possible, etc.). The historian is like an attorney trying a case: she marshalls her evidence, develops her arguments, setting forth her reasons for warranting certain claims, and presents her case in the terms that a jury of her peers will find both credible and convincing. While Harvey seems indisposed to warrant any claim that God directly acted in history, if the jury of our peers is willing to accept the possibility of such divine action, then the religious believer can both meet Harvey's criteria for principled historical judgment and stand in faithful continuity with the biblical witness that God has acted and continues to act in human history.

A great deal of unnecessary confusion can be dispelled if we shift our understanding of faith from a willingness to believe or affirm what is often literally unintelligible to a willingness to believe, or trust, that we have correctly inferred the facts of history (as they engage our life in relation to God) as revealing God's character and intentions. As long as God is understood in dualistic or transcendent terms, faith will most often be a catapult by which to hurl our intellect into a realm of 'knowledge' into which the limits of our ontological context prohibit entry as long as we remain within the horizon of cognitive intelligiblity. Faith will be a willingness to 'see' or to 'affirm' what our natural intellect is literally unable to comprehend.

But if faith is trust, then it remains grounded in our ontological context, and wedded to the terms of cognitive intelligibility. We lose, perhaps, the psychological security of absolute cognitive security, but we gain an integration between our thinking and our deepest feelings. Trust is both an intellectual act and a deeply personal commitment. It is intellectual insofar as it requires a careful reading, analysis, and weighing of the evidence, and is deeply personal insofar as the inferences we draw from that intellectual process become the ground upon which our willingness to commit our whole selves to the God we trust has acted for us is based.

The basic question, therefore, for most contemporary Christians is whether there is enough historical data to support the Christian's inferential judgment that God has been at work in the world enacting a purpose to which the contemporary disciple can and should commit his life.

The Importance of An Interpretive Tradition

It is precisely at this juncture that the relation between a secular reading of history and a reading informed by an interpretive tradition begin to diverge, even though both may accept the event, qua event, as having happened. The interpretive tradition begins by placing this event in a narrative sequence of other events, the totality of which constitutes the basis of its belief that in and through this sequence the individual or the community has been acted upon (and responds to) a divine actor. No interpretation begins and ends with a single event. Only a sequence of events can establish the fabric through which an interpretive thread can be woven, unifying the individual parts. If a person whom I have never met looks in my direction and utters the words "It was you," I would have no immediate grounds on which to understand what has just happened. If the individual subsequently explains to me that he has seen my picture in the newspaper as the speaker at a rally who said a number of things with which he violently disagreed, then I can begin to interpret the event of being spoken to more clearly. In other words, every event requires a contextual framework or narrative thread if it is to be understood as having an historical meaning. A previous (or sometimes subsequent) sequence of events must prepare the way for us to place the contemporary event into a coherent context of meaning.

A culture which has never entertained the metaphysical possibility of a singular individual powerful enough to bring about mighty disturbances in nature would have no context into which to place a claim that a particular disturbance was the work of a divine agent. Should such a disturbance occur (e.g., waters parting across a large body of water) it would (and should) first be placed in the interpretive context of a natural event (not an act), which, while stupendous and extraordinary, could be expected eventually to fall under a natural law explanation. Only two things would (and should) suggest a different (or more inclusive) explanation: one, a prior set of equally extraordinary events, already interpreted by others as the work of a divine agent; or, two, a subsequent set of equally extraordinary events that begin to make sense only if they are linked with the first event in an extended narrative sequence under the rubric of divine actions.

Of course, if events in a chain are to be seen as originating from a single agent, either they must literally be seen to be connected with the agent who produced them, or they must manifest a continuity and commonality of intention such that it is reasonable to infer that they are the work of a single agent enacting a single, overarching intention over the course of time. In the first instance, we would be justified in claiming that a single agent authored each act even if there appears to be no unifying or overarching intention behind them, simply because the basis for our claim is physical observation. We might see Sarah yelling obscenities on the street to her clergyperson, tenderly binding up the cuts on a small child's knee, hitting an elderly woman with a baseball bat, and reading an exquisitely sensitive poem about nature to a group of senior citizens. If these were the only acts we saw Sarah perform, it would be hard to deny that she was their author (since we actually *saw* her doing them), but it would be equally difficult to infer any kind of unifying intention behind them. In the second instance, where no visible link between agent and act is present, we would be forced to infer such a link only if we first inferred a unifying intention (or, perhaps, if the kind of acts in question was so unique, e.g., involving unheard of physical force). God has never been observed directly performing an act. Therefore, the claim that God is the author of an act or series of acts must be based on the *inference* that this particular sequence of occurrences makes sense (as a sequence of acts originating from a single author) only because it seems to be held together by a unifying intention. Coupled with the observation that these acts also seem to require a degree of extraordinary power, not known to exist among human beings, this inference has led to the biblical claim that God is the agent behind those acts that shape and inform its understanding of reality. Central to this inferential conviction is the belief, as well, that God's activity will (in the words of Michael Goldberg) "display the fullest possible integration and coherence such that no phase of his actions in the past will ever be abandoned in the present or future but will instead be continually affirmed and advanced in each new act."[15] Or as Thomas Tracy adds, "there will be no inconstancy in God's action—none of the disillusioned reassessments and sudden reversals that may punctuate the life of a human agent."[16]

The existence of a world that seems generally supportive of human development, the liberation of an oppressed people (when realistic assessments of their situation would have justified hopelessness), the settlement and defense of a new land against militarily and politically superior nations, the provision of covenantal laws that held them together against forces that, according to the laws of 'real world' politics, should have destroyed them, the appearance in their midst of an individual who seemed to have remarkable charismatic healing and teaching powers, the resurrection of this individual from the dead, the survival of a community of his followers against persecution and martyrdom, and the thousands of individual experiences of finding strength and healing subsequent to prayer when human resources have collapsed, all seem to make sense on the assumption that there is a single, unifying intention behind or at least involved in each or most of these experiences. That intention seems to be one of nurturing, compassion, empowerment, peace, justice, and community. And this, of course, is precisly the biblical claim: in and through these occurences, God is acting according to an overarching, unifying intention of love. As Ronald Thiemann has put it, "God is identified primarily as the *God of promise* whose promises receive *narrative enactment and fulfillment* in the history of Israel, and the life, death, and resurrection of Jesus."[17]

The biblical witness is that all these events, and thousands of others that have never received canonical status or even been known outside one or a few individuals, make sense if there is a divine agent enacting, or at least involved or co-enacting all of them according to a common underlying purpose. But the biblical witness is, ultimately, an inference—a historical inference drawn from a sequence of occurrences whose meaning is revealed only when they are joined together by the common thread of interpreting them as God's acts in history. And an inference is not *proof*, nor is it immune to historical revision or rejection by persons who do not read the evidence the same way (even assuming they are open to the metaphysical possibility of divine action).

Is the Bible Internally Consistent?

Like the problem of evil, however, securing a victory for the credibility of belief in specific divine action brings with it the messy
problem of trying to decide if the biblical witness to God's acts is
inconsistent with itself. Michael Goldberg has recently argued that
from within a Jewish framework of meaning, there are more *dis-
continuities* between the acts of God inferred by Jews as recorded
in the Hebrew Scripture and the acts inferred by Christians as found
in the New Testament. For Jews, God's promised fulfillment of the
covenant depends upon the cooperation of its human partners. As
he reads the New Testament, it seems to suggest that God's promises are fulfilled entirely by God alone, with no human cooperation at all, "God acting absolutely *unilaterally*, God acting *completely graciously.*"[18] Conversely, "In Jewish eyes, were God to have
acted in the way ascribed to him by Matthew's story, he would,
through his very actions, have radically undermined—even reneged
on—the terms of the agreement [the Covenant]. For in attempting
to effect salvation in the very person of Jesus of Nazareth, God
would have in essence been playing both parts—his own and that
of humanity—consequently usurping the role previously accorded,
for better or worse, to humankind alone."[19]

Goldberg's observations reveal clearly that even a common belief
in an acting God does not necessarily lead to a common inference
about *which* acts God has performed or about the intention behind
those acts. Goldberg reminds us that no proof of God's acts and no
identification of only one intention behind those acts can be simply read from the narrative text. Inference is always tricky and risky.
It must always be supplemented with personal experience in which
one feels, both singly and in community, the presence of God as
a living agent. A dialectic then emerges in which the feeling of
divine presence is checked against the narrative inference and the
narrative inference is given weight and credibility by one's personal
or communal experience.

At the heart of the Christian faith, therefore, is the ultimate
conviction that Christians have somehow gotten the right inference
about history because that inference makes sense of their present
experience of being acted upon by a God whose character seems
perfectly consistent with the character of the God inferred from the
historical narrative of those acts. And what is that inference? What
is the confidence (or trust) that Christians have established through
the integration of their personal and communal experiences with

their reading of God's acts in history? In a word it is that God is calling the entire created order into community with itself and with God. God is the agent who has been (and continues to be), in the words of Paul Hanson, "active in all history to guide the human family to a common life of justice, compassion, and shared prosperity on a mended and peaceful earth."[20]

Christians and Jews share a common conviction that God is intending a universal community of all persons living together in harmony with nature. Nevertheless, they also believe that God has acted in particular ways in their histories to effect that intention. These particular acts of God are the substance of the biblical narrative. At the same time, however, few would deny that God has also acted in the histories of other peoples, even though the people within biblical communities lack the narrative stories of divine acts in other religious traditions. In other words, Jews and Christians believe both that God has acted in their midst in dramatic and decisive ways and that these acts do not exhaust the whole range of divine actions that have shaped the course of human development worldwide. What Jews and Christians do insist upon, however, is that in the divine deeds that constitute their histories, they see a true and decisive revelation of God's intention and character, one that God's acts in other histories cannot ultimately contradict.

It would be impossible, in this book, to rehearse the whole range of the biblical story and the textual analysis that confirms it as a picture of God's overarching intention to achieve community. What is possible for us is a closer look at how some of the biblical witness undergirds and complements our understanding of God as divine Agent.

Liberation from Oppression

First, it is clear that the biblical belief in God as Agent is predicated on the specific and dramatic act of liberation from oppression experienced by the Hebrew slaves in Egypt. As a people, their subsequent history was always traced back to this formative sequence of events, beginning with the call to Moses and continuing through the epic crossing of the Red Sea, the establishment of the Covenant with God at Mount Sinai, the wandering in the desert, and the eventual settlement in the land "flowing with milk and honey." In the light of those events, the Hebrew people were then able to reconstruct, perhaps to a large degree only imaginatively, a history prior to the events of Exodus, including God's creation of the world, the Noahic covenant, the call to Abraham, and so forth. But the central event, the liberation from political and economic oppression in Egypt of the people called by God into community through covenant at Mount Sinai, gave the people the basis from which to draw the essential inference as to God's character and intention: the God they know is the one who liberates and cares enough to bind Godself to them.

This character trait was to remain constant throughout all subsequent inferences of God's acts in history, extending into the Christian era as well. God was understood as the Agent who acts to bring liberation from oppression and compassion in time of trouble. What eventually distinguishes Jews from Christians is a lack of consensus as to not only whether in Jesus God was continuing to enact God's intention of liberation, but also whether in the events surrounding the life, death, and resurrection of Jesus, God had acted decisively to bring about the ultimate guarantee of liberation, even from death itself. Despite this disagreement, however, Jews and Christians are one in holding that the overarching divine intention is liberation and that God has performed some specific historical acts to further that intention.

Personal Experience of Divine Presence

In addition to those dramatic historical acts, however, Christians also claim an ongoing, present experience of God's acts in history, namely the experience in their own lives or in the lives of those whose witness they are willing to credit, of divine grace, presence, comfort, and healing. These experiences, as we have suggested, provide the indispensable counterpart to any attempt to find evidence of God's acts in previous histories. But wherever we find sustained and sustaining communities of love, we believe, we find continuing evidence of God's work in the world, precisely because those communities seem to be the underlying, continuing, constant intention of God throughout all of biblically recorded history.

This is not to say that God's acts *alone* create community. It is part of the biblical record that God has chosen, for the most part, to enact God's intention only with the cooperation of God's human partners. Community in the bible is built on the response of those in whose midst God has acted. Community is never forced upon persons. In fact, the very concept of community presumes the conscious and willing commitment of all its members. Most acts of

God call for human response if their underlying intention is to be fully realized.

Divine Coercion or Persuasion

Process theology has rightly recalled this point to our attention. Process theologians argue that God acts by persuasion, not coercion, by 'calling' or 'luring' people to respond in such a way to God's vision for them so as to further its historical development. This belief in the importance of divine persuasion is an appropriate counterpoint to traditional dualistic claims that, as omnipotent, ultimately God *must* determine all that happens, no matter how subtly God utilizes 'secondary causation' (i.e., human action) in carrying out that determination. But I would not want to rule out the possibility that *some* of God's acts are coercive, at least in the sense that in those acts God simply brings about the effect God intends without willing cooperation from human (let alone nonhuman) agents. This certainly could be the case with respect to nonhuman entities. (If) God parted the waters of the Red Sea, God did so directly (whether as a basic act or through a sequence of acts that eventuated in the parting. See chapter 6 for a fuller discussion of this issue). The concatenation of natural forces (whether speeded up, condensed, etc.) that constitute the operation of the parting of the waters was brought about solely by God's intention in that specific situation. It may also be the case, however, that, from time to time, God coerces human beings directly as well (e.g., God's hardening the heart of Pharoah).

But divine 'coercion' is an option (not a necessity for all divine acts) if God is an agent, literally understood. It is an option that God apparently chooses to exercise on some occasions and not on others. It may even be the case that over time God's coercive action becomes either very infrequent or perhaps even ceases entirely. (See the earlier reference to Ludwig Kohler's claim that God only 'guides' human wills.) It has sometimes been held against the biblical picture of divine action that the God of 'miracles' (e.g., of creation, water-parting, manna-bestowing, virgin-birthing, resurrecting, etc.) simply doesn't seem to do that kind of stuff anymore. From the absence of divine 'miracles' (I use the word hesitatingly because, as we have seen, it is not necessary to refer to 'miracles' in describing God's acts in history, any more than we use it to refer to human acts), it has been concluded by some that God *never* acted miraculously and by others that if God did, and doesn't now, then God is for all intents and purposes, dead.

A third option is that God has acted both coercively and persuasively but that the particular forms of God's action have changed over the course of history, moving from a time in which coercion prevailed to a time when persuasion, or at least very subtle coercion, predominates. This option seems more in line with the biblical picture as a whole, culminating in Jesus' wrestling in the garden of Gethsemane with his own acceptance of God's intention. It is possible to read that episode as one in which God wants to make the best out of a tragic situation. It is not self-evident that Jesus' crucifixion was 'necessary' for God's subsequent resurrectional action. In fact, if it had been necessary, then we would be forced to view Jesus' death as part of God's coercive activity, which would certainly take something away from the historical freedom of both Jesus and the other human agents in the events surrounding his death, a freedom that seems essential to the full meaning of those events and to the record of God's willingness to wait upon the free human response to God's initiatives. But if God chose to refrain from coercive action at that point (either upon natural objects or human wills), that choice might well mark a turning point in the way in which God will, from that moment on, deal with God's created order.

Jesus and the Problem of Evil

This possibility takes us back to one response to the problem of evil. God may have felt that in and through Jesus God had revealed as clearly as was possible (not overriding the always present human freedom to reject that revelation) the true meaning of human fulfillment. In Jesus God embodied or incarnated (literally made fully human) the fullest, most decisive, example of what a whole, healthy, integrated, reconciled, and fulfilled human life could be. In short, in Jesus, God can be understood to have given us God's own intention fully humanized: God's own inner will and truth were given flesh and blood instantiation. This act (the bestowing upon Jesus of, or the creation of Jesus with, the divine intention) could be understood as coercive in that Jesus may not have had a choice as to whether he would bear that intention. Understood in this way, the act that *is* Jesus retains its traditional interpretation as God's act (and makes the identity between God and Jesus easier to understand). On the other hand, the presence of the divine intention in Jesus could be understood as a persuasive act by God in that God presents God's intention to Jesus and Jesus chooses to accept it (this interpretation seems to have the weight of biblical evidence in its favor, at least in some of the Gospel stories). (Either way of understanding the incarnation, incidentally, might provide a metaphysically sounder and more credible alternative than the traditional one shaped by Hellenistic metaphysics in which two ontologically different 'natures' form a single 'person'.) In that act of incarnation, God might have decided that God had given humanity enough evidence of what human life should look like, how it should be (in)formed by the divine intention of love, peace, and justice, so as to be a sufficient guide for all future human conduct. Having incarnated God's intention in this way, God could then have decided not to act *in that way* ever again. In other words, God, as Agent, could have chosen to stop acting in the ways that seem to have characterized God's actions prior to Jesus, namely, as the doer of 'mighty', overtly public historical acts. Instead, God might have chosen from then on to act less dramatically upon the public stage of history and more quietly upon and in the private and personal lives of individuals and smaller intentional communities that have chosen to be together bound with God.

To put it somewhat baldly, God might have said after Jesus, "Look, I've given you in Jesus' life, death, and resurrection, all the information you need (i.e., I've revealed it as best I can) to enable you to know how to live a fulfilling life in community with yourselves, your world, and me. From here on out, it's up to you to choose to live by the examples I've given you. I won't interfere in the traditional ways in your public history ever again because to do so would be to override the very freedom I want you to use in choosing my ways, which I have been preparing you to use since I first created you, and which, in Jesus, I have shown you how to use most responsibly. I will be present with you in the deepest parts of your hearts and minds as you struggle to live as my disciples, I will comfort and console and inspire and uplift you, but I will not again interfere publically with the history you now will be responsible for, in all its consequences, trivial, horrendous, and joyful. I have spent most of your history interfering with your world in order to give you ample evidence as to my intentions for you. Many of you have read that evidence correctly and believe that I have been at work in the world for good, liberating, redeeming, and reconciling. But in Jesus, I gave you, in your own terms, the terms of the body and blood of a fellow human being, the fullest, most complete, most decisive, embodiment, realization, and incarnation of what I intend the fulfilled human life to be. Now you have both the freedom and the power to realize that life for yourselves and your communities. Many of you will make mistakes; you will even wander so far from my intention as to create some of the most vicious, cruelest, diabolical forms of evil my world has ever witnessed. But I will not interfere, except as comfort, because I now am giving the responsible running of history over into your hands. You know what that responsibility entails and you have the freedom to act responsibly. Only if you can accept that responsibility and learn to create loving, peaceful, and just communities by your own power, will you fulfill my intentions for you and for all creation."

This imagined divine soliloquy suggests one Christian response to the evils of our own time, including the horrors of the Holocaust. It could be said that in Jesus God chose to *be with* those who suffer, even to the point of death, but not to act publically in order to eliminate any of the means of bringing about death and suffering that human beings in their willful freedom choose to create, become complicit with, or indifferent to. This answer will be of little or no comfort to the Jew who simply does not see any compelling evidence that God was acting in Jesus in the way I've imaginatively reconstructed it or feels God's presence only in the strangled cry of a boy being hanged by the Nazis.

But for Christians, who have made the risky historical inference and now trust that they know what God intends and that God can be trusted to abide by that intention, this answer can make sense of a number of their deepest convictions. First, it can provide an explanatory context for Jesus' own death on a cross, in which he moves from a cry of despair (Eli, Eli, why hast thou forsaken me?) to an affirmation of deep confidence (Into thy hands I commit my spirit). It can make sense of their own suffering (God has not chosen to remove the evil before me but has given me the strength to deal with it). And it can make sense of continuing evil in the world (we have fallen away from God's intention and, in our sin, have not used our freedom or our power to counter the evil wills of those who are working actively against it).

God and the Evil of the Holocaust

Perhaps the most troubling aspect of a belief that God *can* act in history and that God *has* acted in the past, is God's apparent failure to act now in specific personal or global situations so as to remove or deflect evil. In some ways, God's 'decision' to permit the Holocaust and other human acts of genocide and oppression in the present can be accepted if we accept the reality of human freedom and our responsibility to use it for good. At least evil acts can be traced back to human beings acting evilly or they are the accumulated consequence of human beings acting over a long period of time without due attention to those things that create evil intentions and permit evil acts to occur. We do reap what we have sown, both as a race and as individuals. And if we are to grasp the full meaning of communal responsibility we must understand that communal indifference to the conditions that stunt the capacity for love will ultimately produce people whose intentions more often realize the capacity for fear, hate, and destruction than they do for love and compassion. God's calling to God's people through the prophets is a clear example of how God was constantly reminding the people that they must bear much of the responsibility for their own survival or destruction. It was their work for peace and justice as a people, and not just as individuals, that would, in large part, determine their future state. The evils that befell them in exile were largely of their own doing (or failure to do what they should have done).

More difficult to accept is God's 'failure', at least on numerous occasions, to intervene to prevent or deflect personal tragedies due not to evil actions but to natural causes, such as death at an early age through fatal illness, disease, or accident. We can all imagine concrete personal situations in which a single divine act would have prevented profound human suffering and tragedy. (God might only have to have eliminated one cancerous cell from a baby's bones, or twisted the hands of the drunk driver so that his car did not hit and kill someone.) The problem is made even more intense if we add the factor of human prayer, which we have not mentioned until now. Prayer, especially intercessory prayer, is a form of direct communication from the individual person or community to God. Some prayers ask God to do certain things, to perform certain acts in order to bring about certain effects or to prevent other effects from occurring. If God *never* acted specifically in response to intercessory prayer, then such prayer would literally be meaningless (except perhaps as a form of therapy through the psychological self-delusion of mythical thinking).

Response to Prayer

But there are thousands of Christians who believe they have experienced the actions of God in direct response to their or others' prayers. If we accept the possibility that God has acted in response to some of these prayers as the intercessors hoped God would (or acted in ways that the intercessors did not specifically intend but that were, nonetheless, ultimately beneficial to the one who asked), then isn't God culpable for not acting upon all such prayers, especially those that ask God simply for delivery from the worst kinds of evil? It is not necessarily blasphemous to expect God to respond to prayers for delivery from evil since Jesus himself taught his followers to pray for that. One does not have to expect God to provide everything one asks for (since much of what we ask for can be frivolous or irrelevant to the kind of fulfilled life God wants for us), but if we can expect nothing from God in response to prayer, then we are really not dealing with a God who is actively bound together with us in love.

The Status of Divine Action in the Present

There are some extremely devout Christians who believe that God simply does not intervene at all anymore, either in big historical ways or in private, personal ones. They believe God has so acted in the past, and could so act now if God wanted to, but it is part of their faith that God will not act now because God has, in effect, given the world entirely over into our hands until such time as God decides to bring the Kingdom in its fullness. This view corresponds to Dietrich Bonhoeffer's notion that during this 'penultimate' phase of history (from Jesus' resurrection to the coming of the Kingdom in its fullness) we are on our own to respond freely to God's initiative, without expecting divine intervention.[21] From this perspective, it is not really a problem of culpability if God does not act to "deliver us from evil" in specific ways.

The problem with this view, however, is that it often mixes inperceptibly with a second view, which holds that even though God no longer does the big public acts or the direct interventions in private lives in response to prayer, God does provide strength, consolation, inspiration, and the capacity to bear the worst kinds of evil. This second view, while denying God's intervention generally, does hold to a particular kind of intervention, namely one in which God somehow 'causes' in us a *psychological effect* in which we feel strength or consolation in time of grief or trouble. If one does not accept any part of this second view, and holds strictly to the consequences of the first view, one is left maintaining that God does not act *at all*, even to aid and comfort those who mourn. And a God who does not act at all is virtually no God at all. It would be hard to know why prayer or praise is appropriate if directed to a God who does literally nothing in and for the persons who love God.

I would argue that if we believe that God acts to comfort us or to give us the strength to deal with adversities (even if we deny to perform 'mighty' acts), then we *do* believe that God acts in specific ways, if only in the inner recesses of the hearts and minds of individual persons. Now if God acts only in these ways, the notion of God as Agent is still credible, but the proof that God has chosen to act only in these ways would be hard to develop conclusively, especially for public scrutiny. One would also have to deal with the question of why God had decided to limit God's action only to the recesses or interstices of the human brain and not, for example, to the somewhat larger genetic structure, or the physical order of nature as such. And given the immense complexity of the neurological processes of the brain, it would be virtually impossible for human investigation to determine which synaptic firings (for example) were interfered with by God and which continued to operate by the regular causal processes of the natural infrastructure. These difficulties do not, of course, in themselves, rule out the possibility that it is precisely and exclusively in these ways that God is now still acting. But they do make the claim of such action extremely difficult to substantiate in practice, if not in theory.

The Mystery of Divine Action

But there is another alternative to understanding divine action now. It appeals to the dimension of mystery in all human intentional action, rather than to an explanatory scheme for unpacking the mechanisms of divine action. It suggests that God does in fact act now, and in a variety of ways. God acts sometimes interstitially in the brain, sometimes in the genetic structure, sometimes in more public, global ways. Some of God's acts are more easily inferable than others. And, of course, there is always the mystery of exactly *how* God acts in any given instance (the same *kind* of mystery, though to a degree virtually unimaginable, as how human beings act). But there is an even deeper mystery, and that is the mystery of *why* God chooses to act in this way now and in that way then and, apparently, in no way at all on other occasions. Why do some people's prayers receive apparently direct and hoped-for responses and others seem to go unanswered? Why does it seem appropriate to give praise to God for the safe return from a perilous journey and yet not blame God for not intervening to save the life of a dying child? How is it possible to give praise to God for the emergence of the nation of Israel and not accuse God of failing to save God's people during the Holocaust? Even in a single person's or community's life, how is it possible to give thanks to God for comfort in one situation and not hold God accountable when such comfort is not forthcoming in another?

These are the deepest possible kinds of questions from inside the existential life of each believer who feels together bound with God. They not only do not go away as the mind becomes convinced that God can act, but they become more intense and difficult. And it is here, at this juncture in the life of faith, that the believer comes up against the deepest mystery of the love of God. It is not primarily the mystery of conceptual understanding; it is not the paradox of trying to understand two rationally incompatible ideas, or of trying to cross the border between two ontologically different contexts. It is the mystery of relationship, the mystery of why love expresses itself in so many perplexing ways. Love is never susceptible to complete rational predictability or modeling. Love is, by its very nature, surprising, transrational, and confusing. But it is not, for all that, irrational or absurd.

Love is not blind faith: it accepts the necessity of trusting in what it does not now see fully, but it bases its trust on the experience of the (at least partial) fulfillment of previously announced promises and intentions by the one(s) in whom we place our trust. In any love relationship, the partners who go on loving each other have a shared history of fulfilled expectations. They have received love from each other. These grounded experiences become the basis for the trust that in the future the acts of their partner(s) will continue to embody loving intentions. And it is this past set of experiences that provides the context for trusting that when some of those future acts occur in ways that are ambiguous, or fail to live up to one's expectations, there is still, somehow, genuine love behind them (or, at least, that genuine love will surmount them).

If a husband who has demonstrated his love for his wife repeatedly over twenty-five years fails to remember the twenty-sixth anniversary, or doesn't get for his wife just what she asked for on her birthday, or neglects to call when he is out of town for a few days, his wife is justified in trying to understand these 'failures' of expectation within the context of the previous twenty-five years of demonstrated love. She is justified in trusting that somehow these failures are compatible with the love her husband has shown her over the course of a quarter of a century. This does not mean that she knows *how* to explain her husband's most recent acts, but it does mean that she has a justifiable basis on which to trust that they *are* explainable and will at some point get explained. (It may be that her husband has suffered memory loss, or is, in an attempt to be humerous, trying to surprise her with a totally unexpected gift.) And, of course, it may also be the case that her husband has genuinely stopped loving her. Well-grounded trust is no guarantee that what one is trusting will turn out, in this instance, to be true.

Nevertheless, the analogy with the believer's relationship with God is not far removed from the situation of the love between husband and wife. Those within the Jewish and Christian faiths believe they have a strong, extended historical as well as personal record of God's demonstrated love toward them. This record is found in the Scriptures, traditions, and history of their respective religious communities as well as in the experiences of each individual who belongs to them. This record and these experiences form the well-grounded basis of trust by which to confront the absence or failure of God to be visibly responsive to those situations in which God's presence would normally be expected and desired. The believer simply does not know *how* these situations are compatible with God's love. There is no obvious way in which they can be reconciled with the divine intention to be empowering, comforting, and redeeming. This is why all attempts to 'explain' the Holocaust or the death of children have been and always will be ultimately fruitless. But being together bound with God means that one has a lifetime of experiences (both individual and communal) in which God has been empowering, comforting, and redemptive. And these experiences constitute the justifiable basis for continuing to affirm God's trustworthiness in the future in the face of evil. The mystery of God's love is not resolved or dissolved. It continues and permeates the relationship of being mutually bound with God in love.

The Importance of Community

This does not, of course, as in the human case sketched above, rule out the possibility that if one goes through a long enough (as determined experientially, not chronologically or statistically) period of God's absence or failed expectations, one will, and perhaps should, justifiably abandon the belief that God cares. It would be insensitive in the extreme to argue on purely rational grounds with someone who has been the victim of sustained abuse by others, and has suffered a lifetime of innumerable tragedies, that he or she should simply 'have faith' and go on loving God. That kind of argument simply doesn't respond to the experiential failure of God's love to make itself manifest in that person's life. But this is where the experience of the community that is also together bound with God becomes crucial. While each person must experience the love and mystery of God in his or her own existential situation, the communal experience (stretching back in time to the recorded beginnings of God's interaction with humankind) helps to put those individual experiences in a larger context. The community reminds the individual that she is not alone, that God is working as much through the community as God is working directly (or apparently not working) in the life of the single person. Her comfort, empowerment, and redemption are also the work of her community. Her losses and fears and frustrations are their concern as well as God's. In giving herself to the community, therefore, she is already being given one of God's greatest and most decisive acts in history: namely, the creation of a community of love called into being in order to manifest God's intention of love for all humankind in fellowship. It is one of the strongest ontological claims of the Christian faith that ultimately reality is such that if persons (even ones horrendously scarred by abuse and neglect) give themselves into the safekeeping of a community formed by the bonds of love, they will be healed. Christians believe that God created the world in such a way that in the long run no actions that embody love can ultimately be frustrated or fail to be realized. This belief is so basic, both to the meaning of the Christian faith and to reality itself, that it forms the foundation of the hope that sustains the Christian community in the midst of its present journey through affliction: the hope that Christians are together bound with God as they are bound for glory.

Notes

1. Paul D. Hanson, *The People Called: The Growth of Community in the Bible* (San Francisco: Harper and Row, 1986), p. 528.

2. Ibid., p. 531.

3. Wolfhart Pannenberg, *Jesus: God and Man*, trans. Lewis L. Wilkins and Duane A. Priebe (Philadelphia: Westminster Press, 1968), p. 91.

4. Ibid., pp. 99, 109.

5. Ibid., p. 98.

6. Ibid., p. 105.

7. William J. Abraham, *Divine Revelation and the Limits of Historical Criticism* (New York: Oxford University Press, 1982), p. 91.

8. Ibid., p. 109.

9. Ibid., p. 111.

10. Van A. Harvey, *The Historian and the Believer: The Morality of Historical Knowledge and Christian Belief* (New York: Macmillan, 1966), p. 39.

11. Ibid., p. 42.

12. Ibid., p. 48.

13. Ibid., p. 51

14. Ibid.

15. Michael Goldberg, "God, Action, and Narrative: *Which* Narrative? *Which* Action? *Which* God?," *Journal of Religion* 68 (January 1988): 40.

16. Thomas F. Tracy, *God, Action, and Embodiment* (Grand Rapids, Mich.: William B. Eerdmans, 1984), p. 136.

17. Ronald F. Thiemann, *Revelation and Theology: The Gospel as Narrated Promise* (Notre Dame, Ind.: University of Notre Dame Press, 1985), p. 100.

18. Goldberg, "God, Action, and Narrative," p. 50.

19. Ibid., p. 54.

20. Hanson, *The People Called*, p. 5.

21. Dietrich Bonhoeffer, *Letters and Papers From Prison* (enlarged edition, ed. Eberhard Bethge) (New York: Macmillan, 1972). See especially the letters from April through June of 1944.

10

The Challenge
and Possibility
of Christian Community

It is clear from a biblical point of view, that one of God's most decisive and sustaining acts is the creation of human community. It can even be said that the establishment and continuation of community is God's ultimate intention in all of God's historical action. We need, in this final chapter, to spell out more fully the meaning of that community, its relation to the development and fulfillment of the individual person, and its place within the life of a world in which community is daily denied by injustice and the absence of peace. Finally, we need to say something about the role that the understanding of community plays in the life of those persons who are engaged in the ministries and discipleship of peace and justice as they await, in hope, the consummation of God's kingdom on earth as it is in heaven.

The Ideal of Community

John Macmurray, in his major study of community, *Persons in Relation*, claims that the inherent ideal of the personal is a "universal community of persons in which each cares for all the others and no one for him[sic]self. . . ."[1] This is an audacious and even startling claim, both because it runs counter to the inherited wisdom of theologies of sin and secular ideologies of realism and because it seems to undermine the development of each person's unique gifts and individuality. But its superficial audacity hides a deeper truth, which rests squarely on the biblical insight that God's intention for the world is the creation of a community of genuine and full mutuality. In addition to giving meaning to the biblical understanding of God's action in the world, that truth might well provide an essential complement to one of the more intractable issues in the recent debates among social philosophers over communitarianism versus individualism as well as within contemporary feminist thought over the degree to which women ought to enter into a community in which they would be expected to share power only recently won against men. Both debates are relevant to a religious understanding of community because religious communities now exist in secular societies alongside and within forms of association that can both challenge as well as undermine what these religious communities take to be essential to the fulfilled life. At the same time, the religious community needs to stake its claims about the reality of God and divine action in the face of secular claims that no such reality exists.

While much of the ink spilled in the debate between individualistic liberals and organic communitarians has been over whether persons are essentially social or individualistic, a deeper issue has received little attention, namely *what specific kind* of community is best for persons if they are more than private atoms in contractual relationship with others. There are many forms of human association (one of which contractarian liberals accept), and until communitarians become clear about which form(s) are more appropriate to the essentially social nature of persons, the debate will remain stagnant.[2]

Community in Feminist Thought

Within feminist thought there is also a debate, closely paralleling the communitarian/liberalist one, about the status women should aspire to in any association of persons. Some feminists, suspicious of the domination men have exercised when they had a monopoly of power, have argued for women's right to countervailing power, understood as that power by which women will be able to achieve their own advancement and fulfillment, often without support from men. Fearful of losing their recently acquired access to political and economic power in an organic soup of indiscriminate 'oneness', and distrustful of being lulled into new forms of submission by calls to merge their lives with others in an overarching 'community', these feminists are wary of any social forms that entail dependence on or equality with the very power wielders who have excluded them for centuries from the benefits which power secures. When they hear the call to identify with the needs of others before themselves, it reminds them of men's tendency to exploit women by viewing them solely as care-givers who should spend themselves on others (especially children and husbands) and leave the realms of political and economic power to men.

Nevertheless, there are other feminists who are concerned that as women celebrate their hard-won access to the freedom to exercise power, they may be celebrating what is increasingly being seen as a life of meaningless and unfulfilling competition with other power wielders. As Jean Bethke Elshtain has said, the concept of a 'community' based on the liberal freedom to compete for scarce goods, "while celebrated, has remained mostly an empty term—for there is no way to create real communities out of an aggregate of 'freely' choosing adults,"[3] (just as the communitarians have claimed in their arguments against the notion of a liberal society of atomistic individuals).

Macmurray's claim (and the Bible's) that the fullest experience of one's personhood is found in centering one's concern on others may well provide the metaphysical foundation for articulating the form of a specific kind of community called for by liberal critics of communitarian rhetoric and for a way to get around the fear some feminists have of submerging their newly won individuality in the congealing quicksand of new dependencies. Nevertheless, to establish that claim may require one element not usually given credibility in the contemporary discussion—human interaction with a divine being who acts in their midst.

Self-Interest and Two Forms of Association

One basic assumption about human nature has, of course, traditionally checked any tendency to regard Macmurray's claim as anything but naive. It is the assumption that human beings are essentially motivated by self-interest. Theologians discuss this human characteristic under the rubric 'sin', and secular theorists under the label 'realism'. Persons may have social impulses, but they will always act, as Reinhold Niebuhr put it, by "contradicting and defying the law of love".[4]

Historically two forms of human association have emerged from this 'negative' view of human nature. One is the liberal, individualistic (or the atomistic/contractarian) society in which persons, each driven primarily by self-interest, rationally contract with each other so as best to minimize the threat each poses to the fundamental autonomy of the other.[5] Adam Smith's 'invisible hand' sees to it that in such an individualistic association, self-interest will work for the benefit of all.[6]

The other form of association to emerge from self-interest is what I have called the organic/functional.[7] It is based on the claim that the nature of persons is to be profoundly interdependent, as organs related to each other and to the whole organism of which they are a part. The worth of each person is determined by his or her functionality within and for the whole. But even this interdependent view, in one sense the polar opposite of the independence extolled by the atomistic/contractarian position, ironically winds up reflecting the latter's belief that the chief end of relationship is primarily to advance one's own self-interest. It simply regards organic interdependence and cooperation as a more effective (and thus more 'natural') means for doing so. Karl Marx, one of the most eloquent representatives of the organic/functional view, even when he is extolling the virtues of sociality rather than individualism, still speaks positively of the 'appropriation' of others by the self for its own interests. My association with others, he claims, is "an organ for *expressing* my own *life.*" Other persons become my "objects," who confirm and realize my being.[8] Self-realization thus seems as much a primary goal in Marxian cooperative community as it does in Hobbesian atomistic society. Both assume the interests of others must be calculated in terms of how they will serve the interests of the self. They differ primarily in how they make that calculation, that is, through the enforcement of a contract or through the fraternity of cooperation. If the only alternative to a liberal society is a vague concept of 'community', no movement toward a genuinely mutual community similar to the biblical vision can occur.

A specific form of community with the potential for moving the debate forward is that of a mutual relationship between persons whose union is for the sake of their love for, enjoyment of, and delight in each other. A view of community as a mutuality of communion seems to find virtually no place in the atomistic/contractarian view because mutuality is almost literally irrational. It also finds little place in the organic/functional view because even cooperation is seen as a means to the real end of relationship—namely self-realization. And cooperation is clearly not the same as love: it is a way of working together for a common end, whereas love is a form of *being together* as an end in itself. And interdependence is not the same as mutuality: the former is a biological or sociological given, whereas the latter must be a matter of will, something continually intended by the persons in relation. Too often contemporary writers have been so attracted to any cooperative alternative to the individualism of atomistic forms of association, and in particular to the organic/functional imagery of cooperation, that they have failed to discern the differences between cooperation and love.

This is sometimes the case with some feminist writers who have rightly rejected the individualistic models of relationship associated historically with male domination. Some writers are attracted to the organic view just because it seems to overturn hierarchy for organic interdependence. But within the organic model we often hear calls for "forms of collective life in which each member is empowered to actuate [his or her] potentialities to the mutual benefit of self and community . . . keeping hierarchy always in service to the empowerment and development of all participants in a collectivity."[9] As Hinze has noted, however, this appeal only makes sense within a traditionally 'liberal' individualistic view "which focuses on the rights of individuals to pursue their divergent interests, [and] views liberty in terms of maximum freedom from constraint. . . ."[10]

Feminists are right, however, in raising the question of whether, in our search for a genuinely loving community, as Jean Baker Miller puts it, we can "create a way of life that includes serving others without being subservient [to them]"?[11] We need a view of the person-in-relation that does not submerge her under the domination of others in an individualistic free-for-all, or dissolve her identity in an organic pool in which all individual gifts and traits are washed away, or define her primarily in terms of her 'role' or function within a subsuming organic whole.

A New Model of Community as Mutuality

We need a model of personal relationships in which the unique gifts of each person are celebrated and nurtured, and in which the celebration and nurturing of others are the primary intentions of all the members. That new model seems to be what the Bible calls *koinonia*, the intentional community of persons who, under God's grace, look after each other in and through the deepest kind of love, or *agape*. Paul's letter to the Philippians says, "fill up my cup of happiness by thinking and feeling alike, with the same love for one another, the same turn of mind, and a common care for unity. . . . You must *humbly reckon others better than yourselves. Look to each other's interest and not merely to your own*" (Phil. 2:1–4).

Heterocentrism and Self-fulfillment

If we look more closely at Macmurray's version of *agape*, namely 'heterocentrism' (the placing of the self's interests *primarily* in the other—'hetero'—rather than in itself), it may seem paradoxical, and therefore inconsistent, to claim that fulfillment comes from placing the interests of others ahead of one's own. Isn't fulfillment essentially a manifestation of or a hope built upon self-interest? Doesn't the self want to be fulfilled and therefore tries to find what will fulfill it? And if it happens to discover that heterocentrism is an effective means for doing so, isn't other-regarding action simply a useful device in securing the self's own interests? Isn't the prior and basic motivation one of seeking my own self-fulfillment and isn't cooperation, therefore, simply a means to that end? Isn't the biblical vision of community simply unrealistic, or to the extent that it is realistic, isn't it identical to the organic/functional view?

There is much truth in these observations. Persons obviously wish for their own fulfillment. We might say that persons are always *motivated* by the desire for self-fulfillment. But what is wished for may not be what is primarily intended. One may *intend* one thing, hoping all the while that something else (not inconsistent with what one intends) will *also* occur. One's intention may subsume one's motivation without contradicting it. As Macmurray reminds us, motives are not intentions. Motives are felt, not thought, and are often unconscious. A motive determines movement or orientation, whereas an intention 'takes control' of that movement and consciously directs it toward an end deliberately chosen by the agent.[12] Thus what one intends may or may not contradict how one is motivated to behave. One may be motivated by self-interest and intend the interest of others first and foremost. And one may find that what one is motivated toward arrives as a gift precisely because one is not intending it in the first instance. We may be enjoined to love our neighbors as ourselves. But this could be taken to mean that we are motivated to love ourselves as a matter of fact, and that we should *intend* actions that direct that love primarily toward others. This intention does not contradict one's motivation or desire, but it does surpass, override, or subsume it, and, paradoxically, ultimately fulfill it precisely because it does not *primarily* intend it.

An individual can suffer from high blood pressure and be motivated (and hope for a way) to reduce it. However, acting on a primary and overriding intention to reduce it may well have the unintended side-effect of actually elevating it, especially since fussing and fretting about changes in life-style may bring on such anxiety that the problem is not only not relieved but aggravated. On the other hand, intending something entirely different, such as devoting more time to one's family or hobbies, may result in what one hopes for (the lowering of the pressure) without actually intending it in the first instance. We have not, strictly speaking, *achieved* a lowering of the pressure, but it has come to us nonetheless. We have not denied our self-interest (it remains active throughout as a motivation), but it has been made secondary to the primary intention of loving others first.

There is enough in this analogy to suggest that one might hope for self-fulfillment while primarily intending the fulfillment of others. It is certainly logically conceivable that one could devote oneself fully to the nurture of others and, as a result and without it having been one's overriding intention, find oneself fulfilled as well. In this conception, the nurturer does not deny her desire for personal fulfillment (as some versions of self-abnegation would urge), but neither does she act primarily on an intention shaped by that desire.

This leads, of course, to the question of why self-fulfillment would occur when a person is primarily intending the fulfillment of others. And the logical answer can only be if the others are primarily intending *her* fulfillment at the same time. In other words, only within a community of mutuality, marked by the heterocentric intentions of each member toward all the others, can the fulfillment of all occur even though each member is not primarily intending his or her own fulfillment in the first instance.

Mutual Gifts

One important dimension of such a community of mutuality is that the members have various 'gifts' to offer to the others (e.g., of sensitivity, skill at ordering things, insight, leadership, and so forth). At the heart of Paul's understanding of the church is the sharing of gifts; Rom. 12:6 says, "The gifts we possess differ as they are allotted to us by God's grace, and must be exercised accordingly". But quite often the exercise of these gifts is most effective when the employer of them is not focusing on his or her possession of the gift but on its use in service to the others instead. If one discovers a gift for singing, one wants to exercise it and usually receives greater satisfaction when one sings for the enjoyment of others than when one sings alone. Particularly important in community is the gift some people are said to have of 'being there' for others, that is, of being especially sensitive and attentive to their needs. And it is a trait of this kind of gift that it works best in those situations in which the one with the gift is not consciously focusing upon it, precisely because one is focusing upon the others by means of the gift. This gift seems to flow from the person's very center even as she seems so unattentive to it because she is attentive to the one who is the recipient of her gift. And the more we exercise our gifts, the more we often want to exercise them and the more fulfilled we are in exercising them. Fulfillment, in short, can come from the use of something received as a gift, not from the mere possession of something achieved as a reward for hard work.

Now if we put this logical conception in the context of Christian theology we might get something like the following. Assuming the desire or motivation of all persons is to be fulfilled, it might be the case that the conditions for fulfillment have been established (by a divine power) in such a way that this desire can be realized only in and through a community of heterocentric mutuality. Given the theological insistence on sin, however, how can a sinful self (namely one driven primarily by egocentrism) begin to intend and act heterocentrically? If a mutual community presupposes that each member is sufficiently fulfilled such that he or she *can* override his or her sinful egocentrism enough to intend the fulfillment of others before his or her own, how is such sufficient fulfillment possible?

The answer can only be through a gift of what we might call sufficient or minimal fulfillment from an Other who is so maximally fulfilled that it can intend the fulfillment of others before its own.[13] A self that is totally egocentric simply cannot act for others, except as a calculated means to its own fulfillment. (This is the truth in the philosophy of individualism.) But there is no reason why fulfillment cannot be a process that passes through various stages of completeness. Thus a self might move from minimal fulfillment toward greater and greater degrees of fulfillment.

But can a self move by itself from a complete lack of fulfillment (assuming that is what sin entails) to minimal fulfillment by
its own efforts? The Christian tradition has clearly heard many
voices on this issue, even though the Augustine-Luther-Calvin-
Niebuhr camp has generally determined the orthodox position that
only by God's grace (gift) can the power to act lovingly toward others be given or restored to the sinful self. Nevertheless, it is at least
conceivable that one could hold that God has, as a kind of initial
cosmic gift, as distinct from individual gifts to particular persons,
implanted in the structures of reality, including the constitution
of sinful selves, the ontological possibility of initiating heterocentric
intentions. But in either case, the development of the self's fulfillment would require its membership in a community of mutuality,
intending the fulfillment of others and receiving fulfillment from
them as their gifts to him or her.

Through God's gift (structural or individual) of initial fulfillment
the self is empowered to love others primarily for their sakes, and
not for its own. Now if other selves have been similarly 'gifted' or
empowered by the same divine Creator, then those selves can (and
desire to) enter into relationships with others in which each cares
primarily for the other and not for himself. These relationships
become reciprocal and mutually reinforcing. The more one cares
for others the more one feels fulfilled since one is exercising a gift
that the conditions of reality support and empower. And if others
are exercising their gifts of caring, reinforcement from the conditions of reality proceeds apace. The self begins to discover that it
enjoys others for their sakes and that it is being enjoyed for its own
sake by them. Fulfillment is a completely reciprocal, mutual occurrence. It is, in short, the result of *mutual heterocentrism*: *agape* in
koinonia, the manifestation of the mutual receipt and exercise of
gifts in which all are fulfilled precisely because all are givers and
receivers at the same time, though in different respects. If all give
to others in the context of a mutual community, then necessarily
all receive from others. There is no *achievement* of fulfillment by
individual selves, but rather their mutual receipt of fulfillment
through heterocentric action. No one gives love who has not initially received it from God and from other persons, and yet the
receipt of love is not the primary intention (despite its being the
underlying hope) of those who are loving others on the basis of their
receipt of the gift of love. The Gordian knot tying 'realism' to the
primacy of self-interest is cleanly sliced by the claim that the basic

interest (motivation) of the self is realized for the self by others who
have taken the self as their primary interest, just as it has taken
them for its primary interest.

But have we avoided the problem of the organic subsumption
of all within a tepid soup from which all differentiating individuality has been removed? Yes, if we understand that a primary intention to love others for *their* sakes entails necessarily a concern to
help them develop what is unique to each one of them. Love for
another means affirming, nurturing, and celebrating those things
about the other that deepen that other's uniqueness. A genuine
community of mutuality would be one in which a diversity of gifts
and talents manifested in the particularities and peculiarities of
individual persons is celebrated and empowered. Gifts, as Paul
Camenisch has pointed out, have a unique capacity for calling forth
from their recipients "untapped potential, [and] . . . new challenges
for growth and enrichment."[14] How else could real love be shown
for another except through a desire that the fullness of the other's
character be expressed? This means, at least in part, that individuals *can* enjoy the fruits of their labor (their achievements), provided
that those achievements are the primary intention of the others,
not of oneself. If my speech to the loving group is well received,
the group has, in effect, acknowledged my achievement and through
that acknowledgment given me the essential reason to enjoy and
take deep satisfaction in what I have done. In addition, I will be
extremely happy that my work has found fruit in the enjoyment
and development of others. But without the receipt of my work by
the community, it remains barren and unfulfilling. In this way we
avoid the potentially drab organic pool in which diversity is washed
away or in which each person's unique traits are made merely functional for some higher organic purpose. A community of mutual
heterocentrism results in the full development of each individual
but, unlike a society of atoms, it does so through intending the
development of others first and receiving the full development of
oneself as a gift from those others.

This receipt of the gifts of others leads to what Enda McDonagh
has called the "highest moral response," namely the "mutual celebration of the presence of others as gift."[15] Morality in this context
is based not on obligation but on trust—the trust that those who
are gifted will desire to "share things as well as themselves with
one another, the desire to enrich one another's life, to bring them
joy and pleasure, to express their affection for one another."[16] Trust
is the essential condition on which the moral relation of a loving

community is established. Trust is also, in the biblical sense, the fundamental basis for belief in God. Trust constitutes the meaning of faith: the trust that God will remain committed to God's covenant of being together bound with God's people in the sustaining of community.

Mutual Trust and Altruism

Trust, however, only makes sense in a context in which persons genuinely intend to care for others and to believe that such care is justified morally as well as ontologically (that is, by the structures of reality as underwritten by God). Trust in an association of self-interested individuals is essentially an expectation that others will be deterred from acts that are harmful to one because potential doers of harm are afraid of the negative consequences of violating the laws regulating human interaction. Trust in a loving community is based on one's conviction that others are generally trustworthy and, even in those specific instances when they are not, that the underlying structures of reality will ultimately support and reward trusting behavior.

That such trust is warranted is the conviction underlying Laurence Thomas' recent argument that altruism, which he defines as an unconditional love for others, is a more basic source of moral behavior than self-interest. Thomas' claims support the argument of this study even though they fly in the face of the inherited wisdom of recent moral philosophy. Thomas holds that there "has to be more altruism in our bones ... than contemporary moral philosophers have allowed."[17] He goes on to argue that our capacity for altruism is in part a biological heritage or a natural talent.[18] His use of sociobiology is at least consistent with my earlier claim that God may have 'wired into' reality the conditions that would support heterocentrism. But like a talent, or gift, Thomas points out, the capacity for altruism needs to be nourished by our social environment or it grows stale. While Thomas makes no use of the notion of a grace-ful God, his observation coheres with my other claim that God may act upon individuals (either directly or through the supportive environment of a loving community) to provide the gift of initial or minimal fulfillment such that they can begin acting heterocentrically.

Thomas makes a convincing case that in a community of love (especially that represented by the parent-child relationship), the child experiences a basic psychological security that she is loved regardless of how she performs some kind of 'function'.[19] She is, in our terms, the object of an unqualified heterocentric love, which empowers her to love herself (because she is loved for her own sake) and thus to love others for their own sakes (and not because they serve her self-interest). Thomas argues that fear need not be a primary motivation for the child if the parental or communal support is genuinely loving toward her. The child may love the parents simply because she respects them and wants to help them flourish just as and because she has been respected and helped to flourish by them.

Finally, Thomas argues, as one discovers how much one is loved by others, one discovers one's own worth. In this sense, self-love is the result, not the source, of love for and by others. Because one is loved for oneself, one comes to desire the realization of one's talents and gifts. And despite this concern for one's own self-realization, as Thomas puts it,

> neither the desire to realize one's talents nor the desire to be treated equitably entails always preferring one's interests, however small, to the interests of others. On the contrary, both desires are compatible with taking considerable delight in the flourishing of others. Indeed, the love that persons have for others is at its best when persons realize both dimensions of self-love in their lives. For then their attachment to their loved ones is not born of insecurities, the need for praise, and the like. . . . I take love to be more basic than self-love . . . because it is love that gives rise to self-love.[20]

Thomas does not rely upon any religious arguments in his defense of altruism. But his developed position is fully consistent with my conception of a mutual community of love whose 'realism' is grounded in the structures of reality and, at least in some instances, the action of God in the lives of persons and communities. His understanding of the conditions of fulfillment corresponds to the Christian claim that divine grace empowers its recipients to love one another as Christ loves them. Scripture is replete with references to the empowering grace of God, the renewal and transformation of hearts and minds, through which communities of *agape* or *koinonia* are created and sustained. Scripture simply does not talk about the 'achievement' of the ability to love or about loving as a means employed by the self-interested individual for securing happiness. Love is always a heterocentric act, primordially the act of God toward God's creation, which empowers the other precisely because the lover regards the other as the primary object of his love. And those who have been empowered by divine love are then inspired to use their newfound power to empower others. As Camenisch puts it, the gratitude that follows upon the receipt of the gift of self will produce a community living "with a joyful sense of the interrelatedness of things whereby life is enriched by the generosity of persons or powers outside of themselves. Their lives will reflect the conviction that the goodness of life is not grounded primarily in themselves, . . . [but rather] in the uncoerced, undeserved bounty of other agencies well-disposed towards them."[21]

The Realism of Community

And so we are back to the realism or naivete of the Bible's and Macmurray's claim that genuine community is one in which each cares for the other and no one for himself. The claim can be understood as realistic if and only if mutual heterocentrism is possible. And, as we have argued, it is possible if and only if the capacity for it is received as a gift, not achieved solely by individual effort. Therefore, the realism of the claim boils down to the question: Is there a being of sufficient power, whose nature is sufficiently whole and healthy, who has the intention to love others for their own sakes, who has the capacity to act upon those others in order to carry out his or her intention, and who has, in fact, so acted and still acts despite recalcitrance and obstruction from those whom he or she is seeking to love? And the answer to that question, clearly, lies at the heart of biblical theology. Christians obviously believe there is such a being—namely the God of Abraham, Isaac, Rachel, Jacob, and Jesus. And they believe that this God is the basis for affirming the realism of Macmurray's claims about human love and mutual community. The only thing at stake, therefore, is the reality of God as so described. This means that Christian theology has a right to demand that its claims about God's relation to community be taken with the same seriousness as one takes purely secular claims about what constitutes human associations.

Theology's claims about God are not to be confused with perfectionism or with the notion that sin is gradually disappearing under the onslaught of education or the maturation of the moral sentiments. Theology does not assume that persons, once gifted with the capacity to begin loving others heterocentrically, will always and in every instance act solely on the basis of *agape* love. Sin is real and so is our freedom to manifest it. The claims about mutual heterocentrism rest on a different foundation. They are based on a theo-logic of relationship, which requires only that the primary affirmation of others be *possible* provided that the affirmer has already been affirmed by the divine Agent (and through that affirmation, empowered to affirm others). It may well be true that the vast majority of human beings either refuse the divine affirmation or choose to misuse it. The freedom to misappropriate the gift is never taken away by the donor. But just because sin may be universal does not make the logic of mutual heterocentrism impossible.

That logic rests, finally, on a claim about God's power to act graciously in the present on individuals and upon a record of such acts in the past. The structures within which individuals live, especially those based on a belief in the primacy of selfishness, obviously act as a barrier to the development of alternative structures built on a different assumption about our intentions with respect to other persons. It is at least conceivable that alternative social structures, such as those associated with intentional Christian communities, might mitigate some of the worst forms of selfish behavior as well as open up possibilities for heterocentric behavior not dreamed of in the prevailing forms of social relationships. The hegemony of social structures based on 'realism' (political 'realpolitik') has the effect, as Vernard Eller has said in commenting on Reinhold Niebuhr's view of God, of closing off to consideration "possibilities which simply are not calculable by sinful man [*sic*] as being options under history's conditions of sin."[22]

Utopianism

In this regard, the theo-logic of mutual heterocentrism dovetails nicely with recent theological reflections on the meaning of 'utopianism'. Gustavo Guttieriez has said that utopia "necessarily means a denunciation of the existing order" and an annunciation of "what is not yet, but will be; it is the forecast of a different order of things, a new society."[23] And as Paul Ricouer has noted, the denunciation involved in utopian thinking must be concretely allied with specific commitments to live out a new consciousness and new relationships.[24] And this in turn requires a leap of imagination, a break with traditional ways of thinking, a refusal to remain complicit with the prevailing wisdom of what is possible in and through human relationships. The moral consequence of thinking from the point of view of life and self as gift will lead, as Camenisch puts it, to a "distinctive mode of life . . . in which the giftedness of our total existence comes to color our entire outlook,"[25] one that is not reducible to traditional moral relationships based on contractual obligation and duty alone. Christian hope underlies utopian thinking, a hope for a divine kingdom in which *agape* will prevail.

Two Radical Changes

But the logic of mutual heterocentrism does demand two radical changes in our traditional way of thinking: one, it requires that we accept ourselves (and the power through which we can act heterocentrically) as gifts received, not accomplishments achieved. Without that change, we will have no alternatives but those that atomism and organicism offer us. We will remain stuck in the debate between those who assert the necessity for the self to be free from any dependent or interdependent bonds with others and those who argue for a resubmersion of the self into a larger cooperative organic whole in which only our functionality is important. Neither feminists who want to wrest power from those who exploited them nor communitarians who want a viable alternative to liberal individualism can make much progress without some notion of a specific form of community in which interdependence does not mean either subservience or the use of others for private ends.

But a second radical change requires that we take seriously, and not simply metaphorically, the claim that God can (and does) act in history and that God will continue to act upon individuals in order to bestow the enabling gift of love. I believe that much of liberal theology's reluctance to believe in the power of other-affirmation and the realism of heterocentrism is ultimately due to its failure of nerve in affirming the reality of God's gift of love in the human heart. God has become for much of modern theology either an austere, semi-remote, quasi-Deistic being or an ineffable ground of being to whom homage can be due for God's creation and maintenance of the general order of the universe or on whom feelings of mystery and awe can be centered. But belief in God's ability to act concretely in the world has virtually disappeared. Such belief has, as I have tried to show in this study, metaphysical support and rational credibility. But only if we can come to believe in God's capacity and willingness to act, and God's performance of real acts of empowerment to love, will we have the metaphysical basis on which to defend the realism of heterocentrism and break the stranglehold of the 'realism' of the primacy of self-interest. If Christians truly believe that God is real and has acted with power in the world, then they should be willing to introduce that belief into the debate over community that presently remains stuck within purely secular parameters. Until those parameters are broken to allow the divine reality to be a living force in human life, there will be no way to sustain genuine mutual heterocentrism and viable new ways of being in relationship.

Notes

1. John Macmurray, *Persons in Relation* (New York: Harper and Brothers, 1961), p. 159.
2. See especially Bernard Yack, "Liberalism and Its Communitarian Critics: Does Liberal Practice 'Live Down' to Liberal Theory?," in Charles H. Reynolds and Ralph V. Norman eds., *Community in America: The Challenge of Habits of the Heart* (Berkeley: University of California Press, 1988), pp. 147–69.
3. Jean Bethke Elshtain, "Feminism, Family, and Community," *Dissent* 29 (1982): 442.
4. Reinhold Niebuhr, *Man's Nature and His Communities* (New York: Charles Scribner's Sons, 1965), p. 39.
5. Frank G. Kirkpatrick, *Community: A Trinity of Models* (Washington, D.C.: Georgetown University Press, 1986).
6. For a popular and influential development of the deleterious effects of this view on American self-understanding, see Robert Bellah, et al., *Habits of the Heart: Individualism and Commitment in American Life* (Berkeley: University of California Press, 1985).
7. Kirkpatrick, *Community: A Trinity of Models.*
8. Karl Marx, *Economic and Philosophical Manuscripts of 1844,* edited and with an introduction by Dirk J. Struik. Translated by Martin Mulligan (New York: International Publishers, 1964), p. 140.
9. Christine Firer Hinze, "Structuring Power Releations: The U.S. Constitution and Its Latter-Day Daughters" (Paper read to the Ethics Section of the Annual Meeting of the American Academy of Religion, December 6, 1987) pp. 22, 24.
10. Ibid., p. 32.
11. Jean Baker Miller, *Toward a New Psychology of Women* (Boston: Beacon Press, 1983), p. 44. Miller's work parallels that of Carol Gilligan and Nel Noddings, both of whom suggest that for women the 'moral problem' is essentially one of caring-for others rather than being primarily one of rights and rules. It is a morality grounded in relationality rather than rational justice, as such. Nevertheless, Gilligan is not about to sacrifice some deep sense of individuality at the altar of relationality. She does not want to define caring, for example, as nothing more than self-sacrifice.

What I am suggesting is that Macmurray's notion of community provides the metaphysical foundation for the full development of morality as 'caring-for' in relation which also enhances and celebrates the individuality of each person in that relation. See Carol Gilligan, *In A Different Voice* (Cambridge, Mass.: Harvard University Press, 1982, and "Remapping the Moral Domain: New Images of the Self in Relationship," in T. C. Heller, et al., eds., *Reconstructing Individualism* (Stanford: Stanford University Press, 1986), pp. 237–52; and Nel Noddings, *Caring* (Berkeley: University of California Press, 1984).

12. See John Macmurray, *The Self as Agent* (London: Faber and Faber, 1957), pp. 193–95.

13. The question of whether God is no longer in need of or cannot increase God's own degree of fulfillment does not need to be taken up here. Nevertheless, process theology has spoken persuasively on this point. I see no reason why God's enjoyment of the fulfillment of others cannot be quite real for God and, in this sense, God can be said to increase God's degree of fulfillment as God is the 'recipient' of the love of others. In fact, it might be argued that God's enjoyment of those gifts is all the greater because God does not 'need' them in some ontologically basic way. The doctrine of the Trinity might also contain the potential for exploring the notion of God's fulfillment in relation to others with whom God is intimately bound in and through mutual love. This is one clear implication of the notion of God as together bound with God's creation.

14. Paul Camenisch, "Gift and Gratitude in Ethics," *The Journal of Religious Ethics* 9, no. 1 (Spring 1981): 17–18.

15. Enda McDonagh, *Gift and Call* (St. Meinrad, Ind.: Abbey Press, 1975), p. 86, quoted in Camenisch, "Gift and Gratitude," p. 15.

16. Camenisch, "Gift and Gratitude," p. 19.

17. Laurence Thomas, *Living Morally: A Psychology of Moral Character* (Philadelphia: Temple University Press, 1989), p. viii. It is not insignificant, I believe, that Thomas, a black American moral philosopher, writes out of the historical context of a religious/cultural community that has been characterized by love, compassion, and concern for others far more than have the kinds of secular communities from which many of the moral philosophers who espouse self-interest seem to come. This may suggest that arguments based on self-interest reflect at least as much one's social and economic privilege as they do the conclusions of ahistorical rational argument. This in turn may suggest that one's willingness to believe in the possibility of a mutual community has as much to do with one's moral experience as it does with the logic of claims that such a community is impossible 'given human nature'.

18. Ibid., p. 72.

19. Ibid., p. 61.

20. Ibid., pp. 193–94.

21. Camenisch, "Gift and Gratitude," p. 25.

22. Vernard Eller, *The Promise: Ethics in the Kingdom of God* (Garden City, N.Y.: Doubleday, 1970), p. 87.

23. Gustavo Guttieriez, *A Theology of Liberation*, translated and edited by Sister Caridad Inda and John Eagleson (Maryknoll, N.Y.: Orbis Books, 1973), p. 233.

24. As referred to by Guttieriez, *A Theology of Liberation*.

25. Camenisch, "Gift and Gratitude," pp. 24, 23.

Appendix

Bibliography of Sources on Act(s) of God in the World

Alston, William P., "Divine and Human Action." In *Divine and Human Action: Essays in the Metaphysics of Theism*, edited by Thomas V. Morris. Ithaca, N.Y.: Cornell University Press, 1988, pp. 257–80.

——. *Divine Nature and Human Language*. Ithaca, N.Y.: Cornell University Press, 1989.

——. "God's Action in the World." In *Evolution and Creation*, edited by Ernan McMullin. Notre Dame, Ind.: University of Notre Dame Press, 1985, pp. 197–220.

——. "Functionalism and Theological Language." *American Philosophical Quarterly* 22, no. 3 (July 1985): 221–30.

Blaikie, Robert J. *"Secular Christianity" and God Who Acts*. Grand Rapids, Mich.: William B. Eerdmans, 1970.

Brummer, Vincent. "Farrer, Wiles and the Causal Joint." *Modern Theology* 8, no. 1 (January 1992): 1–14.

Dilley, Frank. "Does the 'God Who Acts' Really Act?" In *God's Activity in the World*, edited by Owen C. Thomas. Chico, Calif.: Scholar's Press, 1983.

Ellis, Robert. "God and 'Action'." *Religious Studies* 24 (December 1988): 463–81.

——. "The Vulnerability of Action." *Religious Studies* 25 (June 1989): 225–33.

Farrer, Austin. *God Almighty and Ills Unlimited*. London: Collins, 1966.

Gill, Jerry H. "Divine Action as Mediated." *Harvard Theological Review* 80, no. 3 (1987): 369–78.

Hansson, Mats J. *Understanding an Act of God: An Essay in Philosophical Theology.* Uppsala, Sweden: University of Uppsala Press, 1991.

Hebblethwaite, Brian. "Providence and Divine Action." *Religious Studies* 14 (1978): 223–36.

Hebblethwaite, Brian, and Edward Henderson, eds. *Divine Action: Studies Inspired by the Philosophical Theology of Austin Farrer.* Edinburgh: T&T Clark, 1990. Includes the following essays: Alston, William. "How to Think About Divine Action," pp. 51–122; Forsman, Rodger. " 'Double Agency' and Identifying Reference to God", pp. 123–42; McLain, R. Michael. "Narrative Interpretation and the Problem of Double Agency," pp. 143–72; Thomas, Owen. "Recent Thought on Divine Agency," pp. 35–50; Tracy, Thomas F. "Narrative Theology and the Acts of God," pp. 173–96.

Jantzen, Grace. *God's World, God's Body.* Philadelphia: Westminster Press, 1984.

Kaufman, Gordon. *God the Problem.* Cambridge, Mass.: Harvard University Press, 1972.

———. "On the Meaning of 'Act of God'." *Harvard Theological Review* 61 (1968): 175–201.

King, Robert H. *The Meaning of God.* Philadelphia: Fortress Press, 1973.

Mason, David R. "Can We Speculate on How God Acts?" *Journal of Religion* 57 (1977): 16–32.

Peacocke, Arthur R. *Creation and the World of Science.* Oxford: Clarendon Press, 1979.

———. "God's Action in the Real World." *Zygon* 26, no. 4 (December 1991): 455–76.

———. "God's Interaction with the World." In *Theology for a Scientific Age.* Oxford: Basil Blackwell, 1990.

Polkinghorne, John C. "Creation and the Structure of the Physical World." *Theology Today* 44 (April 1987): 53–68.

———. "God's Action in the World." *Cross Currents* (Fall 1991): 293–307.

———. "The Nature of Physical Reality." *Zygon* 26, no. 2 (June 1991): 221–36.

———. *One World: The Interaction of Science and Theology.* Princeton: Princeton University Press, 1986.

———. *Science and Providence: God's Interaction with the World.* Boston: New Science Library, 1989.

Schwobel, Christoph. "Divine Agency and Providence." *Modern Theology* 3, no. 3 (1987): 225–44.

Thomas, Owen C., ed. *God's Activity in the World.* Chico, Calif.: Scholar's Press, 1983.

Tracy, Thomas F. "Enacting History: Ogden and Kaufman on God's Mighty Acts." *Journal of Religion* 64 (1984): 20–36.

———. *God, Action, and Embodiment.* Grand Rapids, Mich.: William G. Eerdmans, 1984.

Wiles, Maurice. *God's Action in the World.* London: SCM Press, 1986.

Wood, Charles M. "The Events in Which God Acts." *Heythrop Journal* 22 (1981): 278–84.

For process views see:

Cobb, John B. Jr. *A Christian Natural Theology.* Philadelphia: Westminster Press, 1965.

Cobb, John B, Jr., and David Ray Griffin. *Process Theology: An Introductory Exposition.* Philadelphia: Westminister Press, 1976, pp. 41–62.

Ford, Lewis. "Divine Persuasion and the Triumph of Good." In *Religion for a New Generation,* edited by Jacob Needleman, A. K. Bierman, and James A. Gould. New York: Macmillan, 1977, pp. 287–304.

Griffin, David Ray. *God, Power, and Evil: A Process Theodicy.* Philadelphia: Westminster Press, 1976.

Hartshorne, Charles. *The Divine Relativity: A Social Conception of God.* New Haven, Conn.: Yale University Press, 1948.

Ogden, Schubert. *The Reality of God and Other Essays.* New York: Harper and Row, 1966.

Williams, Daniel Day. "How Does God Act? An Essay in Whitehead's Metaphysics," in *Process and Divinity,* edited by William L. Reese and Eugene Freeman. LaSalle, Ill.: Open Court, 1964.

Bibliography

Abraham, William J. *Divine Revelation and the Limits of Historical Criticism.* New York: Oxford University Press, 1982.

Alston, William P. "Can We Speak Literally of God?" *Divine Nature and Human Language.* Ithaca, N.Y.: Cornell University Press, 1989.

Aquinas, St. Thomas. *The Summa Theologica.* In *Basic Writings of Saint Thomas Aquinas,* edited by Anton C. Pegis. vol. 1. New York: Random House, 1945.

Bellah, Robert, et al. *Habits of the Heart: Individualism and Commitment in American Life.* Berkeley: University of California Press, 1985.

Bonhoeffer, Dietrich. *Letters and Papers From Prison* (enlarged edition, edited by Eberhard Bethge). New York: Macmillan, 1972.

Brummer, Vincent. "Farrer, Wiles and the Causal Joint." *Modern Theology* 8, no. 1. (January 1992).

Bultmann, Rudolph. *Jesus Christ and Mythology.* New York: Charles Scribner's Sons, 1958.

Burrell, David B. *Aquinas: God and Action.* Notre Dame, Ind.: University of Notre Dame Press, 1979.

———. *Knowing the Unknowable God: Ibn-Sina, Maimonides, Aquinas.* Notre Dame, Ind.: University of Notre Dame Press, 1986.

Camenisch, Paul. "Gift and Gratitude in Ethics." *The Journal of Religious Ethics* 9, no. 1 (Spring 1981).

Coreth, Emerich. *Metaphysics* [English edition by Joseph Donceel]. New York: The Seabury Press, 1973.

Danto, Arthur. "Basic Actions." *American Philosophical Quarterly* 2 (1965): pp. 141–48.

Davidson, Donald. "Actions, Reasons, and Causes." in *The Philosophy of Action*, edited by Alan R. White. Oxford: Oxford University Press, 1968.

Davies, Paul. *God and the New Physics*. New York: Touchstone Books, 1983.

Davis, Lawrence. *Theory of Action*. Englewood Cliffs, N.J.: Prentice-Hall, 1979.

Dean, William. *History Making History*. Albany: State University of New York, 1988.

Dyck, Grace M. "Omnipresence and Incorporeality." *Religious Studies* 13 (1977): 85–91.

Eller, Vernard. *The Promise: Ethics in the Kingdom of God*. Garden City, N.Y.: Doubleday, 1970.

Ellis, John M. *Against Deconstruction*. Princeton: Princeton University Press, 1989.

Elshtain, Jean Bethke. "Feminism, Family, and Community." *Dissent* 29 (1982).

Farrer, Austin. *Faith and Speculation*. London: Adam and Charles Black, 1967.

————. *The Freedom of the Will*. London: Adam and Charles Black, 1958.

Fischer, John Martin, ed. *God, Foreknowledge, and Freedom*. Stanford: Stanford University Press, 1989. Includes the following articles: Marilyn McCord Adams, "Is the Existence of God a 'Hard' Fact?"; John Martin Fischer, "Freedom and Foreknowledge"; and Nelson Pike, "Divine Omniscience and Voluntary Action."

Gilkey, Langdon. "Cosmology, Ontology, and the Travail of Biblical Language." *Journal of Religion* 41 (1961).

Gilson, Etienne. *The Christian Philosophy of St. Thomas Aquinas*. New York: Random House, 1956.

Goldberg, Michael. "God, Action, and Narrative: Which Narrative? Which Action? Which God?" *Journal of Religion* 68 (January 1988).

Guttierez, Gustavo. *A Theology of Liberation*. Translated and edited by Sister Caridad Inda and John Eagleson. Maryknoll, N.Y.: Orbis Books, 1973.

Hanson, Paul D. *The People Called: The Growth of Community in the Bible*. San Francisco: Harper and Row, 1986.

Hansson, Mats. *Understanding an Act of God: An Essay in Philosophical Theology*. Uppsala, Sweden: University of Uppsala Press, 1991.

Harrison, Jonathan. "The Embodiment of Mind or What Use Is Having a Body?" *Proceedings of the Aristotelian Society* n.s. 74 (1973–74).

Harvey, Van A. *The Historian and the Believer: The Morality of Historical Knowledge and Christian Belief*. New York: Macmillan, 1966.

Hasker, William. *God, Time, and Knowledge*. Ithaca, N.Y.: Cornell University Press, 1989.

Hawking, Stephen W. *A Brief History of Time*. New York: Bantam Books, 1988.

Hein, Hilde. *On the Nature and Origin of Life.* New York: McGraw-Hill, 1971.

Hick, John. "Mystical Experience as Cognition." In *Understanding Mysticism,* edited by Richard Woods. Garden City, N.Y.: Doubleday Image Books, 1980.

Jantzen, Grace. " 'Where Two Are to Become One': Mysticism and Monism." In *The Philosophy in Christianity,* edited by Godfrey Vesey. Royal Institute of Philosophy Lecture Series, no. 25 Supplement to Philosophy, 1989. Cambridge: Cambridge University Press, 1989.

Jones, James W. *Contemporary Psychoanalysis and Religion: Transference and Transcendence.* New Haven, Conn.: Yale University Press, 1991.

Kaufman, Gordon. "On the Meaning of 'Act of God'." *Harvard Theological Review* 61 (1968).

Kenny, Anthony. "Divine Foreknowledge and Human Freedom." In *Aquinas: A Collection of Critical Essays,* edited by A. Kenny. Garden City, N.Y.: Doubleday Anchor Books, 1969.

Kirkpatrick, Frank G. *Community: A Trinity of Models.* Washington, D.C.: Georgetown University Press, 1986.

Kohler, Ludwig. *Old Testament Theology.* Trans. A. S. Todd. Philadelphia: Westminster Press, 1957.

Laszlo, Ervin. *Introduction to Systems Philosophy: Toward a New Paradigm of Contemporary Thought.* New York: Gordon and Breach, 1972.

Macmurray, John. *Persons in Relation.* New York: Harper and Brothers, 1961.

———. *The Self as Agent.* London: Faber and Faber, 1957.

Marx, Karl. *Economic and Philosophical Manuscripts of 1844.* Edited and with an introduction by Dirk J. Struik. Translated by Martin Milligan. New York: International Publishers, 1964.

Mascall, Eric. "The Doctrine of Analogy." *In Religious Language and the Problem of Religious Knowledge,* edited by Ronald E. Santoni. Bloomington, Ind.: Indiana University Press, 1968.

McDonagh, Enda. *Gift and Call.* St. Meinrad, Ind.: Abbey Press, 1975.

McLain, F. Michael. "On Theological Models." *Harvard Theological Review* 62 (1969).

Miller, Jean Baker. *Toward a New Psychology of Woman.* Boston: Beacon Press, 1983.

Morris, Thomas V., ed. *Divine and Human Action: Essays in the Metaphysics of Theism.* Ithaca, N.Y.: Cornell University Press, 1988. Includes the following articles: William P. Alston, "Divine and Human Action"; and Peter Van Inwagen, "The Place of Chance in a World Sustained by God."

Munitz, Milton. *Cosmic Understanding.* Princeton: Princeton University Press, 1986.

Neville, Robert C., ed. *New Essays in Metaphysics.* Albany: State University of New York Press, 1987. Includes the following essays: George Allan, "The Primacy of the Mesocosm"; Nicholas Capaldi, "Coper-

nican Metaphysics"; Charles Sherover, "Toward Experiential Metaphysics: Radical Temporalism"; and Carl G. Vaught, "Metaphor,
Analogy, and the Nature of Truth."

Niebuhr, Reinhold. *Man's Nature and His Communities.* New York:
Charles Scribner's Sons, 1965.

Nof, Doron, and Nathan Paldor. "Are There Oceanographic Explanations
for the Israelites' Crossing of the Red Sea?" *Bulletin of the American
Meteorological Society* 73, no. 3 (March 1992): 305–14.

Otto, Rudolf. *The Idea of the Holy: An Inquiry into the Non-rational
Factor in the Idea of the Divine and Its Relation to the Rational.*
Trans. John W. Harvey. New York: Oxford University Press, 1958.

Pannenberg, Wolfhart. *Jesus: God and Man.* Trans. Lewis L. Wilkins and
Duane A. Priebe. Philadelphia: Westminster Press, 1968.

Peterson, Michael, et al. *Reason and Religious Belief: An Introduction to
the Philosophy of Religion.* New York: Oxford University Press, 1991.

Polkinghorne, John. *One World: The Interaction of Science and Theology.*
Princeton: Princeton University Press, 1986.

———. *Science and Providence: God's Interaction with the World.* Boston: New Science Library, 1989.

Pols, Edward. *The Acts of Our Being: A Reflection on Agency and Responsibility.* Amherst: University of Massachusetts Press, 1982.

———. "Human Agents as Actual Beings." *Process Studies* 8, no. 2 (1978).

———. *Meditation on a Prisoner: Towards Understanding Action and
Mind.* Carbondale: Southern Illinois University Press, 1975.

———. "The Ontology of the Rational Agent." *Review of Metaphysics* 33,
no. 4 (June 1980).

———. "Power and Agency." *International Philosophical Quarterly* 11,
no. 3 (September 1971).

———. *Radical Realism: Direct Knowing in Science and Philosophy.*
Ithaca, N.Y.: Cornell University Press, 1992.

Shepherd, John. *Experience, Inference, and God.* New York: Harper and
Row, 1975.

Stace, Walter T., "Subjectivity, Objectivity and the Self." In *Religion for
a New Generation,* edited by Jacob Needleman, A. K. Bierman, and
James A. Gould. New York: Macmillan, 1977.

———. *Time and Eternity.* Princeton: Princeton University Press, 1951.

Strawson, P. F. *Individuals: An Essay in Descriptive Metaphysics.* Garden City, N.Y.: Doubleday-Anchor, 1963.

Swinburne, Richard. *The Coherence of Theism.* Oxford: Clarendon Press,
1977.

Theimann, Ronald F. *Revelation and Theology: The Gospel as Narrated
Promise.* Notre Dame, Ind.: University of Notre Dame Press, 1985.

Thomas, Laurence. *Living Morally: A Psychology of Moral Character.*
Philadelphia: Temple University Press, 1989.

Tillich, Paul. "Being and God" and "The Reality of God". In *Systematic
Theology.* Chicago: University of Chicago Press (1951). 1:211–89.

————. *The Courage to Be*. New Haven, Conn.: Yale University Press, 1952.

Tracy, Thomas F. *God, Action, and Embodiment*. Grand Rapids, Mich.: William B. Eerdmans, 1984.

Urban, Linwood, and Douglas N. Walton. "Freedom within Omnipotence." In *The Power of God: Readings on Omnipotence and Evil*, edited by Linwood Urban and Douglas N. Walton. New York: Oxford University Press, 1978.

Viladesau, Richard. *Answering for Faith: Christ and the Human Search for Salvation*. New York: Paulist Press, 1987.

von Wright, Georg Henrik. *Explanation and Understanding*. Ithaca, N.Y.: Cornell University Press, 1971.

Wainwright, William J. *Mysticism: A Study of Its Nature, Cognitive Value and Moral Implications*. Madison: University of Wisconsin Press, 1981.

————. *Philosophy of Religion*. Belmont, Calif.: Wadsworth, 1988.

Weiss, Paul. "The Living System: Determinism Stratified." In *Beyond Reductionism*, edited by Arthur Koestler and J. R. Smythies (The Alpbach Symposium, 1968). Boston: Beacon Press, 1969.

Whitehead, Alfred North. *Process and Reality* [Corrected Edition, edited by David Ray Griffin and Donald W. Sherburne]. New York: The Free Press, 1979.

Wiles, Maurice. *God's Action in the World*. London: SCM Press, 1986.

————. *Working Papers in Doctrine*. London: SCM Press, 1976.

Wolterstorff, Nicholas. "God Everlasting." In *God and the Good*, edited by Clifton J. Orlebeke and Lewis B. Smedes. Grand Rapids, Mich.: William B. Eerdmans, 1975.

Yack, Bernard. "Liberalism and Its Communitarian Critics: Does Liberal Practice 'Live Down' to Liberal Theory?" In *Community in America: The Challenge of Habits of the Heart*, edited and introduced by Charles H. Reynolds and Ralph V. Norman. Berkeley: University of California Press, 1988.

Index

DATE DUE

DEC 12 97			
			Printed in USA